MORAL RIGHTS
IN THE
WORKPLACE

MORAL RIGHTS
IN THE
WORKPLACE

Edited by:

GERTRUDE EZORSKY

James W. Nickel, Advisory Editor

Published under the sponsorship of the
National Society for Philosophy and Public Affairs

State University of New York Press

Published by
State University of New York Press, Albany

For information, address State University of New York
Press, State University Plaza, Albany, N.Y., 12246

Library of Congress Cataloging in Publication Data

Moral rights in the workplace.

"Published under the sponsorship of National Society
for Philosophy and Public Affairs."
 1. Quality of work life—United States. 2. Civil
rigths—United States. 3. Industrial relations—United
States. I. Ezorsky, Gertrude, 1926–   . II. Nickel,
James W.
HD6957.U6M67   1986   331.25   86-6949
ISBN 0-88706-362-4
ISBN 0-88706-363-2 (pbk.)

10 9 8 7 6 5 4 3 2 1

CONTENTS

3 FREEDOM, COERCION, AND THE RIGHT TO PRIVACY

4 THE RIGHT TO ORGANIZE

8   WORKERS' SELF-MANAGEMENT

INTRODUCTION

FREEDOM, FAIRNESS, AND THE GENERAL GOOD

This book focuses on moral problems that arise for people who labor in ordinary workplaces, in factories, mines, stores and on farms.

While modern moral philosophers have often cited the plain person's views, they rarely refer to moral issues that develop where plain persons spend an important part of their lives—in the workplace. Yet appeals to moral values are often heard during controversy over workplace policy. In this book, appeals to three such values predominate: (1) freedom, (2) fairness, and (3) the general good.

The first value, freedom, is endorsed both by those who criticize and those who defend the capititalist organization of the workplace. Thus a critic, Kurt Nutting, claims that the employer's right to determine working conditions (which in the United States includes the right to discipline or discharge workers even for discussing their political beliefs) is inherently coercive (chapter 3). By contrast, for libertarian philosophers such as Tibor Machan, the establishment of working conditions by management is the outcome of a *free* exchange in the marketplace between employers and workers (chapter 2). Thus, according to libertarians, government regulations, such as laws that require a safe and healthful workplace, interfere with the freedom of both employers and workers. Hence, Machan suggests that one should not "be morally concerned with working conditions which are fully" accepted by workers in a "free agreement."

However, Norman Daniels, a critic of this libertarian view, argues that a worker's acceptance of a hazardous job because it is her only alternative to unemployment is not a free act (chapter 2). He tags such worker acceptance as *quasi-coerced*. Here is why. Compare the hazardous job or unemployment case with a standard coercion case: A mugger says, "Your money or your life." In the mugger case, the choices before the victim have been reduced in a dramatic and *direct* way. In the hazardous job or unemployment case, the worker's choices have also been reduced, but in an *indirect* way: by unfair social practices, such as an educational system that fails to provide sufficient job training opportunities for workers lacking marketable skills. Given such training opportunities, many workers would have alternatives other than destitution or a life-threatening job.

When the choices of a worker have been indirectly reduced due to unfair social practices, then, according to Daniels, her acceptance of a hazardous job is not free, but quasi-coerced.

The value of freedom is also invoked in the controversy over compulsory union membership. Some analysts claim that workers should not be forced to join a union even if compulsory membership brings them economic benefits by increasing the union's bargaining power.

However, Burton Hall argues that compulsory membership is required by the obligation of the union to represent all unit workers, members and non-members, at the bargaining table (chapter 4). Only as union members can workers democratically influence union bargaining policy. Outside the union they have no real power to affect their working conditions. Hence, the important freedom requiring protection is freedom of workers within the union to advocate dissident views on union policies.

The second value, fairness, is invoked in the controversy over affirmative action. After the 1965 Civil Rights Act, affirmative action measures taken by employers contributed in the progress toward a fair share of employment benefits for minority persons and women. However, during the recession beginning in the 1970s, many of the jobs filled by affirmative action were wiped out by seniority-based layoffs. Hence, progress toward fairness for minorities and women has been reduced by the operation of seniority systems that tend to privilege the more senior, white males hired before affirmative action efforts began. Thus, a conflict in moral values exists between today's claims to fairness made by minorities and women and the claims of white males for recognition of their seniority entitlements.

Note that, here, fairness for minorities and women is in conflict not with the immoral workings of prejudice, but with union-instituted seniority systems that have brought significant moral benefits to the workplace. Seniority systems protect workers against arbitrary dismissal occasioned by the whim, malice, or prejudice of the employer. Strengthened by such security, American workers have gained in dignity. They can visibly expect to be treated with a measure of respect. Moreover, in many union-organized workplaces, seniority has become a standard for advancement. As a consequence of advancement by seniority, a workplace can become more humanized; harmony, cooperation and solidarity among employees replace an ugly scramble to win over one's coworkers.

Given the value of seniority systems, their conflict with affirmative action requirements is not easy to resolve. In chapter 7 three types of remedies for this conflict are explained. First, in *Firefighters* v. *Stotts,* the Supreme Court ruled, in effect, that affirmative action cannot take precedence over existing seniority systems. Second, in *Vulcan Pioneers* v. *New Jersey Department of Civil Service,* the court gave priority to affirmative action. According to that policy, some white males may be laid off in order to retain less senior minority persons and women. But the court was sensitive to the situation of the white males who would, in effect, be singled out to pay for past discrimination. Such singling out—while others more responsible for past hiring discrimination, such as employers, pay nothing—seems manifestly unfair. Hence, the court stated that these more senior white males are entitled to compensation for their loss. Howard Glickstein offers a historical precedent for such compensation: Several years ago the federal government compensated New York waterfront workers whose jobs were wiped out by an automation program.

The third remedy, advocated by the former U.S. Commission on Civil Rights in 1977, is work-sharing. Suppose, for example that a one-fifth work force layoff is mandated by a decline in business. A work-sharing remedy would place *all* employees on a four day workweek. (They could collect unemployment compensation for the fifth day.) This remedy distributes the layoff burden over the entire work force, instead of singling out some persons (white males) to bear the whole burden. Hence, the worksharing remedy makes a strong claim to fairness.

The third value invoked by writers in this book is the general good. Utilitarian philosophers believe that usefulness in promoting that general good should be the only moral standard for adopting a policy in the workplace.

In "A Kantian Utilitarian Approach," R.M. Hare construes the general good as the greatest satisfaction of everyone's preferences, impartially calculated (chapter 4). Hare suggests that the nineteenth century laws that benefitted trade unions passed this preference-satisfaction test by improving working conditions and creating greater equality of wealth, power and status. According to Hare, present disputes about rights in the workplace, for example the right to *not* join a union, should be tested in the same way: by impartially estimating the preferences of all individuals involved—workers, employers and the general public.

However, some critics of utilitarianism would fault Hare's preference test. They might argue that, in at least some cases, the greatest general satisfaction, impartially calculated, should be sacrificed in order to respect the rights of particular individuals.

Suppose, for example, that a small group of older women work as underpaid and exploited housecleaners. They earn barely enough to live on, have no medical benefits, receive no sick pay, and so forth. Each woman works one day a week for a different employer. Note that in this case their employers constitute the *majority* of the community. This majority wants to continue paying the cleaning women the same miserable wages. Thus, in an impartial calculation of everyone's preferences, the policy that favors the exploitation of these women wins out. Yet the women surely have a moral right to decent pay and working conditions.

Some philosophers might put the matter this way: There are good and bad preferences. Exploitation of these women is bad, no matter how many people prefer it.

Articles by G. A. Cohen, Joseph Des Jardins, Gerald Doppelt, Gertrude Ezorsky, Burton Hall, Michael Harrington, Tziporah Kasachkoff, R.M. Hare, Charles Landesman, Donald Levy, Judith Lichtenberg (in its entirety), Dan Lyons, Tibor Machan, Larry May and John C. Hughes, Diana Meyers, Kai Nielsen, Kurt Nutting, and Laurence Thomas are published here for the first time.

I should like to express my appreciation to the National Society for Philosophy and Public Affairs for the support they have given this volume.

the Editor

PART 1 _____

THE RIGHT TO MEANINGFUL WORK

Night Shift in A Pickle Factory*

Steve Turner _____

The same choice came to me as to all the other people out of work in the dying old factory towns here: either go along the river with the migrant crews, picking the tobacco and vegetables, or sign on at the pickle cannery. I've done both kinds of work before, and you can have either one for fertilizer as far as I'm concerned. But the bugs and heat are especially bad here in August. And I really don't have the right body for stoop labor anymore. . . .

They hired me for the night shift: 4:00 P.M. – 12:00 A.M., with two fifteen-minute breaks and a half-hour for dinner. Minimum wage plus ten cents shift differential. Hot stuff. It's not a union shop. Not yet. . . .

So I go on into the production area, where the day shift is still working. . . . Everyone has on white plastic aprons and head-deforming hair-nets. Tired, sweaty people. Their glazed eyes scan me and then move on to the clock. Tufts of what look like cotton stick out of most ears, and I understand why as I move into the first room and noise engulfs me: the rattle of conveyors and chuff-sigh of a big pneumatic packing machine, and the whining hum of many motors, and a major roaring from a device that is vacuum-cleaning jars—which are themselves hustling and clinking on the conveyors like a million glass chickens.

Also bathing me now is the breath of the place, thickly humid and warm but not (hurray!) as pungent as I feared. There is vinegar in the air, indeed, but not enough to overcome the dull smell of cut cucumbers—which litter the floor everywhere, with water puddling and flowing around them. Water seems to be running, spraying, or dripping from all equipment. Looking below conveyors I see that everybody has soggy footwear and pants wet to the knees.

---

* Reprinted from Steve Turner, *Nightshift in a Pickle Factory* (*Singlejack Books, San Pedro, California* 1980), Copyright © by Steve Turner by permission of the publisher.

3

And I see glass: dense, sparkly scatterings of it blended here and there with the vegetable scrap and water in a horrible stew, thicker around my feet as I slog toward the production office. Can this really be the Great Shiny Kitchen where our nation's canned foods are made? . . .

It's my second night. I'm out of shape for this: stiff back, sore body, desperate knees. But I'm surviving. . . . I share with a worker named Johnson T. the joy of poling the dipper. This task is the factory's answer to a little flaw in the mechanization. Once the cucumbers are on the conveyor, they go mighty fast. But getting them on there is a problem, because they are floating in a ten-foot by four-foot tub of rinsewater. Solution? A basketball-size net on a six-foot pole. Alternating every two hours, Johnson T. and I stand on a wobbly platform beside the tub and dip them out, 20 to 40 pounds per netful, and dump them in the hopper at the end of the conveyor. Dip and dump enough to keep a flow going that will bring—even with all the rejects culled out—four dozen jars' worth every minute through the spray washer to the packing machine, a dandy big robot that cuts off the ends of the pickles, slices and inserts them, two cucumbers into each pint jar. Watching all this shiny automation carry away my laboriously lifted netfuls, I am reminded of the old cartoon of the fancy car with its hood up, and instead of an engine inside it has a cage of squirrels with a treadmill.

Alternating on stints away from the dipper, Johnson T. and I work beside the two sorters, who are assigned to catch and discard rejects as the belt speeds the cucumbers past them. . . .

The sorting job is not as hard as dipping, but just standing there and doing it really gets to the knees. Also it is a total wet pants job: the conveyor has an open-mesh belt, so all the rinsewater from the cucumbers, and the drain-off from the spray washer runs right down on us as we work. A simple splash-guard at the work zone would help a lot and probably a lot of people have asked for one, but that's the sort of thing the management here doesn't install. Sometimes we get cardboard boxes from where the glass is unpacked, flatten them out and hang them from the conveyor rails to deflect the constant shower. They soon sog through. By the end of the shift we are usually too tired to care.

I find solace in the memory of another cannery where I worked years before. They were running a 10-hour day shift and a 12-hour night shift, packing peas. I was stacking the finished product there instead of sorting, and glad for it. Sorters had to search an endless fast moving stream of shelled peas to find—and pinch out—bad ones, gravel, poison belladonnas and other undesirables. They weren't wet all the time like at Brogan's, but they were worse off. Periodically they went pea-happy and began smashing the stock. I haven't eaten canned peas since.

I'm feeling more fit on my third night, which is good because this evening we experience our first High Management Official (HIMO). He appears with a small flotilla of subordinates, all wearing hard hats and no aprons. This makes us feel even sillier with our heads misshapen by the hairnets. I am poling the dipper. Johnson T. is sorting. The line is really rolling. The HIMO peers into the reject tote, grabs out a little cucumber, and holds it up for Johnston T. to see.

"What criteria are you using to discard this pickle?" the front office man asks. (Inside the factory, cucumbers tend to be called pickles whether they are yet or not.)

Yes, the HIMO wants Johnson T. to explain to him the fate of this one of tens of thousands of cucumbers we will handle tonight. Johnson T. immediately understands that this is a military situation. He snaps to attention. "Sir," he shouts, "criteria for pickle discarding, sir." Hands of the other two sorters accelerate desperately in the sudden overload created by the absence of Johnson T's.

"None under four inches, sir," yells Johnson T. "None too fat to go through the measuring ring. None too whopping large, sir, nor the sick nor broken." The HIMO's eyes begin to glaze over. Johnson T. snatches up and brandishes a huge, J-shaped mutant from the passing swarm. "None too curvy, sir," he shouts, "none too bent!"

"This one is more than four inches," hisses the HIMO. He holds it against the length-measure tape on the sidewall of the conveyor, and it is four-and-one-half inches long. Johnson T. gestures silently to the fast mass passage on the belt, inviting HIMO to demonstrate his rare binocular skill in action. The other sorters are keeping careful poker faces but have begun doing exaggerated slumps and acting out other signs of despair.

"Just keep a sharp eye," says the HIMO, returning the reject to the tote as he leaves. Johnson T. salutes his departure with the mutant, and goes back to work. I have had to keep on dipping throughout the exchange, but stop now to applaud. Later I start to laugh from the recollection. By break time I realize that I am finished with my new-guy adjustment. Like most, if not all the others, I am no longer upset about being unable to do the job right at the speed they run the line. . . .

Tonight our crew moves to the big time: we're running the main packing line. But my job—I'm mixing the spices—is mostly removed from the conveyor and is less noisy, less hectic than the rest, though it has its own drawbacks to make up for it. . . .

On my list of things we haven't got that we need, I put stools. Even for jobs such as hand-packing, where the work is perfectly suited to sitting, there are no stools. Besides finding it hateful to be forced to stand still in one place for hours at a time, I have been told that it injures legs and feet and helps cause varicose veins. . . .

I nab the production manager as we are all heading out to go home, and I ask him how come no stools? He tells me that if some workers had stools to sit on, all would want them! It is on the tip of my tongue to tell him— angrily—that out on the production line we are not so dumb as to be unaware of the difference between stationary work and work that requires movement. But I keep my mouth shut, not wanting to get on his list, and merely file a request for further consideration of stools. He promises nothing.

Meanwhile, workers all over the cannery have adopted the use of overturned slop buckets for seats. They're low, so in most jobs you can't work from them, and they are wet, and they have sharp edges on the bottom. But using them beats the alternative, which is nothing, by about 75%. The line bosses warn us that if any HIMOs catch us sitting down we will be disciplined (and the pails will be taken from us), but people simply ignore that advice. I think we all know, on both sides of the issue, that there would be trouble if someone came and kicked us off our buckets. . . .

Another crew boss is short two bodies tonight, so I am sent to work in the zoo. Am I being punished? This is a wild, dimly-lit area of torment at the head of the warehouse, where the product emerges from the pasteurizers to be labelled, boxed and stacked. The main line pasteurizer emits slow but unstoppable waves of jars, in rows of up to 24 wide, which funnel down into a high-speed stream through the labeller to a pair of desperate women who have to get them into boxes.

These are an unmatched pair of people: one tall, sleek and powerful, the other short and compact but very quick. But they are working well together. In fact, they are working harder than anyone else in the cannery, although they are standing still. Their arms make a kind of blur in the poor light. Their bodies from the hips up bend forward and back, forward and back— sometimes in sync, sometimes not—like cammed parts of an engine. Both have adopted pony tails (no hair nets needed out here) to let the air get to their necks. Sweat streams down their faces, drips from their noses and chins. They do not bother to wipe it off. And except where lifted by breasts, their T-shirts are soaked with sweat also. Each has a jar of water (refilled by the forklift drivers) stashed on nearby stacks of boxes, and they grab drinks on the fly whenever they can—which isn't often.

The thing is that in order to keep up with the conveyor these two women have to snatch four jars (two in each hand) every three seconds and fit them into compartmented boxes. If they don't keep up, the oncoming product quickly overwhelms their work table.

So they work with a kind of exuberant intensity—which is the only real alternative to an anger that would force them to quit. They have no time for talk. The tall woman particularly shows the strain. It's in her face, eyes wide and blank, lips pulled back in an unchanging expression like a slight grin (when she goes for break I see her slump by stages as she walks away). The short woman, by contrast, keeps her head down with a frowning face, arms mechanically moving in and out, hands smacking down onto the jar tops with a sharp, persistent sound that I can hear even through the insistent background clatter of the conveyor.

Periodically, though, the frustration of the job gets to them. One or the other will throw back her head and whoop or shriek to vent the pressure of the sustained work speed. And these cries set off a sort of chain reaction: the tail-off-crew—three men stacking all the boxes that the two women fill—tend to echo the women's yells with bellows and shouts of sympathy and shared strain. And the cries of the tail-off crew, in turn, trigger rebel yells or cracked-voice yodels from the forklift drivers who shuttle the pallets of stacked cases into the warehouse.

Listening to this clamor—which echoes in the rafters like sounds in a Monkey House—I sense that I am among people who are on the edge of unbridled action of some sort. And it comes when the two women, after difficulty with a collapsing box-divider insert, fall seriously behind. As the jars swarm in, they suddenly begin to slash through the accumulating pack with their forearms, uttering fierce karate yells as the glass smashes to the floor. They will repeat this performance several times during the shift—with their line boss standing nearby in each instance, afraid even to speak to them. Watching, I get a rush of satisfaction. . . .

The speedup rate set last night is still on: it is the new rate. Our wages, of course, remain the same. . . .

Our line is making an average $4,500 per hour in product value—while our total wages for the same period, including an estimate for supervisors, come to about $100. The sense of a bad ripoff festers in the gap between.

"But you got to count for glass and pickles, and like that," says Motor-mouth.

Hell, give them $2,000 an hour for that, I say, and they still make $25,000 extra from this crew every shift. The slower work on the other lines yields less, but there are three crews minimum working both shifts while the harvest lasts. Take out all the rest of the overhead, there's still a big bundle left for the owners to play with. Our work pays for everything in the end, but it pays us least of all.

There is a short silence. Then Mandrake says, "Ain't that some shit?"

"Cream's gonna rise unless you homogenize," someone says.

We sit there with the sweat cooling, watching the evening come on.

"It's not right, this way of doing things," Alfred says. And I think by this point everyone on the shift would second that, even though there are different opinions about what ought to happen instead. It's just that there isn't anyone among us who doesn't resent how the factory is operated so fast and sloppy, because there's no way to respect what we're doing and what we're making.

In fact, most people here like it best when things don't work right and production goes to hell, and I'm right along with them. And that's a crummy way to waste your working time.

Meaningful Work*

Robert Nozick _____

Often it is claimed that being subordinate in a work scheme adversely affects self-esteem in accordance with a social-psychological law or fundamental generalization such as the following: A long period of being frequently ordered about and under the authority of others, unselected by you, lowers your self-esteem and makes you feel inferior; whereas this is avoided if you play some role in democratically selecting these authorities and in a constant process of advising them, voting on their decisions, and so on.

But members of a symphony orchestra constantly are ordered about by their conductor (often capriciously and arbitrarily and with temper flareups) and are not consulted about the overall interpretation of their works. Yet they retain high self-esteem and do not feel that they are inferior beings. Draftees in armies are constantly ordered about, told how to dress, what to keep in their lockers, and so on, yet they do not come to feel they are inferior beings. Socialist organizers in factories received the same orders and were subject to the same authority as others, yet they did not lose their self-esteem. Persons on the way up organizational ladders spend much time taking orders without coming to feel inferior. In view of the many exceptions to the generalization that "order following in a subordinate position produces low self-esteem" we must consider the possibility that subordinates with low self-esteem begin that way or are forced by their position to face the facts of their existence and to consider upon what their estimate of their own worth and value as a unique person is based, with no easy answers forthcoming. They will be especially hard pressed for an answer if they believe that others who give them orders have a right to do so that can be based only upon some *personal* superiority.

* Reprinted from Robert Nozick, "Meaningful Work," *Anarchy, State, and Utopia,* no. 8 (New York: Basic Books) by permission of the publisher. Copyright © 1974 by Basic Books.

Technology and the Humanization of Work*

Gerald Doppelt _____

There is a paradox at the core of modern economic development. On the one hand, enormous material progress has been made possible since the Industrial Revolution by a series of dramatic, ingenious revolutions in the nature and organization of work—the specialized division of labor, differentiation of functions, mechanization, automation, numerical control, and so forth. On the other hand, during the last few decades, there has been a tremendous upheaval concerning productivity and the very quality of work life. This upheaval is summarized in *Work in America,* a report to the secretary of Health, Education, and Welfare:

Significant numbers of American workers are dissatisfied with the quality of their working lives. Dull, repetitive, seemingly meaningless tasks, offering little challenge or autonomy, are causing discontent among workers at all occupational levels. This is not so much because work itself has greatly changed; indeed, one of the main problems is that work has not changed fast enough to keep up with the rapid and wide-scale changes in worker attitudes, aspirations, and values. A general increase in their educational and economic status has placed many American workers in a position where having an interesting job is now as important as having a job that pays well. Pay is still important: it must support an "adequate" standard of living and be perceived as equitable—but high pay alone will not lead to job (or life) satisfaction.

There have been some responses to the changes in the work-force, but they have been small and slow. As a result, the productivity of the worker is low—as measured

* This paper was presented in a 1981 symposia series on "The Humanities and Business" at National University in San Diego, organized by Ann-Marie Feenberg and funded by the *California Council for the Humanities.* I wish to express my appreciation to Professor Feenberg and the California Council.

by absenteeism, turnover rates, wildcat strikes, sabotage, poor-quality projects, and a reluctance by workers to commit themselves to their work tasks. Moreover, a growing body of research indicates that, as work problems increase, there may be a consequent decline in physical and mental health, family stability, community participation and cohesiveness, and "balanced" sociopolitical attitudes, while there is an increase in drug and alcohol addiction, aggression, and delinquency.[1]

I

This upheaval surrounding workers' dissatisfaction indicates that modern work is no longer experienced *solely* as a financial necessity. Rather, it is increasingly believed that work ought to possess intrinsic interest and rewards. These expectations indicate the extension of liberal-democratic values from social and political life into the workplace. As the general educational and cultural level has risen, more of us expect to exercise responsibility, self-direction, and skill in work life. The individuality and dignity prized in our society increasingly shape the attitudes of workers to their roles in the division of labor.

These liberal-democratic, individualistic aspirations clash with a division of labor, largely hierarchical, undemocratic, and coercive. The following inequalities stand out: (1) Inequalities in decision-making powers concerning what is produced, and under what working conditions; owners and managers primarily make these decisions and give orders, which others must simply carry out. (2) Inequalities in opportunity for autonomy, control, and discretion within one's particular job definition (e.g., managerial perogatives versus unskilled, assembly line work). (3) Inequalities in the interest and challenge of jobs and unequal opportunities to use one's mind and skills. (4) Inequal opportunities to work with others in a cooperative and mutually respectful manner.

Contemporary resistance to this hierarchical division raises my key question: Is our division of labor rational? Does the resistance to it rest on false hopes, or does it contain the promise of a more human conception of labor? Put differently, are we witnessing a catastrophic disintegration of the work-ethic or a potentially healthy redefinition of its meaning?

These questions raise the underlying issue: Are there feasible alternatives to our division of labor that might humanize work? A predominently negative answer prevails in our most influential circles: owners, management, unions, government, academics, and so forth. They claim our hierarchical division of labor is necessary because it provides the inescapable framework of all economic progress.

Let us examine the view that our division of labor is *necessary* in order to determine its meaning and rationality.

II

Is our division of labor necessary in the sense that it has been caused by inexorable laws of nature, operating independently of human choice? Perhaps the emergence of modern hierarchical work patterns is the consequence of large-scale forces we cannot understand and control. In that case, we have no choice but to adjust ourselves to the dictates of moder work organization, much as we adapt to inclement weather.

Undoubtedly large-scale historical phenomenon, such as development of the modern labor process, give rise to some social consequences that no one can foresee or control before the fact. Nonetheless, the hierarchial division of labor is a man-made thing, various aspects of which were intentionally introduced and developed by individuals pursuing their goals. For example, entrepreneurs shifted from home-based to centralized manufacturing to minimize costs of transporting raw materials and finished products and to better control labor force output. Another example: firm owners introduced middle-strata foremen and supervisors because their firms became too large for effective personal, direct control over the labor process and work force. In sum, the modern hierarchical division of labor is not the outcome of uncontrollable historical forces, but rather, the outcome of countless past and present human decisions to introduce or develop modes of work organization for specific ends.

But perhaps these decisions were themselves dictated by existing technology. In that case, there are unavoidable technological imperatives necessitating our current work organization.

But this "technological-determinism" view of the division of labor should be rejected. First, existing technology typically permits a range of possibilities concerning division of required tasks among workers and between various job classifications. Thus, many American job-rotation experiments require no alteration or under-utilization of technology; for example, the utilization of an assembly line technology does not *by itself* dictate either (1) that one particular task on the line must be the exclusive job of any given worker for the entire workday *or* (2) that assembly line work itself must be the exclusive job of any given worker or occupational classification for the entire day. Another example: consider the recent revolutionary development of numerically controlled contouring machine tools: a technology that automates machine tools by transferring the skills of the machinist onto a program or tape, so that any given machine tool can be automatically adapted to make any one of a large range of machine parts simply by inserting a different program into it.[2] Given this technology, certain tasks are required—programming and machine-tending functions. But *nothing* inherent in this technology determines whether or not programming and machine-tending are assigned to different people (management and workers) or to the same people who master both functions. In short, the technology of numerical control dictates only that programming and machine-tending must be done; it does not dictate that there must be programmers, on the one hand, and machine-tenders on the other. The latter was a mangement decision taken in light of its goals.

Second, existing technology does not dictate how decision-making powers and opportunities are divided up. For example, an assembly line technology does dictate that once the pace of the line has been designed or set, individual lineworkers cannot control it. But nothing in this technology dictates who will determine the speed of the line at the outset any more than it dictates how the lines tasks required will be distributed among job classifications. Furthermore, decision making often can be democratically shared in a workplace without affecting technology (e.g., decisions about hiring and firing, grievances, the physical work environment, production goals and so on).[3] Of course, a given technology does require specific knowledge and training. Yet even this does not dictate how such knowledge and expertise will be divided among job definitions or occupations and to whom it will be accessible in the decision-making process. It may or may not be most advantageous to have a division of labor where certain forms of technical knowledge and expertise are monopolized by special employees, who consequently also enjoy relevant decision-making perogatives; in any case, this social division of knowledge and expertise is justified not by technology itself, but on some other basis.

Third, existing technology embodies a range of technical possibilities other than what is physically realized at any moment in the established array of hardware and required methods of production. Every physically embodied technology represents the confluence of various layers of knowledge, techniques, mechanical subsystems, inventions, and so forth. These elements can be altered, restructured, or improved so as to generate alternative technologies. Indeed, technological innovation involves just such a process: decision makers consciously choose to develop and utilize one technology over other more or less feasible alternatives. Thus, at the point numerical control was developed, existing technology also allowed the development of an alternative technology for the automation of machine tools called "record playback." Management decided to utilize numerical control and abandon record playback, but not because of technical feasibility. Rather, the decisive difference between the two technologies concerned the division of labor and control. With record playback, the traditional machinist, with his or her special skills, is still required at the outset in order to make the original magnetic tapes, which subsequently take over his or her work. With numerical control, the tapes can be made without relying on the machinist at any point, and thus the whole process can be controlled by management.

In this manner, existing technology allows a range of technological alternatives that respectively make possible different divisions of labor, among them more or less humane, democratic, and interesting forms of work. *Work in America* and other reports describe firms that successfully transformed their embodied technology in order to humanize and enrich the division of labor.[4] These examples and the above considerations seem to refute the view that there is a fixed "technology" that rigidly determines our hierarchical division of labor.

III

It may be replied that, while technology *by itself* does not dictate the hierarchical division of labor, efficient use of technology requires it. Thus, according to an influential view, the existing hierarchical division of labor is practically necessary. But what is the nature of this "efficiency" that should dictate our way of working? Does efficiency determine the choice of technology, the path of technological innovation, and the hierarchical division of labor? Suppose we think of efficiency or productivity as the ratio of physical to material input, the value produced relative to value used up in its production. Then the choice of technology and division of labor would be dictated by efficiency—the capacity to produce more with less expenditure (of time, energy, money, etc.) than would otherwise be required.

Understanding efficiency in this natural way, it is clear that in our society the choice of technology and work organization is not primarily dictated by efficiency. A simple example brings my point home.[5] Imagine that a given technology and division of labor, A, makes it possible for an average worker to produce ten units of X in a workday, but also gives workers the power to set the pace of their work. A second technology and division of labor, B, only makes it possible for an average worker to produce eight units of X in the same workday, but gives management power to set the pace of the work. Strictly speaking, A is more efficient than B, but B is the typical choice of management in our society, for the obvious reason that B allows management to establish the pace of work and thus control the absolute size of output at an unvarying and reliable rate. Under method A, while each worker could produce ten units of X a day, he or she may only produce seven units a day; while under B, it is guaranteed that he will typically produce eight units a day. Assuming that A and B involve the *same* costs or purchased inputs, B results in greater output and profitability than A, even though A is more efficient.

This example shows that maximal profitability, not pure efficiency, motivates the choice of technology and work organization. In some cases, the most efficient method will also be the most profitable, because it also allows management as much or more control over the pace of work as in less efficient alternatives. Nonetheless, the choice in our society to develop technological innovations such as the assembly line or numerical control are not made on grounds of pure efficiency, in the above sense. Rather, these forms of technology allow a new measure of hierarchy in the division of labor that gives management new modes of control over the pace and quality of work; it thereby increases their power to maximize output and profits.

Abstractly there is nothing wrong with maximizing output or profits. In this vein, we might once again redefine "efficiency" to overcome the problem raised above: the most efficient technology and division of labor is, all things considered (workers' motivation, performance, possibility of management control, and so on), *whichever* one of the feasible alternatives *in fact* maximizes output, given a fixed material input. On this new definition, in our above example, method B—the one typically chosen in our society—does turn out to be more efficient than method A. For, given the same material inputs, B in fact reliably yields a greater output and profit than A. This is what many persons mean when they defend our division of labor and technology as dictated by the imperative of maximal efficiency.

To evaluate this claim, we need to examine the notion of efficiency as what maximizes output per given unit of material input. For this to be a usable measure of efficiency, we need some way of determining what counts as output and inputs. In our society, where the main goal of firms is profit, the measure of efficiency, inputs, and output is reduced to a matter of money; the most efficient method is the one that maximizes the output of marketable commodities relative to a given unit of *purchased* inputs or monetary costs to the firm. Thus, a technology and division of labor, B, that yields the same marketable output for smaller per-unit costs or expenditures to the firm, than some alternative, A, is the more efficient.

Now we approach the heart of the upheaval surrounding workers' resistance to our existing hierarchical division of labor. That division and technology may well maximize output while minimizing the firm costs—at least, its existence is largely due to managements' belief that it satisfies the imperative of efficiency—but can the costs of this way of working be identified with the monetary costs to the firm. Can input simply be reduced to employer expenditure? Consider our above example where some method of working, B, (e.g., the assembly line, or numerical control) is chosen over an alternative, A, because it allows management to control and indeed maximize the pace of work without incurring additional expenditures. From the standpoint of management, more output results from the same input. But B may involve greater "wear and tear" on the bodies and minds of the workers; B may require them to work in a way that is harder, more tedious, and more frustrating. Indeed, B may involve greater health risks and dangers for workers than A. Yet none of these inputs and costs are immediately represented as employer costs, although they constitute great costs to individual workers, their families, and society both in monetary and human terms.

Thus, we can see that the established conception of efficiency ignores all costs not translatable into the firms' expenditures. The contemporary upheaval concerning work questions this conception of efficiency. The revolt against work signaled by strikes, large rates of worker turnover and absenteeism, declining productivity represents a growing attitude on the part of workers; they are less willing to assume the personal costs of a hierarchial division of labor and technology that may otherwise maximize profit, economic growth, or even their wages. The penetration of liberal-democratic culture into the world of work has raised working people's expectations, as well as their awareness of the hidden price they pay for dehumanizing working conditions.

Work in America argues that dehumanizing work takes a serious toll on the health and well-being of the working public, which in turn contributes to our most ominous social problems—crime, alcoholism, delinquency, welfare-dependency, escalating health costs, unstable family life, and political alien-ation.[6] These social costs are costs in two senses. First, they require a tremendous expenditure in the form of tax payments by the public sector for social welfare, crime control, subsidized health care, alcoholism, and social programs. Such social problems also constitute public costs because they threaten social and cultural disintegration and undermine the quality of life.

The human costs of a hierarchial division of labor to working people have affected employers costs also. Absenteeism, turnover, sabotage, apathy, slow-downs, strikes, shutdowns, shop-floor limits on productivity, cost the firm a pretty penny. This suggests that job enrichment and participatory management may lower costs and heighten sagging productivity.

Nevertheless, humanization of work and maximazation of output and profits (or even maximazation of wages) remain *distinct, independent* goals; as such they frequently conflict, even though in some circumstances one may serve or coexist with the other. This basic situation explains why most employers and managers have not "bought" the argument for humanization advanced in *Work In America.*

On the one hand, improving the quality of work life does generally raise the morale and productivity of workers—at least in the short-run. On the other hand, such attempts can be a very costly and risky venture for capital. They often involve large outlays of initial capital for retooling, retraining, absorbing the losses of an initial transition period, and so forth. These experiments may generate resistance from middle-management and technicians who have a stake in the existing division of labor. Beyond these potential costs and risks, experiments in the humanization of work may eventually generate expectations in workers for additional changes; thus, owners and managers often perceive these experiments as possibly unleashing a challenge to their most basic managerial perogatives and goals.

Despite widespread dissatisfaction, there is presently no major group that challenges the established division of labor or is pursuing alternatives. I have suggested why management is not interested, but we must frankly admit that unions, political parties, and other organizations are not any more interested. Thus, the costs of dehumanizing work are still primarily experienced by individuals as personal fates and local conditions. If they are less and less willing to bear these costs, the democratic public's task of acting on behalf of an alternative, more human form of work has still to be invented!

Work and Self-Respect*

Diana T. Meyers _____

Meaningful Work and Self-Respect

To understand what makes work meaningful, it is necessary to ask what makes life worthwhile. But the latter question seems to have almost as many answers as there are people. For one person, it's becoming an astronaut; for another, it's caring for a child; for another, it's helping to alleviate world hunger; for still another, it's composing a popular song. Since this list could go on indefinitely, it might seem futile to seek a single, comprehensive account of what makes life worthwhile. But the concept of self-respect provides a unifying theme.

Despite the remarkable diversity of their pursuits, people agree that self-respect helps to give life value. As John Rawls puts it, "Without it (self-respect), nothing may seem worth doing, or if some things have value for us, we lack the will to strive for them."[7]Self-respect protects people from despair while it enhances their resolve to carry out their plans and intensifies their satisfaction in fulfilling these plans. In view of this multiple function, the prevailing consensus that self-respect is desirable comes as no surprise. Still it is not at all obvious how self-respect is related to the myriad occupations that people engage in.

A person who has self-respect is able to lead a more rewarding life than a person who is burdened by self-contempt. But how do people gain self-respect? Part of the explanation lies in our upbringing. Attentive, supportive parenting fosters self-respect. Yet since we have no control over this childhood experience, it is important to consider how as adults we can build upon this early care or, if necessary, overcome the lack of it. In this essay, I shall argue that personal integrity is necessary for self-respect and that rights can promote self-respect by allowing for personal integrity. Applying these results to the work world, I shall urge that employers ought to recognize certain work-related rights. For the right to employment, the right to equal opportunity, and the right to participate in job-related decisions encourage personal integrity. In so doing, these rights give persons the chance to make their work meaningful.

Personal Integrity and Self-Respect

Self-respect appears to be a particularly elusive good. Like happiness, it is not the kind of thing that one can will into existence. Each person chooses to act in this way or that, to associate with this acquaintance or that, to strive for this virtue or that—in sum, to live a certain kind of life. Along the way, self-respect or self-contempt may accrue. There is no formula guaranteed to bring about one or the other. Still, since it is hardly accidental that some people have self-respect, we must consider how self-respect is gained.

To have personal integrity, a person must have stable beliefs and feelings that he or she expresses in practice. Personal integrity contrasts both with fickleness and with hyprocrisy. Lacking firm convictions and abiding affections, the chameleonlike person tailors his or her views to fit changing circumstances. And though the hypocrite has lasting convictions and emotional bonds, this individual belies them in his or her conduct. Because of their respective failings, neither the chameleon nor the hypocrite can have self-respect.

A self-respecting person reflexively affirms the value of being a unique individual, that is, of having a distinctive mix of characteristics. Among them are the person's beliefs and feelings. Though Susan may share many convictions with others, she combines them in her own way. Like her friend James, Susan believes that more women should seek jobs in the construction industry; however, unlike James, Susan is fond of Linda. To respect herself, then, Susan must have beliefs and affections that taken together differentiate her from other individuals, and she must act in a manner that affirms the worth of this package.

Someone might object that because stable beliefs and feelings obstruct growth and improvement, they are inimical to self-respect. A self-respecting person must be free to develop his or her potential, and, to be free in the requisite way, a person must be open and flexible. Strong convictions and passions can freeze the self in foolish or outdated modes.

This objection confuses stability with rigidity and fanaticism. Saying that a self-respecting person's beliefs and feelings must be stable is not equivalent to saying that once formed they must never change. If Linda stops reciprocating Susan's friendship, Susan's warm feelings for Linda will gradually disappear, and rightfully so. Stability is not immutability. But if Susan never felt any ongoing affection for Linda, her friendship was not genuine in the first place, and stability could not be an issue.

If a person's beliefs and feelings shift constantly, the person can still approve or disapprove of these fleeting attitudes. However, momentary self-satisfaction is not self-respect. Quite the contrary, self-respect is a steady self-acceptance that endures through occasional self-blame, as well as occasional self-congratulation. This foundational valuation would not be possible if personal characteristics all varied wildly. For only if the main lineaments of a person's character are stable can continuing acceptance (or continuing rejection) of the self be warranted. While the scope of a self-respecting person's convictions and affections could be extremely narrow—it could be limited to dedication to a single cause or attachment to a single person—no one could have self-respect without at least one enduring belief or feeling. After all, self-respect requires a self to respect. An individual devoid of convictions and affections may be an experiencer but is not a self.

It is important to recognize that a self-respecting person's conduct need not be predetermined and routinized. A person might believe that in some areas it is better not to form judgments, but, instead, to feel one's way and cope intuitively. However, this allowance for spontaneity does not license the hypocrite's wiles. The hypocrite has lasting beliefs and feelings, but does not hew to them in action. In order to curry favor with others, the hypocrite pretends to share their views; thus betraying the ones he or she really holds. This self-suppression prevents hypocrites from respecting themselves.

Frequently when a person silences beliefs or feelings, the reason is self-doubt. But a person can suppress beliefs or feelings in order to shield them from unsympathetic or even cruel audiences. John, who is gay, may deny these inclinations because he is ashamed of them and does not want to become the target of what he regards as others' justified disdain. Or he may deny them because he cherishes them and does not want them to be eroded by what he regards as others' unjustified disdain. In the former case, it is clear that John suffers from self-contempt. In the latter case, John's strategy may effectively preserve his integrity despite widespread hostility to his predilections. Provided that John is part of a supportive community in which he is free to discuss and act on his sexual preferences, his selective self-censorship may well help him to retain his self-respect. Unrelieved self-censorship, however, would be an entirely different matter.

We have seen that a person who has no stable beliefs and feelings cannot have self-respect because this individual lacks the kind of self that can be respected. The trouble with the person who has stable beliefs and feelings but relentlessly supresses them is that this individual cannot know himself or herself well enough to have self-respect. Without self-knowledge, a person's respect would be directed at an imagined self rather than at the real self.

Consequently, self-respect would be illusory. It would be like falling in love with a character in a movie, but mistakenly believing it is the actor whom you love. Since self-knowledge is necessary for self-respect, the conditions under which self-knowledge is possible must be indicated.

Introspection alone is not sufficient for self-knowledge. Suppose Ann prides herself on being, at heart, an acute social critic and a steadfast supporter of oppressed minorities. Yet suppose also that Ann chooses never to reveal any of her insights to anyone else and deliberately hides her antagonism to racism. She has reason to doubt her self-concept. People discover who they are in part by observing themselves in action. To form a self-concept without the benefit of this testing ground is to run the risk of substituting a fictional self for the real one.

Both aspects of personal integrity—enduring convictions and affections and the expression of these beliefs and feelings in conduct—are inextricable from self-respect. Accordingly, self-respect is a highly individual good. Since no two persons have identical convictions and affections, no two persons can maintain their integrity and gain self-respect by following the same life plan. This explains why there can be no universal program for achieving self-respect and also why the private good of self-respect is often linked with the public good of liberty.

Self-Respect and Rights

Human rights are commonly characterized as rights that all persons have simply in virtue of being human. The idea is that by itself humanity is a dignified station deserving of respect. Human rights articulate a set of moral requirements that specify the forms of respect humanity is owed. People have a right to life because of their capacities as human beings, not because of their personal talents or accomplishments. To respect a person's human rights, then, is to respect that person as a person.

Since compliance with a person's rights is obligatory regardless of special merits, rights may seem irrelevant to self-respect. As I have emphasized, self-respect presupposes intimate knowledge of the self and honors the unique self. We do not respect ourselves for being members of the human species, but rather for our distinctive qualities and achievements.[8] Though it is difficult for a person to maintain self-respect if everyone else despises him or her, the fact that others accord a person his or her dignity as a human being cannot secure self-respect. What, then, is the contribution fundamental rights make to self-respect?

Rights give right-holders prerogatives in regard to specified benefits. A person who has a property right in a piece of land may use the land as he or she pleases, and a person who has a right to free speech may voice whatever ideas he or she chooses. Although right-holders are forbidden to violate others' rights while exercising their own, rights provide the persons who possess them with options. Even rights that do not explicitly confer liberties, such as the right to medical care or to decent housing, nonetheless afford persons a measure of discretion. Right-holders may avail themselves of existing rights-implementing facilities. They may demand improved programs to deliver the objects of their rights, or they may decide not to take advantage of their rights at all.

The prerogatives rights afford are the key to the way rights support self-respect. We have seen that personal integrity is necessary for self-respect and that personal integrity requires that individuals form lasting convictions and emotional ties that they act on. But without freedom, persons are likely to adopt the views and attitudes the authorities prescribe. Moreover, if they have nonconformist ideas, they will be forced to hide them or risk penalties. Only when people are free to discover themselves and to express their distinctive personalities can personal integrity flourish. Because every right secures a measure of such freedom, each right serves to foster self-respect.

It might be objected that the superabundant freedom that rights grant is detrimental to self-respect. When people are confronted by an unlimited array of possibilities, they are apt to be uncertain and distraught about which direction to take. People need self-confidence before they can use their freedom to secure personal integrity. For self-confidence gives people the courage to express themselves. But to have self-confidence, it could be urged, people need to know their social role and what society expects of them. A person's secure knowledge that he or she belongs in an assigned social role and shares socially condoned values reinforces this person's self-confidence. Once this base of self-assurance is established, a person can begin to form and carry out his or her own ideas and feelings. Without this base, confusion and anxiety will preclude personal integrity as well as self-respect.

Undeniably, self-confidence is necessary for personal integrity. Nevertheless, funneling people into predetermined social roles and imposing values on them is neither the only nor the best way to build self-confidence. Child-rearing methods emphasizing delight in diversity, familiarity with a common heritage, and emotional openness in a supportive atmosphere nurture self-confidence. Also, associations of adults whose talents and interests overlap help to sustain this sense of personal worth.[9] In contrast, enforced social roles and values expand the self-confidence of some at the expense of the personal integrity of others. For example, Jane, who embraces the conventional feminine stereotype, may find it gratifying to know that society applauds her activities as a housewife and mother. But social ridicule may compel Brian, who would prefer a life as a homemaker and father, to play the traditional masculine role of provider. Rigid social attitudes rend Brian's personal integrity, and social tolerance would not necessarily dissolve Jane's self-confidence.

The freedom human rights afford does not present people with so bewildering a selection of options that self-confidence is inevitably destroyed. First, each person's rights are limited by others' rights. Though some rights may be exercised competitively, everyone has rights that prohibit, among other things, assault, deception, and coercion. Since rights do not authorize persons to overturn these constraints, rights themselves set ground rules that narrow right-holders' prerogatives. Furthermore, to the extent that parents and teachers give children practice at imagining and evaluating options, adults become more adept choosers. They become accustomed to deciding what to believe and whom to associate with, and they automatically consult their own convictions and feelings in deciding how to act. The worry and frustration many people suffer when faced with free choice in strange situations can be alleviated through education.

Widespread agreement about the importance of rights that allow for individuality goes hand in hand with respect for dissent and idiosyncrasy. Accordingly, conduct based on self-generated beliefs and feelings is not as likely to meet with reflex condemnation in a society concerned with insuring human rights. Insofar as self-confidence depends on popular acceptance, then, a greater variety of people will be able to enjoy this good if their rights are firmly established. Both by protecting self-confidence and by guaranteeing freedom, rights promote personal integrity and, along with it, self-respect.

Rights and Meaningful Work

In authorizing persons to exercise a range of prerogatives, rights invite right-holders to act in accordance with their settled beliefs and feelings. Unlike duties, which impose requirements, rights issue permissions. Each of these permissions defines an arena in which individuals may set personal objectives and standards and seek to fulfill them. To the extent that right-holders grasp these opportunities and succeed in projecting their values and inclinations, they gain personal integrity and strengthen their self-respect. Though rights cannot endow persons with self-respect—no social mechanism can—denial of persons' rights can crush self-respect. For this reason, it is important to consider how rights support self-respect in major areas of life. Since work consumes a large part of most people's lives, it is especially urgent to determine how rights figure in work.

The concept of work is an evolving one. Work is traditionally associated with onerous labor, and people work mainly in order to earn a living. Nevertheless, history reveals a broadening range of activities that count as

work. During the Middle Ages, workers were sharply differentiated from the
nobility with their stations in life as well as from the clergy with their callings
to God's service. Workers performed physical, often dirty tasks, while the
nobility wielded political power and patronized the arts, and the clergy studied
and prayed. Vestiges of these divisions persist; however, with the democra-
tization of political, intellectual, and religious pursuits came an expanded
concept of work. Today, government officials, teachers, and spiritual leaders
all work alongside servants, factory workers, and farm hands. The category
of work thus includes any socially useful occupation.

Accompanying this enlargement of the concept of work has been a
humanization of the purposes work is thought to serve. As we have seen, a
variety of personally rewarding occupations is now considered to be work.
Also, unionization and labor law have provided greater job security and better
salaries for many employees, while public education has afforded many people
a more egalitarian perspective on life. As a result, many people are not
content to devote most of their time merely to earning a wage, and many
workers have begun to demand more fulfilling work arrangements. Still, the
problem of meaningful work has not been solved. Though meaningful work
has become a widely discussed issue, many people remain unemployed or
stuck in tedious jobs. I shall argue, however, that full implementation of
three rights would make the work world much more conducive to self-respect.

The first difficulty a person encounters vis-a-vis work is finding employment.
In our society, gainful employment is a badge of respectability; however,
since World War II the official unemployment rate has never been lower
than 2.8 percent and has ranged as high as 10.6 percent. Moreover, these
government statistics do not count as "unemployed" those individuals who
are unemployed because they have given up looking for jobs or have never
wanted jobs. This distinction—the distinction between an unwilling, defeated
dropout from the job market and a willing, happy dependent of another
person or the state—is crucial to the issue of self-respect. For a willing
dependent does not need employment to respect himself or herself, but
enforced unemployment is a direct threat to an unwilling dropout's personal
integrity. The latter individual accepts conventional economic values, like effort
and self-sufficiency. But a surplus of job candidates combines with rigidity
in the economic sphere to prevent him or her from acting on these beliefs.
Structural unemployment compels its victims to jettison their values or sacrifice
their self-respect.

The right to employment is primarily a right to a fairly remunerated
position. However, in a society where unemployment is chronic, it is important
to see that this right implies a right to be recognized as a member of the
work force. As such, it provides right-holders with two kinds of leverage.
First, this right entitles persons to the training they need in order to find a

niche in the job market. Second, it justifies persons in demanding innovation in patterns of job and income distribution, such as part-time positions that pay decent wages and provide essential health and retirement benefits. Thus, the right to employment denies that a class of permanently jobless, though able people is inevitable, and it authorizes right-holders who have been excluded from the job market to stand up for their values.[10]

The standard argument against the right to employment is that society cannot afford it: Training programs are costly; reliance on part-time labor is only feasible when it can be bought cheap; the economy would falter because people would not strive to get ahead if jobs were guaranteed. The economic issues raised by this objection are too complex for adequate treatment here. Nevertheless, it should be said that it is an open question whether the proposed programs would be prohibitively expensive. In their support, it can be said that savings on welfare and increased productivity would help to offset these costs. Moreover, trimming the military budget could release funds to implement the right to employment. Finally, it must be stressed that the right to employment would not eliminate competition for jobs. Though everyone would be assured of some job, candidates would compete for the more interesting and better paying positions. Accordingly, there is no reason to suppose that the right to employment would weaken the incentive to work.

At this point, the problem of how to distribute the more desirable positions arises. The right to equal opportunity comes into play in education preparatory to work, in the search for employment, and in consideration for promotion and raises. At each of these stages, this right guarantees that no one's opportunities will be limited by discrimination on grounds of race, creed, sex, or other irrelevant characteristics. In other words, this right requires that the best qualified applicant be chosen for each available opening.

An obvious way in which the right to equal opportunity bears on self-respect is that this right shields persons from arbitrary and humiliating rejections. Victims of discrimination may perceive that they are not being judged fairly, yet it is difficult to avoid succumbing to self-doubt when one's endeavors meet with repeated failure. The right to equal opportunity removes this source of self-contempt. Moreover, in assuring all candidates that their credentials will be reviewed impartially and taken seriously, this right implicitly affirms that self-respect properly hinges on a person's effort and attainment, not on the accidents of one's birth. In effect, this right calls on individuals to assess their abilities, envisage a suitable career, and strive to bring it about. The right to equal opportunity releases people from tradition-bound assumptions about the social niches befitting them and offers them the chance to work at jobs of their own choosing, if not their own design. Thus, a notable function of the right to equal opportunity is to guarantee the possibility of self-expression in a person's initial choice of an occupation.

Now it might be objected that self-respecting persons need not regard their jobs as reflections of their selves. Persons can gain self-respect from performing a socially designated task well. Perhaps, insisting that one's work match one's personality is evidence of self-indulgence, not self-respect, for no viable economy can accommodate such adamant individualism. Whatever the merits of equal opportunity, the objection concludes, workers must accede to the time-honored compromises and strictures of the work world.

Of course, no right can promise that everyone's dreams will come true. Mature adults modulate their aspirations and expectations in light of a realistic appraisal of what is possible. Graceless weaklings do not yearn to be ballerinas; they turn to other enterprises. Nevertheless, if prejudice forces the members of one social group to discard otherwise sensible career plans, while many individuals who do not belong to discriminated against groups can pursue the careers they prefer, personal integrity in employment goals becomes a privilege of the advantaged class. Notoriously, there was never any good reason to bar the great black pitcher Satchel Paige from major league baseball. The right to equal opportunity prevents maldistribution of a central component of self-respect, namely, personal integrity in career direction.

Other rights protect personal integrity on the job. Prominent among them is the right to participate in job-related decisions. This is a right that is sometimes dismissed out of hand because it seems to conflict with the rights of business owners to delegate authority wihtin their firms as they think best.[11] However, there are various ways to implement this right, and some of them do not usurp property owners' legitimate prerogatives. Moreover, all of these ways support personal integrity in the workplace.

First, it is important to recognize that business owners are not entitled to wield absolute authority over workers during the workday. When laws or union contracts provide for such employee rights as the right to safe working conditions, rest periods, and job security, owners' rights are thereby eroded. Yet since the compelling needs of employees plainly justify many of these arrangements, property rights must yield to them. Likewise, the right to participate in job-related decisions can be instituted in a manner that restricts but does not extinguish owners rights. For example, the right to participate in job-related decisions could be interpreted as requiring procedures for consulting with all concerned employees and a reorganization of work activities. Consultation involves soliciting and paying attention to employees' views before making decisions. Reorganization may involve breaking up assembly lines, eliminating regimented, mass-production formats in offices, and replacing them with work groups that are responsible for handling particular projects. Experience has shown that such reforms can improve efficiency.[12] Also, it is clear that these programs do not preempt owners' rights.

Actually to democratize the workplace would be to grant employees the power to control, through their ballots, a firm's future course. Consultation procedures and reorganized work schedules do not redistribute economic power in so far-reaching a fashion and, therefore, are not tantamount to economic democracy. Nevertheless, a right exacting these reforms could have a marked impact on employees' self-respect since both afford opportunities for constructive self-expression at the workplace.[13] In discussions with supervisors and in cooperation with a self-contained work unit, individuals would be encouraged to reflect on their occupations and to suggest changes. Workers' proposals must pass tests of practicality, but nothing would prevent workers from putting forth sound suggestions based on their own values and feelings. Insofar as allowance for employees' personal integrity can be incorporated into the workplace, self-respect can be promoted in this context. Clearly the right to participate in job-related decisions serves this purpose.

Thinking about their lives, many people sharply divide work from leisure. At work they maintain an appropriate facade, but at home they can be themselves. Needless to say no one is equally at ease with loved ones and comparative strangers, and people will always have to adapt themselves to public situations and be more guarded in this sphere. Still, none of this entails that the good of personal integrity must be confined to the private domain. The right to equal opportunity and to participate in job-related decisions provide employees with the moral leverage they need to break down this compartmentalization of life's reward. In authorizing employees to bring their convictions and feelings to bear on their occupations, these rights respect the unity and independence of persons. In recognizing the autonomy of employees, these rights make work a source of self-respect and, as such, a site of personal meaning.

Alienation and Work

Kai Nielsen _____

Many people are skeptical about moral judgments. They believe no one can really show that something is good or bad, right or wrong. However, a careful look at the workplace will tell us why that skeptical view is problematic.

There is something very paradoxical about ethical skepticism in the face of what we know about our lives. We have experienced destructive wars that achieved no morally acceptable end. The life work of many is useless, frustrating, and not under their own control; still, as bad as their jobs are, given the alternatives, they are fortunate to have them, and hence cling to them—that is the depth of their alienated condition. We see pollution and the destruction of our environment and racism and sexism as pervasive features of our lives, and in the face of all this, we feel powerless.

Are there not certain conditions—those just mentioned—that are plainly wrong and those—their opposites—that are plainly right? It seems to me that we have good reasons for saying that there are some things—things that are a part of the very fiber of our social lives—that are plainly evil.

What are these ills that are so pervasive and so alienating in our society? I believe, if we think concretely and nonevasively about work and the conditions surrounding it, we'll see that there are deep evils in our world that are by no means inevitable or necessary. What I am saying here needs to be concretized and exemplified. Following is an extreme case, but a true one:

When black school children in South Boston were bused into white schools, they were violently assaulted. They saw, as their buses passed through white neighborhoods, black mannequins hung in effigy, white power signs, and, on one school wall, a sign announcing in four-foot-high letters, "Hitler was Right." Inside the school, even with police protection, they were violently attacked by antibusing gangs. It was painfully clear that police sympathies lay with the whites. Even a few teachers were viciously prejudiced. Ask yourself what happens to a young child under such an assault. What must be the effect of such unprovoked hatred on the personality and self-respect of a child? Such actions can have no justification. We know that something is happening here that is morally intolerable.

Like racism, sexism is often grossly obvious and widespread. The hiring and treatment of secretaries is sometimes a dramatic case in point. To be told: "We usually don't hire married girls. We want young, pretty, available girls around the office" is to be evaluated on qualities irrelevant to the position for which you are interviewing. If obtaining a job and advancing within a company means tolerating sexual harassment, then you are being treated merely as an object. Again we have human conditions that are morally intolerable, though often tolerated in our society.

Then there is the plight of the elderly, who because unproductive are expendable. In the extreme, although not statistically insignificant, cases, you will find elderly people living in dilapidated residential hotels with two-burner hot plates and less than minimal food, heat, and hot water. They are isolated, lonely, and fear eviction. Again, we have a widely tolerated but still morally intolerable situation.

People complain about welfare "bums," but there are people in North America and Europe who try but are not able to find work. (In 1983, 35 million people were out of work in the capitalist societies of the West.) Many of the habitually unemployed are caught in an endless cycle of poverty and ignorance. Most come from uneducated and poverty-stricken backgrounds. Deprived of a decent education, they're thrown into the work force at a very young age, with little experience and no training. Because of their lack of education, they're job prospects are very limited, and without a job that pays well, that education may never be achieved. Such people are caught in an endless cycle of poverty that saps the will, undermines dignity, and destroys their lives and the lives of their children. In this way a relatively permanent class of unemployables is created. Again we have a situation of the morally intolerable being routinely tolerated.

Finally, let us look at consumerism and work. Eleanor Langer, in her expose of life inside the New York Telephone Company, points out one very strong, largely socially imposed, motivation for those women working within the company in alienating and emotionally exhausting circumstances.[14] Through social manipulation, they become trapped by their love of objects. Their work affords them no satisfaction or any basis for developing self-respect. A telltale showing of this was in their endless purchasing of new and different wigs. So, with incessant company encouragement, they try to find their identities in consumerism. Theirs is an endless quest for objects. We have—to make a general statement—a pervasive consciousness industry, combined with frustrating conditions at work and in our families, pushing us into largely senseless patterns of consumption. We, in this example, have people being manipulated in a way that is morally unacceptable.[15]

Let us turn to our reflection on work. Work is something in our societies that is for many of us deeply unsatisfying, debilitating, dehumanizing, or, as the catch phrase has it, alienating—though still usually preferable to welfare. As Albert Camus put it, "Without work all life goes rotten." But it is equally plain, as he knew, that when work is soulless—as in an assembly line, a typing pool—"life stifles and dies."To make our lives satisfying, we must have meaningful work. Again we have something that is plainly evil.[16]

Why are these things I have mentioned so deeply embedded and pervasive in our social and working lives, and why are they evil? They are evil because they cause people to suffer needlessly; they undermine our self-respect and autonomy. People are simply used, treated as a means, manipulated, and deceived; their hopes for themselves and their children are destroyed. Their health (both physical and mental) is damaged, and they are exploited by their employers. They have nothing even remotely like equal chances in life.

As study after study shows, there is considerable dissatisfaction of workers with the work in our societies.[17] It is not that people do not want to work at all; it is the particular work they do under conditions of supervision and control, that is so dissatisfying. Yet even when work affords them little satisfaction, most people would prefer to work, as a lesser evil, rather than retirement. They want to continue working not because they enjoy it but, as one worker put it, "only to fill time."[18] A task force report to the secretary of Health, Education and Welfare, *Work in America,* summarized a central conclusion of over a hundred studies done over a period of twenty years: "Workers want most . . . to become masters of their immediate environment and to feel that their work and they themselves are important. . . ."[19] These feelings are crucial elements in self-respect. Yet modern working conditions militate against their fulfillment. Work is very often authoritarian. The very idea of democracy in the workplace is often thought an outrage. Yet the fact is that work typically takes place under close supervision and dictation in an authoritarian atmosphere not unlike the military.[20]

People learn to do routine and fragmented tasks, often having little conception of the overall process. However, when management introduces labor-saving machines—machines that under socioeconomic circumstances could be liberating to workers—the workers must resist their adoption in order to keep their wretched jobs. As Adam Smith recognized before Karl Marx, work under such conditions is a thoroughly dehumanizing experience that "so stunts our understanding and our sensibilities that we generally, if we are formed under such employment, become as stupid and ignorant as it is possible for a human creature to become."[21] Our very human capacities are stunted, and we suffer self-estrangement and alienation.

Our alienation is deepened because we feel powerless to change our situation, to alter the fact that we must sell ourselves in order to work at all. (Recall that while in the middle of the nineteenth century, less than half of all employed people were wage and salary workers. By 1970 only 9 percent were not salaried employees—a drop from 18 percent in 1950. The idea that most of us, if we chose to take the risk, could work for ourselves is pure illusion.[22]

Work is often perceived as meaningless because it contributes very little to our well-being. It certainly does not give us a sense of pride to make products designed to become obsolete. Often workers know they are making junk, sometimes needlessly polluting junk, yet they must continue to make it anyway. They also very frequently make things that are a waste of our natural resources and energy and may even be harmful, for example, electric toothbrushes, snowmobiles (except for very limited purposes), food additives, and valium (in many instances).

Suppose a salesperson sells insurance to someone who doesn't need it or persuades someone to buy a product they don't need to replace a product that is good for them. Or suppose you are a secretary who types documents that teach companies how to avoid taxation or pollution controls. Suppose you are an accountant paid to "doctor" a firm's books. How can such pursuits be considered meaningful work and how could it not undermine your self-respect?

In our societies, workers have very little input into decisions about what is to be produced and how it is to be produced; therefore, a genuine work community never develops, where workers "come together to determine through their social interaction the important decisions governing production."[23] Under such circumstances work becomes drudgery, an instrument for gaining money and material security.

To work under such conditions is alienating and self-estranging. This state is often masked in various forms of self-deception: dissatisfaction with ourselves and with the world. And with this dissatisfaction come feelings of powerlessness, senselessness, and isolation. But alienation has an objective sense as well. Alienation occurs, as Herbert Gintis puts it, "when the structure of society denies you access to life-giving and personally rewarding activities and relationships."[24] When elements in your personal and social life become meaningless, fragmented, out of reach, you begin to feel, as existentialists have stressed, the absurdity and the pointlessness of your life. When this is your situation, you are alienated, though such alienation can take more disguised, less self-conscious forms.

The dibilitating effects of many workers jobs carry over into their personal lives. Alcoholism and drug addiction are very high among many workers. Also, work in which one has little control or responsibility engenders a general passivity. "The worker who is denied participation and control over the work situation is unlikely to be able to participate effectively in community or national decision making, even if there are formal opportunities to do so."[25] Without democracy in the workplace, we are unlikely to achieve meaningful democracy in community affairs.[26] What we too often see are alienated, passive human beings who feel utterly powerless before forces they can neither control nor understand.

Their nonpassivity, like the return of the repressed, comes out in authoritarian behavior at home, a preoccupation with sex—for males a preoccupation with how many women they can seduce—and as is seen on television, a preoccupation with sex and violence. The politically impotent, the supervised and drilled male, can at least be boss in his own bed and home if not at work. In the extreme cases, this often leads to spouse and child abuse. Alienation at work creates deep alienation throughout one's life, destroying the possibility for healthy emotional development.[27] "To be alienated is to be separated in concrete and specific ways from 'things' important to well-being," principally social roles that involve respectful collaboration with others.[28] Whether there are these social roles that are essential for giving sense to one's life depends on the social structures in which one lives. "Alienation arises when the social criteria determining the structure and development of important social roles are *essentially* independent of individual needs.[29] Work relationships are social relationships, and in our society their authoritarian structures dull our sensibilities, intellectual capacities, initiative, creativity, and autonomy.

I have discussed conditions of life in the workplace that, contrary to moral skepticism, are obvious moral evils. Indeed, if any theory were to imply that these conditions were not evil, I would believe the theory to be plainly mistaken.

Notes

1. *Work in America: Report of a Special Task Force to the Secretary of Health, Education, and Welfare* (Cambridge, Mass.: MIT Press, 1973), XV-XVI.

2. This example is taken from David Noble, "Social Choice in Machine Design: The Case of Automatically Controlled Machine Tools and a Challenge for Labor," *Politics and Society,* vol. 8, nos. 3–4 (1978), 313–49.

3. For examples of such democratic decision making in the workplace, see Daniel Zwerdling, *Workplace Democracy* (New York: Harper Row, 1980).

4. *Work In America,* 93–121.

5.   This example is taken from Richard Edwards, "Social Relations of Production at the Point of Production," *Work and Labor: A Special Issue of the Insurgent Sociologist,* vol. 7, nos. 2 & 3 (Fall 1978), 114–15.

6.   *Work in America,* 76–93. The authors develop a conception of "social efficiency" to replace the narrower concept of "industrial efficiency" in our society (pp. 23–28).

7.   John Rawls, *A Theory of Justice* (Cambridge, Mass.: Harvard University Press, 1971), 440 (parenthetical material mine).

8.   For a related view, see Robert Nozick, *Anarchy, State, and Utopia* (New York: Basic Books, 1974), 243.

9.   Rawls, *A Theory of Justice,* 440–42.

10.   The right to employment raises important questions about the activities of homemaking and parenting. Many women perform these services on a full-time unpaid basis; however, it is neither clear that their decisions to assume this role are free nor that their economic dependence on their husbands is desirable. One solution that has been proposed would respect the right to employment by paying these domestic workers. Another solution would be to divide household responsibilities equally and to widen part-time and flexitime employment opportunities.

11.   In this essay, I focus on the conflict between employees' rights and business owners' rights; however, government employees and workers in nonprofit institutions are equally entitled to the benefits of this right.

12.   *New York Times,* 15 January 1984, 1 and 20.

13.   For a helpful related treatment of self-respect, see Thomas E. Hill, Jr., "Servility and Self-respect," *Today's Moral Problems,* ed. Richard A. Wasserstrom (New York: Macmillian Co., 1979), 133–47.

14.   Eleanor Langer, "Inside the New York Telephone Company," *The Capitalist System,* 2d ed., ed. Richard C. Edwards et al. (Englewood Cliffs, N.J.: Prentice Hall), 4–11.

15.   Hans Magnus Enzensberger, *The Consciousness Industry* (New York: Seabury Press, 1974).

16.   See Harry Braverman, *Labor and Monopoly Capital* (New York: Monthly Review Press, 1974); Samuel Bowles and Herbert Gintis, *Schooling in Capitalist America* (New York: Basic Books, 1976).

17.   *Work in America.*

18.   Ibid.

19.   Ibid.

20.   Langer, *The Capitalist System,* 4–11; Harry Braverman, *Labor and Monopoly Capital.*

21.   Adam Smith, *The Wealth of Nations* (New York: Modern Library, 1937), 734.

22.   Gintis, *Schooling in Capitalist America,* 293–317.

23.   Ibid., 275.

24.   Ibid., 276.

25.   Langer, *The Capitalist System,* 267.

26.   Ibid., 267.

27.   Ibid., Gintis, *Schooling in Capitalist America,* 277.

28.   Ibid.

29.   Ibid.

PART 2 _____

OCCUPATIONAL HEALTH AND SAFETY

The Cotton Dust Case*

The Occupational Safety and Health Act of 1970 (Act) requires the Secretary of Labor (Secretary), in promulgating occupational safety and health standards dealing with toxic materials or harmful physical agents, to set the standard "which most adequately assures, to the extent feasible, on the basis of the best available evidence" that no employee will suffer material impairment of health. . . .

. . . The Secretary, acting through the Occupational Safety and Health Administration (OSHA), promulgated the so-called Cotton Dust Standard limiting occupational exposure to cotton dust (an airborne particle byproduct of the preparation and manufacture of cotton products), exposure to which induces byssinosis, a serious and potentially disabling respiratory disease known in its more severe manifestations as "brown lung" disease. Estimates indicate that at least 35,000 employed and retired cotton mill workers, or 1 in 12, suffer from the most disabling form of byssinosis, and 100,000 employed and retired workers suffer from some form of the disease.

Descriptions of the disease by individual mill workers, presented at hearings on the Cotton Dust Standard before an Administrative Law Judge, stated:

When they started speeding the looms up the dust got finer and more and more people started leaving the mill with breathing problems. My mother had to leave the mill in the early fifties. Before she left, her breathing got so short she just couldn't hold out to work. My stepfather left the mill on account of breaching [sic] problems. He had coughing spells till he couldn't breath [sic], like a child's whooping cough. Both my sisters who work in the mill have breathing problems. My husband had to give up his job when he was only fifty-four years old because of the breathing problem. Ct. of App. J. A. 3791.

---

*American Textile Manufacturers Institute, Inc. et al. v. Donovan, Secretary of Labor et al. Certiorari to the U.S. Court of Appeals for the District of Columbia (1981); reprinted from U.S. Reports, vol. 452 (1981–1982): 490, 497.

I suppose I had a breathing problem since 1973. I just kept on getting sick and began losing time at the mill. Every time that I go into the mill I get deathly sick, choking and vomiting losing my breath. It would blow down all that lint and cotton and I have clothes right here where I have wore and they have been washed several times and I would like for you all to see them. That will not come out in washing.

I am only fifty-seven years old and I am retired and I can't even get to go to church because of my breathing. I get short of breath just walking around the house or dressing [or] sometimes just watching T.V. I cough all the time."
Id., at 3793.
. . . I had to quit because I couldn't lay down and rest without oxygen in the night and my doctor told me I would have to get out of there. . . . I couln't [sic] even breathe, I had to get out of the door so I could breathe and he told me not to go back in [the mill] under any circumstances.

The Asbestos Industry On Trial*

Paul Brodeur _____

The hearing records of some twenty death or disability claims that were brought before the California Industrial Accident Commission during the nineteen-thirties, forties, and fifties bear stark witness to the human suffering and tragedy that occurred there. A particular grim episode is described in the record of a death claim that was brought on January 4, 1932, by a woman named Maria Martinez, who filed it against the Celite Company— a Johns-Manville subsidiary that operated the Lompoc plant—and several insurance firms, including Travelers, Standard Accident, and the Pacific Indemnity Company. Maria Martinez's husband, Macedonio, had died in August of 1930, at the age of thirty-three, after working for only two and a half years at the Lompoc plant as a janitor and bag loader. The report of Dr. Milton V. Duncan, of Lompoc, who signed a death certificate listing the cause of Martinez's death as "acute edema of the lungs" reads like a horror story. "I saw Macedonio Martinez on the morning of August 23, 1930, at about 6:30 a.m.," Dr. Duncan wrote. "I was called to his house by a friend and found him sitting on a bed gasping for breath—blood fleck foam coming from his mouth and nose—a half pint of similar fluid in a can beside the bed had been expectorated previously. His expression was that of extreme terror—his face was pale and skin clammy with cold perspiration; pulse about 150 thready; heart sounds indistinct; chest full of bubbling, piping rales. He was talking loudly in Spanish, repeating the word "morir." In a few seconds he began to gasp harder and with a rush of fluid from his nose and mouth he expired."

At a claims hearing that was held in April of 1932, Dr. Duncan testified that he believed Martinez might have been suffering from silicosis, but the assistant medical director of the California Industrial Accident Commission disagreed, ascribing Martinez's death to a cardiovascular lesion, and in July of that year the workmen's-compensation referee in the case denied Maria Martinez's claim. According to the hearing report, she was pregnant when he died, and for six months thereafter she suffered from "a mental state which precluded her giving any thought to business affairs." It is not known what became of her. It is known, however, that seven months before Macedonio Martinez died he was given a physical examination and a chest X-ray during a health survey of the Lompoc plant, which was conducted by two physicians from the University of California School of Medicine, in San Francisco, and that they found him to be suffering from pulmonary dust disease.

Many of the other early Lompoc compensation claims reveal similarly dismal stories of sick and dying men who were suffering from silicosis but whose ailment was often misdiagnosed by medical doctors retained by insurance companies, whereupon the men were denied benefits for disability by referees of the Industrial Accident Commission. This state of affairs would probably have continued if the California Department of Public Health had not threatened to shut down the Lompoc mill and quarry in 1952, forcing Johns-Manville to institute dust-control measures and employee-health programs there, and to place warning labels on insulation products containing diatomaceous earth. By that time Macedonio Martinez had been dead for more than two decades.

• • • • • • • • •

The Fifth Circuit Court of Appeals' 1973 landmark decision upholding the trial court's verdict in *Clarence Borel* v. *Fibreboard Paper Products Corporation et al.*—the first product-liability lawsuit involving asbestos insulation in which the plaintiff won a jury verdict—triggered the greatest avalanche of toxic litigation in the history of American jurisprudence. . . .

The landmark opinion was written by Judge John Minor Wisdom, who pointed out that Section 402A of the "Restatement of the Law of Torts"—a comprehensive redefinition of tort law that had been published in 1965—required a manufacturer to disclose the existence and the extent of reasonably foreseeable risk involved in the use of his product, and went on to declare that "an insulation worker, no less than any other product user, has a right to decide whether to expose himself to the risk." . . .

In reaching our decision in the case at bar, we recognize that the question of the applicability of Section 402A of the Restatement to cases involving "occupational diseases" is one of first impression. But though the application is novel, the underlying principle is ancient. Under the law of torts, a person has long been liable for the foreseeable harm caused by his own negligence. This principle applies to the manufacture of products as it does to almost every other area of human endeavor. It implies a duty to warn of foreseeable dangers associated with those products. This duty to warn extends to all users and consumers, including the common worker in the shop or in the field. Where the law has imposed a duty, courts stand ready in proper cases to enforce the rights so created. Here, there was a duty to speak, but the defendants remained silent. The district court's judgment does no more than hold the defendants liable for the foreseeable consequences of their own inaction.

. • • • • • • • •

Baldwin's closing argument in *Jackson* v. *Johns-Manville* is considered by many plaintiff attorneys to have been one of the most dramatic summations ever given in an asbestos trial. After pointing out that there was overwhelming evidence to show that insulation products made by Johns-Manville and Raybestos-Manhattan had been widely used in the Ingalls shipyard, Baldwin reminded the jury that neither company had placed warning labels on any of those products. At that point, he set a large crayon-drawn chart on a viewing board and told the jury that it listed sixteen acts of gross indifference on the part of Johns-Manville—five of which had been joined in by Raybestos-Manhattan. He then ran through some of the highlights of these acts, and, in doing so, delivered a comprehensive summation of wrongdoing by the two companies.

"You know that by 1933 they began to have lawsuits," Baldwin said, referring to the first asbestosis lawsuits against Johns-Manville, which had actually been brought in 1929 and 1930. "They settled eleven in the year 1933, but, more important, when they settled those eleven lawsuits in 1933, they bought the lawyer. They made him agree not to bring any more lawsuits against Johns-Manville. To me that was a signal of things to come. It is like finding a dog's tooth in a bowl of chili. It suggests something to you."Baldwin went on to remind the jury that in 1934 Vandiver Brown, the corporate attorney for Johns-Manville, persuaded Dr. Lanza, of Metropolitan Life, to delete some unfavorable references to the disease-producing potential of asbestos in a study that was published by the United States Public Heath Service; that in 1935 Brown and Sumner Simpson, the president of Raybestos-Manhattan, exchanged letters in which they agreed that it would be beneficial if no articles about asbestosis appeared in the asbestos industry's trade journal; that in 1947 the Industrial Hygiene Foundation, an organization financed in part by the two companies, failed to publish a study showing that about twenty percent of the workers in two of their asbestos-textile factories had developed asbestosis; that in 1949 the medical director of Johns-

Manville's Canadian subsidiary advocated a policy of not informing workers of X-ray changes showing that they were developing this incurable lung disease; and that during the nineteen-fifties Johns-Manville made efforts to suppress public knowledge of the link between asbestos exposure and the development of cancer.

• • • • • • • •

The Speake case marked a threshold in asbestos litigation, for as the information he had unearthed between 1978 and 1982 was added to the crushing weight of incriminating material that had already been amassed as proof of the company's past misconduct juries across the nation began to award punitive damages against Johns-Manville. Indeed, as a direct result of all this discovery, punitive damages totaling more than six million dollars were awarded against the company in ten of some sixty-five asbestos cases involving Manville that were tried in 1981 and during the first half of 1982. What seems ironic is that what had come to light was undoubtedly just a small part of the history of neglect and deceit on the part of the nation's asbestos manufacturers. Thousands of documents had either disappeared or been discarded years before. Among the records that had disappeared were those of some thirteen hundred experimental studies of asbestos and other hazards that had been conducted at the Saranac Laboratory over the decades, along with virtually all the papers that had been presented at the Seventh Saranac Symposium—a week-long meeting on pulmonary dust disease that was held in late September of 1952. Unlike the proceedings of six previous meetings, those of the Seventh Symposium were never published, supposedly for budgetary reasons. Some observers believe, however, that they were suppressed because of pressure from asbestos manufacturers and the insurance industry. If they had not been, the meeting might well have gone down in history as the first major conference ever held on the biological effects of asbestos—an honor that went to the New York Academy of Sciences' conference that was organized twelve years later by Dr. Selikoff. Still, it is known that the Seventh Saranac Symposium was attended by more than two hundred medical doctors, research scientists, state and federal public-health officials, insurance-company executives, and manufacturers, who came from far and wide, and that they heard startling disclosures concerning asbestos disease from some of the leading participants in a drama that had been unfolding for more than twenty years. From England came Dr. E.R.A. Merewether, Medical Inspector of Factories in Great Britain, who had conducted the first epidemiological study of asbestosis, back in 1928, and who now presented data that strongly linked asbestosis and lung cancer. From the Medical College of South Carolina came the celebrated pathologist Kenneth

M. Lynch, who, back in 1935, had been the first to suggest such a link. And from the National Cancer Institute came Wilhelm C. Hueper, who had warned for nearly a decade that asbestos was a potent carcinogen. (Hueper, who was later among the first to warn of the dangers of DDT, was a scientist of remarkable foresight, as can be seen from a stunningly accurate appraisal of the coverup of occupational cancer that he had published in a 1943 bulletin of the American Cancer Society.) "Industrial concerns are in general not particularly anxious to have the occurrence of occupational cancers among their employees or of environmental cancers among the consumers of their products made a matter of public record," Hueper wrote. "Such publicity might reflect unfavorably upon their business activities, and oblige them to undertake extensive and expensive technical and sanitary changes in their production methods and in the types of products manufactured. There is, moreover, the distinct possibility of becoming involved in compensation suits with extravagant financial claims by the injured parties. It is, therefore, not an uncommon practice that some pressure is exerted by the parties financially interested in such matters to keep information on the occurrence of industrial cancer well under cover." . . .

If a significant number of the fifty-odd medical doctors who attended the Seventh Symposium had spoken out or had insisted that its papers and discussions be made public, they might well have blown the lid off the asbestos coverup and saved thousands of lives, untold pain and suffering, and millions of dollars. Instead, with the exception of the wonderfully outspoken Hueper, too many of them remained silent, and the conference simply marked the nadir of a year in which the asbestos industry, with the tacit approval of its insurers, successfully suppressed information about the most important industrial carcinogen the world has ever known. Furthermore, in the years to come a number of these physicians—among them Dr. Cooper, who testified for the defendants in the Tomplait and Borel trials—saw fit to take active roles in support of the asbestos industry. As for those who chose silence, it might be said that they were acting in the time-honored tradition of the American medical profession, whose members, by and large, continue to avoid speaking out on important matters of occupational and environmental health, out of elitist deference to an old-boy network that precludes them from voicing criticism either of one another or of a private-enterprise system that, by contaminating homes, hospitals, schools, and other buildings with asbestos, and befouling drinking-water supplies with toxic chemicals, has created public-health problems of staggering magnitude for the entire nation. In any event, because of timidity on the part of doctors, obtuseness on the part of public-health officials, and complacency on the part of Congress, the asbestos industry not only was allowed to conduct a highly successful coverup of medical and scientific knowledge about asbestos disease all during the nineteen-fifties, sixties, and early seventies but also, because of the bankruptcy Code, has been allowed to continue doing business as usual to this very day. Indeed, only the uncompromising commitment of Dr. Selikoff, who has worked tirelessly for more than twenty years to make his findings known, and the dedication of Ward Stephenson and the plaintiff lawyers who, following his lead, carried on after Borel have brought to light the truth about the suffering wrought by the asbestos industry upon tens of thousands of unsuspecting workers in the United States—a truth that, like the truth Emile Zola wrote about in "J'Accuse," had for years been buried underground, where, growing and gathering force, it had been waiting to burst forth.

Human Rights, Workers' Rights, and the "Right" to Occupational Safety

Tibor R. Machan _____

Introduction

I take the position of the nonbeliever.[1] I do not believe in special workers' rights. I do believe that workers possess rights as human beings, as do publishers, philosophers, disc jockeys, students, and priests. Once fully interpreted, these rights may impose special standards at the workplace, as they may in hospitals, on athletics fields, or in the marketplace.

Human Rights

Our general rights, those we are morally justified to secure by organized force (e.g., government), are those initially identified by John Locke: life, liberty, and property. That is, we need ask no one's permission to live, to take actions, and to acquire, hold, or use peacefully the productive or creative results of our actions. We may, morally, resist (without undue force) efforts to violate or infringe upon our rights. Our rights are (1) absolute, (2) unalienable, and (3) universal: (1) in social relations no excuse legitimatizes their violation; (2) no one can lose these rights, though their exercise may be restricted (e.g., to jail) by what one chooses to do; and (3) everyone has these rights, whether acknowledged or respected by others or governments or under different descriptions (within less developed conceptual schemes).[2]

I defend this general rights theory elsewhere.[3] Essentially, since adults are rational beings with the moral responsibility to excel as such, a good or suitable community requires these rights as standards. Since this commits one to a virtuosly self-governed life, others should respect this as equal members of the community. Willful invasion of these rights—the destruction of (negative) liberty—must be prohibited in human community life.

45

So-called positive freedom—that is, the enablement to do well in life—presupposes the prior importance of negative freedom. As, what we might call, self-starters, human beings will generally be best off if they are left uninterfered with to take the initiative in their lives.

Workers' Rights

What about special workers' rights? There are none. As individuals who intend to hire out their skills for what they will fetch in the marketplace, however, workers have the right to offer these in return for what others, (e.g., employers) will offer in acceptable compensation. This implies free trade in the labor market.

Any interference with such trade workers (alone or in voluntary cooperation) might want to engage in, with consent by fellow traders, would violate both the workers' and their traders' human rights. Freedom of association would thereby be abridged. (This includes freedom to organize into trade associations, unions, cartels, and so forth.)

Workers' rights advocates view this differently. They hold that the employee-employer relationship involves special duties owed by employers to employees, creating (corollary) rights that governments, given their purpose, should protect. Aside from negative rights, workers are owed respect of their positive rights to be treated with care and consideration.

This, however, is a bad idea. Not to be treated with care and consideration can be open to moral criticism. And lack of safety and health provisions may mean the neglect of crucial values to employees. In many circumstances employers should, morally, provide them.

This is categorically different from the idea of enforcible positive rights. (Later I will touch on unfulfilled reasonable expectations of safety and health provisions on the job!) Adults aren't due such service from free agents whose conduct should be guided by their own judgments and not some alien authority. This kind of moral servitude (abolished after slavery and serfdom) of some by others has been discredited.

Respect for human rights is necessary in a moral society—one needn't thank a person for not murdering, assaulting, or robbing one—whereas being provided with benefits, however crucial to one's well being, is more an act of generosity than a right.

Of course moral responsibilities toward others, even strangers, can arise. When those with plenty know of those with little, help would ordinarily be morally commendable. This can also extend to the employment relationship. Interestingly, however, government "regulation may impede risk-reducing change, freezing us into a hazardous present when a safer future beckons."[4]

My view credits all but the severely incapacitated with the fortitude to be productive and wise when ordering their affairs, workers included. The form of liberation that is then vital to workers is precisely the bourgeois kind: being set free from subjugation to others, including governments. Antibourgeois "liberation" is insultingly paternalistic.[5]

Alleging Special Workers' Rights

Is this all gross distortion? Professor Braybrooke tells us, "Most people in our society . . . must look for employment and most (taking them one by one) have no alternative to accepting the working conditions offered by a small set of employers—perhaps one employer in the vicinity."[6] Workers need jobs and cannot afford to quibble. Employers can wait for the most accommodating job prospects.

This in part gives rise to special workers' rights doctrines, to be implemented by government occupational safety, health and labor-relations regulators, which then "makes it easier for competing firms to heed an important moral obligation and to be, if they wish, humane."[7]

Suppose a disadvantaged worker, seeking a job in a coal mine, asks about safety provision in the mine. Her doing so presupposes that (1) she has other alternatives, and (2) it's morally and legally optional to care about safety at the mine, not due to workers by right. Prior to government's energetic prolabor interventions, safety, health, and related provisions for workers had been lacking. Only legally mandated workers' rights freed workers from their oppresive lot. Thus, workers must by law be provided with safety, health care, job security, retirement, and other vital benefits.

Workers' rights advocates deny that employers have the basic (natural or human) private property rights to give them full authority to set terms of employment. They are seen as nonexclusive stewards of the workplace property, property obtained by way of historical accident, morally indifferent historical necessity, default, or theft. There is no genuine free labor market. There are no jobs to offer since they are not anyone's to give. The picture we should have of the situation is that society should be regarded as a kind of large team or family; the rights of its respective parts (individuals) flow not from their free and independent moral nature, but from the relationship of the needs and usefulness of individuals as regards the purposes of the collective.

By this account, everyone lacks the full authority to enter into exclusive or unilaterally determined and mutual agreements on his or her terms. Such terms—of production, employment, promotion, termination, and so on— would be established, in line with moral propriety, only by the agency (society,

God, the party, the democratic assembly) that possesses the full moral authority to set them.

Let us see why the view just stated is ultimately unconvincing. To begin with, the language of rights does not belong within the above framework. That language acknowledges the reality of morally free and independent human beings and includes among them workers, as well as all other adults. Individual human rights assume that within the limits of nature, human beings are all efficacious to varying degrees, frequently depending upon their own choices. Once this individualist viewpoint is rejected, the very foundation for rights language disappears (notwithstanding some contrary contentions).[8]

Some admit that employers are full owners of their property, yet hold that workers, because they are disadvantaged, are owed special duties of care and considerateness, duties which in turn create rights the government should protect. But even if this were right, it is not possible from this position to establish enforcible *public* policy. From the mere existence of *moral* duties employers may have to employees, no enforcible public policy can follow; moral responsibilities require freely chosen fulfillment, not enforced compliance.

Many workers' rights advocates claim that a free labor market will lead to such atrocities as child labor, hazardous and health-impairing working conditions, and so forth. Of course, even if this were true, there is reason to think that OSHA-type regulatory remedies are illusionary. As Peter Huber argues, "regulation of health and safety is not only a major obstacle to technological transformation and innovation but also often aggravates the hazards it is supposed to avoid."[9]

However, it is not certain that a free labor market would lead to child labor and rampant neglect of safety and health at the workplace. Children are, after all, dependents and therefore have rights owed them by their parents. To subject children to hazardous, exploitative work, to deprive them of normal education and health care, could be construed as a violation of their individual rights as young, dependent human beings. Similarly, knowingly or negligently subjecting workers to hazards at the workplace (of which they were not made aware and could not anticipate from reasonable familiarity with the job) constitutes a form of actionable fraud. It comes under the prohibition of the violation of the right to liberty, at times even the right to life. Such conduct is actionable in a court of law and workers, individually or organized into unions, would be morally justified, indeed advised, to challenge it.

A consistent and strict interpretation of the moral (not economic) individualist framework of rights yields results that some advocates of workers' rights are aiming for. The moral force of most attacks on the free labor market framework tends to arise from the fact that some so-called free labor market instances are probably violations of the detailed implications of that approach itself. Why would one be morally concerned with working conditions that are fully agreed to by workers? Such a concern reflects either the belief that there hadn't been any free agreement in the first place, and thus workers are being defrauded, or it reflects a paternalism that, when construed as paternalism proper instead of compassion, no longer carries moral force.

Whatever its motives, paternalism is also insulting and demeaning in its effect. Once it is clear that workers can generate their own (individual and/ or collective) response to employers' bargaining power—via labor organizations, insurance, craft associations, and so on—the favorable air of the paternalistic stance diminishes considerably. Instead, workers are seen to be regarded as helpless, inefficacious, inept persons.

The "Right" to Occupational Safety

Consider an employer who owns and operates a coal mine. (We could have chosen any firm, privately or "publicly" owned, managed by hired executives with the full consent of the owners, including interested stockholders who have entrusted, by their purchase of stocks, others with the goal of obtaining economic benefits for them.) The firm posts a call for jobs. The mine is in competition with some of the major coal mines in the country and the world. But it is much less prosperous than its competitors. The employer is at present not equipped to run a highly-polished, well-outfitted (e.g., very safe) operation. That may lie in the future, provided the cost of production will not be so high as to make this impossible.

Some of the risks will be higher for workers in this mine than in others. Some of the mineshafts will have badly illuminated stairways, some of the noise will be higher than the levels deemed acceptable by experts, and some of the ventilation equipment will be primitive. The wages, too, will be relatively low in hopes of making the mine eventually more prosperous.

When prospective employees appear and are made aware of the type of job being offered, and its hazards they are at liberty to (a) accept or reject, (b) organize into a group and insist on various terms not in the offing, (c) bargain alone or together with others and set terms that include improvements, or (d) pool workers' resources, borrow, and purchase the firm.

To deny that workers could achieve such things is not yet to deny that they are (negatively) free to do so. But to hold that this would be extraordinary for workers (and thus irrelevant in this sort of case) is to (1) assume a historical situation not in force and certainly not necessary, (2) deny workers the capacity for finding a solution to their problems, or (3) deny that workers are capable of initiative.

Now suppose that employers are compelled by law to spend the firm's funds to meet safety requirements deemed desirable by the government regulators. This increased cost of production reduces available funds for additional wages for present and future employees, not to mention available funds for future prospect sites. This is what has happened: The employee-employer relationship has been unjustly intruded upon, to the detriment not only of the mine owners, but also of those who might be employed and of future consumers of energy. The myth of workers' rights is mostly to blame.

Conclusion

I have argued that the doctrine of special workers' rights is unsupported and workers, accordingly, possess those rights that all other humans possess, the right to life, liberty, and property. Workers are not a special species of persons to be treated in a paternalistic fashion and, given just treatment in the community, they can achieve their goals as efficiently as any other group of human beings.[10]

Does OSHA Protect Too Much?*

Norman Daniels _____

The Occupational Safety and Health Act (OSHA) of 1970 requires the Secretary of Labor to set *standards* for dealing with toxic or harmful materials in the workplace. Such standards specify permissible exposure levels and require various practices, like the wearing of air masks, and means, like monitoring devices, for insuring that exposure does not exceed these levels. . .

A centrally important feature of the 1970 Act is the *criterion* it specifies for acceptable standards: a standard should "most adequately assure, *to the extent feasible,* on the basis of the best available evidence," that no employee will suffer material impairment of health. . . .

OSHA has taken "feasibility" to mean *technological (or technical) feasibility.* A standard must protect workers to the degree it is technologically feasible to do so. . . . We shall refer to the criterion as the *strong* or *technological feasibility criterion.* . . .

I shall consider two lines of argument . . . for OSHA's strong feasibility criterion. . . . Both develop . . . worries about the voluntariness of the choices workers make when they trade daring in handling hazardous materials for hazard pay. . . .

Is it *coercive* to propose that a worker take hazard pay for accepting certain technologically reducible risks in handling carcinogens or breathing dust?

Consider a central case of coercion, the mugger who threatens, gun in hand, "Your money or your life!" The standard analyses all agree that the coercion consists in the fact that the mugger (1) changes the range of options open to the victim, and (2) the change makes the victim much worse off than he would be in some relevant baseline situation.

* Reprinted from Norman Daniels, *Just Health Care,* Philosophy and Health Series, ed. Daniel Wikler (New York: Cambridge University Press, 1985) by permission of the publisher. Copyright © 1985 by Cambridge University Press.

Suppose we take the case of a worker who has a "clean," non-risky job. His employer wants to change the work process and proposes, "Accept hazard pay for these risks or lose your job." Is the proposal coercive? Our first problem is to specify the "normally expected" course of events. . . . Shall we construe the normal course of events quite *locally,* as the continuation of the clean job now held by this worker? Or should we specify the normal course of events by reference to a more *global* baseline, the normal practices and prerogatives of employers, which include the powers to hire and fire in accord with decisions about the profitability of production processes?

If we construe the baseline *locally,* the proposal begins to look coercive. The employer's proposal changes the particular worker's options in a way that makes the worker much worse off. But this result is quite sensitive to the actual array of alternatives (and their utilities) open to this particular worker: it does not just depend on the employer's action. If there is ready access to comparable clean jobs elsewhere, and shifting jobs entails no great losses of benefits, pensions, and so on, then we may just have a case of an unpleasant offer. The "lose your job" part of the employer's proprosal loses its sting, and the employer has not really seriously altered the worker's options for the worse. That is, conditions (1) and (2) of the standard analysis fail to obtain, so the proposal is just an (non-coercive) offer. However, if the alternatives really are "starve your family (go on welfare) or accept hazard pay for cancer risks," then the proposal again meets conditions (1) and (2) and may well be coercive.

Notice how specific this result is to the details of our example. If the worker were already unemployed, and the proposal was, "Accept hazard pay or stay unemployed," then we again have a case that does not meet conditions (1) or (2). After all, the employer's proposal does not worsen the unemployed worker's situation: were the proposal not made, his options would not be improved (just as the victim is no better off if Mugger A refrains and B acts). But there seems to be something wrong with an account that makes the coerciveness of the offer depend on whether the employer is proposing unemployment which is new or merely continued. The employer's more explicit causal role in firing rather than not hiring does not seem to be just what worries us here. To be sure, the proposal to the unemployed worker might be judged exploitive, even if it is not coercive. But intuitions will differ about whether it is *thereby* coercive.[12] For our purposes, if we could agree the offer was exploitive, we might have grounds for viewing it as morally objectionable in ways that might provide a rationale for the strong feasibility criterion. But then the argument would turn on showing why the exploitive conditions undermine autonomy and not on the narrower, more direct judgment that the employer's offer is coercive.

To avoid the charge that the *local* baseline is undully sensitive to accidental details of the example (e.g., making hazard pay offers to employed workers coercive, but not those to unemployed workers), we might consider shifting to a *global* baseline. Such a baseline builds into our description of the normally expected course of events an account of normal practices of employers. Specifically, suppose that normally workers are presented with such choices as are embodied in the employer's proprosal because the employer's normal practices include the making of decisions which force such proposals. Though our employed worker now faces an unhappy choice, between taking unpleasant risks or not having work, and though his particular options are worse than the ones he happened to enjoy before the proposal, they are not worse than the normally expected options specified by the global baseline. That is, workers normally have such poor options, and the employed and unemployed workers are treated similarly. However, conditions (1) and (2) are now not met in either case, and the offer is not coercive.

Unfortunately, in making the baseline less sensitive to putatively irrelevant details, such as whether new or continued unemployment is threatened, we have also made it hostage to the status quo. If the general practices defining the baseline are, intuitively speaking, coercive, proposals which are no more coercive than these practices will be camouflaged: they will blend in and will not appear coercive at all. Indeed, proposals which (intuitively) seem coercive may be welcomed by people who "normally" suffer from practices that are part of a 'coercive' (global) baseline. Nozick discusses the examples of a slave owner who beats his slaves daily.[13] One day he proposes that the slave can avoid his usual beating if he does something disagreeable that the slave master wants done. The proposal seems coercive, but we cannot show it is by baseline of normally expected options: the change from the baseline is here welcomed by the slave. So, if we do not modify or supplement our account of the "normally expected" baseline, we cannot accommodate this kind of example. And yet, it is the kind of example that seems most relevant to our case: the offer of hazard pay for facing cancer risks is most likely to be welcomed by the otherwise unemployed worker.

There are. . . ways to supplement the account of the baseline to accommodate the example of the slave. The first, (one) which Nozick and others adopt, is to suggest we need a second baseline, specified by what is *morally required*. In the slave example, it is morally required that the slave not be beaten, or not be a slave at all. By reference to this preproposal baseline, the master's proposal is coercive, even if the slave welcomes the offer. . . .

The two-baseline theory faces some serious difficulties. First, where the baselines conflict and yield different judgments about the presence of coercion, we need to know which baseline to use, which is problematic in some case.[14] Second, and more important from our perspective, is the fact that the two-baseline theory makes the concept of coercion an intrinsically moral one.[15] That is, on this view, we cannot decide whether a proposal is coercive or not unless, in key cases, we can agree on other judgments, about what is morally required. For these cases, our judgment about the coerciveness of the proposal is no more basic and no more secure than our judgment about what is morally required at the baseline.

Consider the effect of this point on our hazard pay example. Nozick would probably believe that the normal—unregulated—hiring and firing practices of employers do not violate the morally required baseline. Such practices break no prohibitions derived from what is morally required, since they are within the employers' rights, as specified by Nozick's view of individual rights. Others, however, might argue that if the distribution of income or other social goods, like opportunity, is not fair or just, despite compliance with a framework of Nozickian rights, then hazard pay proposals will make workers worse off than what is morally required. Of course, the background injustice may not be the result of actions by the particular employer making the proposal at all: they are systematic and institutional in origin. Notice what has happened: by making coercion a moral notion, we are required to make judgments about justice. The result is that we cannot hope to appeal to agreement on coerciveness, and its *prima facie* wrongness, to undercut moral disagreement about these other issues. Thus we lose one of the advantages that might have resulted if we could provide a rationale for strong OSHA standards that rested on straightforward claims about coercion.

I shall sketch an argument. . . now which, I believe, provides a plausible rationale for OSHA's strong feasibility criterion. To state the argument I will introduce a bit of terminology which will help us capture the underlying intuition. Let us call a proposal *quasi-coercive* if it imposes or depends on a restriction of someone's alternatives in a way that is unfair or unjust; that is, a just or fair social arrangement would involve a range of options for the individual both broader than and strongly preferred to the range in the proposal situation.

The intuition underlying calling unfair or unjust restrictions of options "quasi-coercive" is that they involve a diminished freedom of action of the same sort which is glaring in the central cases of coercion. A central difference may be in the mechanism through which freedom of action is diminished. We do not have the direct and invasive intrusion into the choice-space of the individual which is present in the central cases of coercion, for example, when the mugger exceeds his rights by pointing a gun at my head. Instead, we have an indirect, yet pervasive, erosion of that space as a result of unjust or unfair social practices and institutions. The two share the feature that the restriction is socially caused. It is not the kind of restriction that results merely from misfortune; it is an act or institution of man, not God or nature, that produces it. Moreover, there are just, feasible alternatives.

Notice an important fact: like the slave in Nozick's example, people who standardly suffer from an unfair or unjust restriction of their options may welcome a quasi-coercive proposal. That is, from their perspective, it may represent an offer and not a threat. Locally considered, the proposal may advance their interest. Moreover, its quasi-coerciveness may even seem to be invisible. Not everyone living under an unjust arrangement may be aware of its injustice. Some may even deny its injustice, say through "false consciousness." Indeed, against the background of a familiar and psychologically accepted range of options, however unfair or unjust it is, jumping at the new "opportunity" embodied in such a proposal, say by trading daring in handling carcinogens for hazard pay, may seem the essence of autonomous action. After all, no one is holding a cocked pistol to one's head or threatening prison if one does not take the offer. The quasi-coerciveness of unjust arrangements works in a more subtly restrictive fashion.

There is another way in which the quasi-coerciveness of some proposals may be hidden: it may be only potential, not actual. That is, if we imagine institutionalizing such proposals, then their effect *over time* will be to produce, or to contibute to, actual quasi-coerciveness, even if initially, and viewed locally, there seems to be nothing worrisome about them, and they seem to be the essence of autonomous exchange. There is just such a worry about a hazard pay market for certain kinds of risks when the market is aimed at workers with a severely restricted range of options. Such proposals might seem unquestionably fair at one time: they are the local manifestation of a process of market exchange which seems procedurally fair under certain circumstances. But such markets will tend to greater inequality over time, especially where there is substantial inequality in bargaining power because workers have highly restricted alternatives. Workers who might at one point be able to sell their daring at a relatively high price—as do, say, movie stuntmen—will find that it is worth little or nothing over time. Risk-taking then becomes a condition of getting a job at all, a price only one with an unfair or unjust range of options—one who is quasi-coerced—would accept. This outcome has historically been the lot of the textile mill worker involved in the Cotton Dust Case, and other low-skill workers whose typical work choices involve exposure to health hazards.

The argument for OSHA's strong feasibility criterion can now be sketched as follows (and this is only a sketch): (1) Hazard pay proposals for technologically reducible risks in the contexts OSHA regulated are quasi-coercive or would tend to be over time. (2) Eliminating such proposals (and the market for them) protects workers from harmful consequences, viz. the destruction of their health at a price that only someone under quasi-coercion would accept. (3) Though hazard pay proposals of the sort involved here may be *offers* welcomed by certain workers, the autonomy embodied in accepting them is only illusory, for quasi-coercion undermines true autonomy in much the same way coercion does. (4) Just as people would reasonably contract to permit paternalistic interventions which protect them against the harmful decisions they would make when they are not, or cannot be, adequately informed, competent, or free to make autonomous ones, so too they would reasonably contract to protect themselves against quasi-coerced decisions of the sort involved here. Thus, OSHA's strong feasibility criterion can be viewed as a social insurance policy against quasi-coercive proposals to trade health for other benefits.

I shall restrict my defense of this sketch to comments on several of its controversial features. One issue of considerable concern is that the argument not prove too much: . . . Specifically, it is important to see that the claim about quasi-coerciveness, or potential quasi-coerciveness, assuming we can apply it to OSHA contexts, does not extend readily to hazard pay proposals involving some other kinds of risky work, where we endorse no such stringent regulation. Does the argument cover the right cases? . . .

Consider that the kinds of risks we are most concerned with, the handling of toxins, carcinogens and other hazardous materials, are not risks which are likely to be chosen for their intrinsic desirability, for the satisfaction that might derive from facing danger or using special skills to survive, or for their instrumental connection to highly desirable consequences, like saving lives. Rather, the motivation to take these risks derives entirely from the extrinsic rewards associated with them, rewards like hazard pay or steady employment in areas of limited employment opportunity. Partly as a result of this difference, the choice to be a fireman or stuntdriver is *exceptional,* reflecting a high degree of self-selection: such choices could readily have been foregone for many other kinds of work. In contrast, the choice to be a miner, millworker, or industrial worker facing health hazards subject to OSHA's strong criterion is *typical.* For a large class of workers, these are the primary forms of available employment. Indeed, these are the typical options, or the sole or most attractive ones, facing a class of workers with a significantly restricted range of options. The restrictions on workers' options are the result of various factors: their limited educational opportunity, their array of marketable skills and talents, accidents of geographical location, or their limited economic resources for financing job mobility.

Moreover, this narrowness of the range of options open to the typical worker is compounded by another factor. The riskiness of exceptional jobs (stuntdriver, fireman) can be viewed as stable over time: the worker knows more or less what he is getting into over a standard period of employment. But in 'typical' jobs, changes in manufacturing processes can expose workers to risks not anticipated at the inception of an employment period. To impose the burden of dodging these risks on the worker, given possible losses in benefits, pensions, family disruption, is to overestimate his effective options, to assume he has job mobility where it does not exist.

What this point about exceptional versus typical choices means, then, is that hazard pay proposals in one setting, made to one group of workers, may be, or will tend to be, quasi-coercive without all hazard pay proposals being so. The difference will depend on judgments about the range of alternatives open to one group, rather than the other, and on the reasons for the restricted options. Thus the argument does not force us to treat dissimilar groups similarly.

Moreover, nothing in this argument for strong OSHA regulation implies we ought to intervene similarly in lifestyle choices affecting health, even though by doing so we might prevent comparable harms. Like the stuntdriver's choices, these lifestyle choices are also not generally or potentially quasi-coerced. . . .[16] (There are) some worries about the voluntariness of certain lifestyle choices, noting, for example, the effect of strong sub-cultural influences. But these threats to autonomy are different from quasi-coercion, and arguments based on these more diffuse kinds of influence are not likely to justify comparable interventions. Indeed, they are just the sorts of influence we are fearful of undermining if we respect diversity.

The argument sketched here for the OSHA criterion thus appears to avoid the worries of the libertarian lament that OSHA must be compatible with the liberty to consent to risk, we recognize in other contexts. It turns out that only the appropriate hazard pay proposals are quasi-coercive, or potentially so. It is important to remember that the argument does not require that we already think the range of options open to regulated workers is unjustly or unfairly restricted. It is sufficient that we believe the restricted range of options such workers enjoy, though fair or just now, would tip in the direction of injustice and unfairness over the long run. Moreover, we should be concerned that the 'tipping' might be hard to detect and therefore that the quasi-coerciveness would remain hidden and invisible to many participants in the hazard pay market. Consequently, we should be reluctant to rely on our perceptions of fairness once faced with such situations. Just as some incompetent or uninformed individuals may not be in the best position to detect their diminished capacity for making autonomous decisions, so too we should not wait till we are quasi-coerced to protect ourselves against diminished autonomy. Rather, it is prudent to impose prior, protective constraints on the framework of markets built on exchanges between workers and employers. These constraints are designed to insure that market changes remain within the requirements of justice or fairness.

An important objection to this argument sketch is . . . that the argument straddles a fence. The appropriate reaction to complaints about an injustice, or potential injustice, in the distribution of social goods should be to alter the fundamental institutional arrangements which lead to the unjust distribution. Yet our argument leads us merely to intervene narrowly to block one sort of consequence of such (potential) injustice, the harm that might result from quasi-coerced decisions. This intervention seems to add insult to injury, if the premise about quasi-coercion is correct. We leave all the factors intact which create, or tend to create, the unjust, quasi-coercive setting. Instead, we intervene to stop a vulnerable class of individuals from exercising its own discretion. This paternalism seems vexing because it leaves intact the background conditions which seem to make the intervention necessary. The objection, then, is that worries about injustice should not lead to narrow constraints on autonomy. If the objection is correct, step (4) of the argument sketch is dubious.

I should like to make three points in response to this objection. First, the autonomy that is restricted here is only an illusion if the claim about quasi-coercion is correct. To be sure, the interventions may remain offensive to those who want to accept the offers involved, but if the discussion in earlier sections is correct, we have reason to think the voluntariness of quasi-coerced decisions is diminished in morally significant ways. Second, contrary to the premise of the objection, arguments from justice often involve restrictions on free exchanges among individuals: the restrictions take the general form of restricting some free exchanges to preserve the fairness of others. Does a market which permits quasi-coerced exchanges respect liberty more than one that restricts some exchanges in order to make all exchanges free from quasi-coercion? I would suggest not, but the answer would take us afield into some central questions in the general theory of justice.

My third point is that the modification of distributive institutions involved in OSHA regulations does have an effect on distributive justice, at least if arguments I have made elsewhere about the nature of health care as a social good are at all plausible. No doubt, the importance of health might be argued for in various ways, all of which might justify viewing the trading of health for too low a price as unfair. But on my own view . . . health is of direct relevance to worries about justice because it contributes directly to the distribution of opportunity in society. Compromising health through quasi-coerced hazard pay bargains thus compromises the ability to maintain fair equality of opportunity in a society. The restricted opportunity range of poor or worst-off classes of workers would act, in hazard pay markets, to further undermine fair equality of opportunity. Earlier, I had argued that claims about the special importance of health or health care will not show by themselves why we should not rely on consent to distribute risks to health:

health is not so important we refuse to let people compromise it in various contexts. The argument sketch for the strong OSHA criterion shows, however, why certain hazard pay proposals would depend on a highly questionable form of consent, consent under quasi-coercion, and that is the crux of the rationale offered here.

There is a deeply troubling consequence of the argument offered in the last section, one that is important to bring out in the open. The rationale I offered turned on concern about the actual or potential quasi-coerciveness of certain hazard pay proposals. The quasi-coerciveness of the proposals depended on the fact that the class of workers facing such proposals have, or are likely to have, unfairly or unjustly restricted alternatives. But what if we could agree that the distribution of income and opportunity were really fair or just, and that the distribution would not be tipped toward unfairness over time through the operation of a market for such risk-taking. Suppose, that is, that we lived in a just social arrangement, one that were stable over time. If the rationale for OSHA's strong criterion depends on the claim about quasi-coerciveness, then there would be no need for the strong OSHA feasibility criterion. Perhaps the class of workers receiving these hazard pay proposals might still face a range of options more restricted than more fortunate groups of workers or professionals, but the inequalities here are no threat to justice (we are supposing). In such circumstances, we would still have a role for OSHA: guaranteeing adequate information is present for informed decision-making about risk-taking, and guaranteeing that costs are internalized, so that hazard pay bargains do not free-load on other parties. But the strong OSHA criterion now lacks a rationale.

Some proponents of the strong OSHA criterion might readily agree to this restriction on its applicability: for them, the rationale I have offered would seem to capture their underlying moral view. But some proponents of strong regulation might feel uneasy about the restriction: indeed, I feel uneasy about it myself. It is not clear to me just what follows from this sort of unfocused uneasiness. It could be that there are other components to a rationale which are not captured at all in this argument from justice. Yet, it is not obvious at all what they are. On the other hand, the problem may lie with this methodology for testing a philosophical argument. Intuitions or considered moral judgments about the rightness of a practice, like stringent OSHA regulations, arise in a particular social setting, one which has many forms of injustice or threats of injustice. It is notoriously difficult to clean up and make the principles underlying these intuitions explicit merely by forming counter-factual test contexts in which to deploy them. To be sure, this is standard philosophical method, but its results are often less clear than what we take them to be. Nevertheless, if one cannot show why one is dissatisfied with the kind of "test" of the rationale this hypothetical case involves, then the dissatisfaction will linger to infect the rationale itself. This result should worry proponents of strong OSHA regulation, who must offer an alternative, or more complete, rationale than the one sketched here.

The rationale I have offered, despite these deeper worries that there are still *other* components needed for a complete account, does carry weight wherever we have reason to worry about quasi-coerciveness in our own society. That is, we *do* get a plausible argument for the OSHA criterion as long as we have reason to worry about the fairness or justice of the distribution of options available to the workers most likely to receive the hazard pay proposals in question. But, of course, just such worries are themselves controversial. And differences in moral judgment here depend not only on different estimates of empirical facts, but on different underlying conceptions of what is just or fair. So my rationale also has the strength of locating clearly a source of controversy about the acceptability of the OSHA criterion itself. My rationale will be controversial just where moral controversy about regulation is sharpest in our society. The rationale cannot by itself resolve this dispute. Still, it may help make it clearer what might be needed to do so, given the source of conflict.

Does OSHA protect too much? The answer depends on other moral judgments we make about the justice and fairness of choices open to workers in certain hazard pay markets.

Are Disadvantaged Workers Who Take Hazardous Jobs Forced to Take Hazardous Jobs?*

G.A. Cohen _____

1

We might define *ideology* as thinking that is not just incorrect but that is systematically deflected from truth because of its conformity to the limited vision and sectional interests of a particular social class. We could then say that *bourgeois* ideology is thinking deflected from truth because of the service it performs for owners and managers of capital.

Now according to a theory I reject,[17] the ordinary language spoken in bourgeois society, by bourgeois and nonbourgeois alike, is permeated by bourgeois ideology, and ordinary language philosophy, because it respects our ordinary use of words, is, therefore, a bourgeois philosophy. And so, for example, to treat the ordinary language of force and freedom as substantially unrevisable, as an ordinary language philosopher would, is to subscribe in advance to a bourgeois point of view.

In my opinion, this theory is wrong about the relationship between ideology and ordinary language, and its proponents fail to notice the contribution ordinary language philosophy can make to ideologically infested dispute. I think ideology runs deep, but not as deep as they think. If the theory I oppose were correct, it would be almost impossible for reason and evidence to prevail against ideology, since the very language in which ideologically sensitive questions are phrased would dictate their answers. But I think it manifest that reason and evidence often defeat ideology quite handily.

My different opinion is that, insofar as there is a connection between ideology and ordinary language, ideological distortion is not so much *in* ordinary language as *of* ordinary language: Our ordinary language misleads us not because it is deformed, but because we fail to achieve a perspicuous view of its complex nature. I do not think all philosophy is generated by misunderstanding of language, but I do think much ideology promotes and feeds on such misunderstanding and that thinking about force and freedom is a case in point. Our ordinary language of force and freedom has unexpected logical properties of which it is easy to be unaware and neglect of which facilitates ideological illusion.

Against Marxists who think the ordinary language of force and freedom is bound itself to be bourgeois, I say that the concepts of force and freedom are so fundamental that in their ordinary employment they are secure against ideological takeover: We simply would not know what we were talking about if ideology governed their use. But in our fallible *reflection* on the same concepts, which goes beyond our *use* of them, ideology does lead us astray, and part of the remedy is to pay close attention to what we ordinarily say.

Now someone who agrees that ordinary language is not itself ideological might nevertheless question my confidence in the power of ordinary language philosophy to dissolve ideological illusion, for a different reason. He might say that the delicate conceptual techniques of that philosophy cannot help us to understand and expose ideology, since the source of ideology is class interest, not conceptual error. But the claim that the source of ideology is class interest rather than conceptual error rests upon a false contrast. For the truth is that class interest generates ideology precisely by instilling a propensity to errors of reasoning about ideologically sensitive issues. Class interest *could* not be the immediate source of the ideological illusions from which even reflective thinking suffers, for an illusion will not gain a grip on a reflective mind in the absence of some form of intellectual malfunctioning. And a common malfunction in the case of ideology is conceptual confusion. It is a striking feature of ideological disagreement that, in typical cases, not only does each side believe true what the other side believes false, but each side believes *obviously* true what the other side believes *obviously* false. It is likely, then, that (at least) one side is not just mistaken, but profoundly mistaken. Yet the mistake persists, and what makes it possible for it to endure is, I maintain, its conceptually complex substructure. Class interest, and not conceptual complexity, is the motivating principle of ideology, but conceptual complexity helps to explain why class interest is able to have the intellectual effect it does.

Consider, for example, the conflicting answers persons of different political persuasions will give not to the particular question which forms my title, but to the broader question whether or not the capitalist system promotes human freedom. For some it *evidently* does, and for others it *evidently* does not, and the dispute can take this extreme form, with honest advocacy on both sides, only because the concept of freedom lends itself, in virtue of its complexity, to systematic misconstrual. And since ordinary language philosophy is particularly good at correcting the misconstrual of concepts we know how to handle but are disposed to misdescribe, it follows that it can act as a potent solvent of some ideological illusions. I hope to use it to that effect in section 3 through 7.[18] If I fail to achieve the desired effect, that will not, I think, be due to fault in the method I have commended, but to my unfaultless use of it.

2

I now turn to the title question. It is surely uncontroversial that disadvantaged workers in hazardous industry have less attractive life options than many of the rest of us do. The main controversial questions are, respectively, factual, conceptual, and moral: *I.* Exactly what are the options facing typical disadvantaged workers, and what causes them to be restricted as they are? *II.* How do the concepts of force and freedom apply to such workers, in the light of the answer to *I? III.* Is it morally acceptable that they find themselves situated as they are?

I have nothing distinctive to say about *I.* I shall devote most of my attention to *II,* some to *III,* and some to the relationship between *II* and *III.*

To fix ideas, let us focus on an imaginary worker in an unimaginary situation, namely one of the seven thousand unemployed people in the town of Hazelton, Pennsylvania (population: thirty-three thousand), to which the Beryllium Corporation came in 1956, offering hazardous jobs.[19a] Our worker, whom I shall call *John,* took one. He was confronted with a choice between employment and health, and he chose the former. Was he forced to take the health-endangering job? Did he, in taking it, contract freely? I shall deal with these questions in sections 3 through 7.

3

Leftists will urge that he *was* forced to enter the relevant contract, while Rightists will contend that, in entering it, he exercised his market freedom. I shall argue that, although both tend to think that they thereby contradict one another, they do not in fact, and, moreover, that if the Leftists are right, then so are the Rightists because of a surprising general truth about force and freedom, which I shall call *T: If a person is forced to do something, then he is free to do that thing.* Hence, if the Leftist is right, then the Rightist also is. For it follows from T that if John was forced to contract as he did, then he was free so to contract. When he contracted, he exercised a freedom to contract and, therefore, his market freedom. The right-wing claim is, accordingly, entailed by the left-wing claim it is supposed to contradict, and it, the right-wing claim, therefore lacks ideological force.

I now temporarily leave Left and Right, in order to defend thesis T, that one is free to do whatever one is forced to do. The most direct argument for it is as follows: If you are forced to do A, you do A. But, if you do A, you are free to do A; you cannot do what you are not free to do. So, if you are forced to do A, you are free to do A.

I am not, in that first argument, equating being free to do something with being able to do something. The argument requires that being free to do something is a necessary condition of being able to do it, but not that it is also a sufficient one.[19b] The argument does not equate being free with being able, since it is consistent with the view that I may be unable to do something I am free to do because I lack the capacity to do it. I am, in a clear sense, free to swim the English Channel, but I am nevertheless unable to. If I were a much better swimmer than I am, but forbidden by well-enforced law to swim the channel, then, again, I would be unable to swim it, but because of unfreedom rather than incapacity.

Someone might object to the argument's premiss that whatever you do is something you are free to do. He might say that not any old doing (including, for example, doing something by fluke) proves freedom to do what is done. Though I think this objection is wrong, I can afford to grant that it is right, for I can replace the premiss it contests by a weaker and less controvertible one that still delivers the desired conclusion, namely, that you are free to do what you are forced to do. The sufficiently powerful, weaker premiss is that a person who, knowing what he is doing, intentionally does A, exercises a freedom to do A. Since when you are forced to do A, you standardly do it knowing what you are doing, and so on, the desired conclusion may be obtained even if not *all* doings require freedom to do what is done.

A second argument for the claim that I am free to do what I am forced to do is that one way of frustrating someone who would force me to do something is by rendering myself not free to do it: It follows, by contraposition, that if I am forced to do it, I am free to do it. To illustrate: I commit a crime, thereby causing myself to be jailed, so that I cannot be forced by you to do something I abhor. If you still hope to force me to do it, you will have to make me free to do it (by springing me from jail).

The fact that being unfree to do A renders it impossible for anyone to force you to do it constitutes a nonpaternalistic justification for certain legislative restrictions on freedom. Some people might be forced to sell themselves into slavery, or to work for very low wages, if their freedom to do so were not removed by legislation. Freedom-removing legislation, by making certain forcings impossible, can serve the interests of freedom itself, since, whenever someone is forced to do something, he is less free than he otherwise would be.

Here, finally, is a third argument for the claim that you are free to do what you are forced to do: Before you are forced to do A, you are, at least in standard cases, free to do A and free not to do A. It is natural to suppose that the force removes the second freedom,[20] but why suppose that it removes the first? It puts no obstacle in the path of your doing A, and you therefore remain free to do it.

The conclusion that being forced to do A entails being free to do A will no doubt be resisted, but it is demonstrably true, and I think resistance to it reflects failure to distinguish the idea of *being free to do something* from other ideas, such as the idea of *doing something freely*. I am free to do what I am forced to do even if, as is usually true, I do not do it freely.

I say that it is usually, not always, true that when I am forced to do something I do it unfreely, because I am inclined to accept something like Gerald Dworkin's claim that 'A does X freely if and only if A does X for reasons he doesn't mind acting from,'[21] and on that view some forced action is freely performed: if, for example, I am forced to do something that I want to do and had fully intended to do, then, unless I resent the supervenient coercion, I do it freely. But that is an unusual case. In the standard case forced action is performed unfreely, even though the agent was, because he must have been, free to perform the action he performed unfreely. What a person is free to do is a matter of his situation. Whether or not he does what he does freely is a complex matter of his internal state. Inferences from the first kind of freedom to the second are dangerous, and whereas it is demonstrable that John was free to contract as he did, it is extremely unlikely that he did so freely.

I labor the truth that one is free to do what one is forced to do because of its manifest bearing on the disagreement about John. But the truth also helps to explain the character and persistence of the analogous but more general disagreement of whether wage workers in a capitalist society are, as Marxists say they are, forced to sell their labor power. In opposition to Marxists, bourgeois thinkers celebrate the freedom of contract manifest not only in the capitalist's purchase of labor power but also in the worker's sale of it. If Marxists are right, then workers, being forced to sell their labor power, are in an important way unfree. But it remains true that (unlike chattel slaves) they are free to sell it. The unfreedom asserted by Marxists is compatible with the freedom asserted by bourgeois thinkers. Indeed, if the Marxists are right, the bourgeois thinkers are right, unless they also think, as characteristically they do, that the truth they emphasize refutes the Marxist claim. The bourgeois thinkers go wrong not when they say that the worker is free to sell his labor power, but when they infer that the Marxist cannot therefore be right in his claim that the worker is forced to. And Marxists share the bourgeois thinkers' error when they think it necessary to deny what the bourgeois thinkers say.[22] If the worker is not free to sell his labor power, of what freedom is a foreigner whose work permit is removed deprived? Would not the Marxists who wrongly deny that workers are free to sell their labor power nevertheless protest, inconsistently, that such disfranchised foreigners have been deprived of a freedom?

4

The disputants in section 3 failed to see that if a person is forced to do A, then he is free to do it (thesis T). They tended, indeed, to assert the opposite implication, that if he is forced to do A, then he is *not* free to do to it. The Left, affirming as it did the antecedent of that implication, wrongly therefore affirmed its consequent, while the Right, being certain of the falsehood of the consequent, wrongly inferred that the antecedent is false too. In the present section we shall find Left and Right once again sharing a mistake which structures their disagreement.

A Leftist convinced by the argument of section 3 might say that, although John was free to take a hazardous job, he was not free not to: he was not free to do something else instead. The response rests on the plausible principle that if a person is forced to do A, then there is no B which he is free to do instead. But that principle, though plausible, is questionable, and if it were sound, then Right could exploit it against Left, as follows.

The Right could point out that someone like John can, after all, go on welfare, or beg, or make no provision for himself and trust to fortune, or, perhaps, take a less hazardous job which pays him rather less money. No one would have prevented John from taking these courses. Therefore, he was free to take them. Therefore, on the plausible principle the Left advanced, he was not forced to contract as he did.

But the principle is incorrect, and the Right's inference is therefore fallacious. To infer from the fact that John was free to do other things that he was therefore not forced to take a hazardous job is to employ a false account of what it is to be forced to do something. When a person is forced to do something he has no *reasonable* or *acceptable* alternative course. He need not have no alternative at all.

I think, moreover, that, if not always, then almost always, *when someone is forced to do something there is an alternative to what he is forced to do, which he is free to do* (thesis T¹). Consider two ways in which Smith, who wants Jones out of the room, might contrive to achieve his aim. Smith might drag Jones over to the door and push him out, thereby, as we say, *forcing* him out of the room. Or he might get Jones to leave by credibly threatening to shoot him unless he does. Now in the second case, but not the first, it is natural to say that Jones is forced *to leave* the room. Only in the second case is there something which Jones is forced to *do,* since in the first case he does nothing, or nothing relevant: he's just pushed out. And I suggest that the contrast is connected with the fact that in the second case Jones has an alternative: He is free to stand fast and be shot. And I think this generalizes that whenever a person is forced to do something there is something else that he is free to do instead. Or, if that is not always so, then the exceptions are of a special kind. One kind of exception might be where a threat so paralyses someone's will that choosing otherwise is in some strong sense impossible for him. But I am not sure that he is even then *unfree* to choose otherwise, as opposed to *incapable* of choosing otherwise.

Those who do not agree that Jones is free to stand fast *may* be persuaded by the following argument, which departs from the premiss that Jones might, after all, though credibly threatened, stand fast, out of, say, irrationality or defiance. Now if Jones stands fast, he was free to stand fast: It is impossible to do what one is not free to do.[23] But his being free to stand fast could not depend on his actually standing fast, since there is nothing one is free to do only if one actually does it. If, before standing fast, he is, as he must be, free to stand fast, then that is a feature of his situation whether or not he proceeds to stand fast. So if, in particular, he is forced to leave, and does not stand fast, then standing fast was nevertheless an alternative he was free to perform.[24]

If I am right, to be forced to do A is, at least standardly, to be forced to *choose* to do A. Thus, when someone says, "I was forced to do A: I had no other choice," then the second part of his statement is, in the standard case, an ellipsis for something like "I had no other choice worth considering." Now when Leftists claim that John was forced to take a hazardous job, they are not using "forced to" in a special, unstandard way, and they certainly do not mean that John's situation paralyzed his will.[25] Hence, the fact that John was free to do other things, so far from refuting the Leftist claim, is an entailment of it: the Leftist claim entails that there were other things John was free to do, but that none of them were acceptable alternatives.

5

Sometimes people respond to my defence of the strange but (as they seem to me) true theses T and T¹ by complaining that my arguments dull the distinction between force and freedom, which lovers of freedom should keep sharp. But I do not say that since people who are forced to do things are really free anyway, it does not matter that they are forced to do them. On the contrary, I emphasize that constrained people are, necessarily, free in certain ways in order to prevent those who notice the freedoms disadvantaged workers have from concluding that they are therefore not forced to take hazardous jobs.

If we contemplate the abstract nouns *force* and *freedom* and never pick at the nits and grit of what we ordinarily say when we use the verbs and adjectives that give those nouns their semantic substance, we shall be apt to think that those who enjoy market freedom cannot, in the very course of exercising it, be suffering from appalling constraint. Yet many of them do suffer immense constraint and immense lack of freedom. Note that I never said that he who is forced has freedom *and does not lack it*. I said that he who is forced to do A is free to do A and is free to do some B different from A, but, and this is why he counts as forced to do A, is free to do no C which is an acceptable alternative to A. If that tripartite truth cannot be restated as a simple relationship between force (as such) and freedom (as such), that is not my fault or the fault of ordinary language. Fault lies with those who expect the truth about complicated matters to be both simple and immediately available.

6

If I am right, the Rightist has to show not that John exercised a freedom when he took the hazardous job, nor even that he had alternatives, but that he had an *acceptable* or *reasonable* alternative.

Now the Rightist might grasp that nettle by claiming that John *did* have an acceptable alternative. He might point out that workers whose situations were no better than John's managed nevertheless to escape it by setting up for themselves in (initially) small businesses, or by leaving places like Hazelton for less toxic employment elsewhere. Whoever escapes from a situation like John's is free to escape it, and what makes him free is the existence of an opportunity that he seizes. It is not credible that in John's case *no* such opportunities existed. He was therefore as free to escape as similarly placed people who do escape manifestly are. So he had an acceptable alternative and was not forced to take a hazardous job. Note that the conclusion is not merely that he was free to *try* to escape, for that might have been true even if there had been no actual opportunity to escape. The conclusion is that there existed opportunities for self-betterment which John was free to seize.

I shall deal with three Leftist replies to this argument.

(i) The Leftist might claim that there are fewer escapes from situations like John's than there are people in such situations, so that necessarily most like John will be unable to escape.

But even if that is so, the Leftist is wrong to infer that persons like John are therefore not free to escape. From the fact that not all people like John, taken collectively, are free to escape, it does not follow that each such person is not free to escape. And as long as the number of others who are actually seeking escape is relatively small, so that there exist exits unclogged by would-be escapees, then all, taken distributively, are free to escape, since there is at least one unexploited opportunity for each to exploit.[26]

(ii) The second Leftist reply is to say that it is unrealistic to expect most people in John's situation to escape it through self-employment or emigration since most of them lack appropriate inner resources, skills of self-presentation, and so on. They are consequently unable to seize whatever opportunities to escape there may be.

But the Rightist will answer: precisely so. Some people are not intelligent enough or enterprising enough to exploit opportunities, but that does not mean that they are constrained by their situation. They lack what unjailed mediocre swimmers (see page 64) lack: capacity, not freedom. Accordingly, what the Leftist says here about John does not show that he was *forced* to take a hazardous job.

It is hard to evaluate this Rightist response. Return to the case of the swimmer. If Jimmy is a nonswimmer because he was deliberately denied swimming instruction normally granted to others, is he then, perhaps, not only incapable of swimming, but also unfree to? If the answer is "Yes," then poor provision of education to disadvantaged people might make them count as unfree to do what their educational deprivation makes them incapable of doing.[27]

(iii) The Leftist of (ii) rejects the principle that one is forced to do A only if one has no acceptable alternative, on the grounds that one may be unable to seize an alternative which undoubtedly exists. A different Leftist accepts the stated principle but insists on a more careful way of describing alterntives, with a view to showing that there existed no acceptable alternative for John. This Leftist says that one must consider (as the Rightist did not) the costs and risks attaching to attempts to seize opportunities before judging that they constitute acceptable alternatives. It is dangerous to embark upon self-employment, since fledgling enterprises often fail, and the costs of failure can be very severe; a worker who has tried and failed to establish a small business may be worse off than if he had not tried at all. Similar remarks apply to the drastic and chancy course of leaving family, friends, and community for possible employment elsewhere. Good exits may exist, but, so the objection goes, it is difficult to know where they are, and the price of fruitless search for them is considerable. Accordingly, the expected utility of attempting an alternative is normally too low to justify the statement that workers like John are not forced to take hazardous jobs.[28]

Let us call this the "risk objection." To assess its soundness, let us state the argument it proposes as it would apply to John:

(1) The expected utility to John of trying self-employment (etc.) was less than the expected utility of taking the hazardous job (even if the utility of becoming and remaining self-employed (etc.) was greater than that of taking the hazardous job).

(2) An alternative to a given course is acceptable in the relevant sense only if it has at least as much expected utility as the given course. (The relevant sense of acceptability is that in which a person is forced to do A if he has no acceptable alternative to doing A). Therefore,

(3) The existence of exits of the stated kind does not show that John had an acceptable alternative course. Therefore,

(4) The existence of such exits does not show that John was not forced to take a hazardous job.

The first premiss is a (more or less) factual claim, and the second is conceptual. In assessing the truth of the factual premiss, we must discount that part of the probability of failure in attempts at self-employment, which is due to *purely* personal deficiencies: see the discussion of objection (ii) on page 69. But even if we could carry out the needed discounting, it would remain extremely difficult to tell whether the factual premiss is true, since the answer would involve many matters of judgment, and also information which is not a matter of judgment but which is hard to get, such as the frequency with which enterprises founded by disadvantaged exworkers succeed. I shall, however, assume that the factual premiss is true, in order to focus on the conceptual claim embodied in a premiss (2).

If a person is forced to do A if he has no acceptable alternative, then what makes for acceptability in the required sense? Suppose I am doing A, and doing B is an alternative to that. In order to see whether it is an acceptable one, do I consider only the utility of the best possible outcome of B or do I take into account all its possible outcomes, summing the products of the utility and probability of each, so that I can compare the result with the expected utility of doing A, and thereby obtain an answer?

It seems clear that the best possible outcome of doing B cannot be all that counts, since if it were, then I would not be forced to hand over my money at gun point where there was a minute probability that the gun would misfire. People are regularly forced to do things to which there are alternative with low probabilities of very high rewards.

It becomes plausible to conclude that expected utility must figure in the calculus of constraint. And I think it does figure, but in a more complex way than premiss (2) of the risk objection allows. An alternative to a given course can be acceptable even if it has less expected utility than the given course. Illustration: "You're not forced to rent an apartment in the village, since you can also rent one uptown, though a village apartment is, I acknowledge, a better bet."

Premiss (2) of the risk objection is false, but something similar to it may be true. Reflection on the intuitive data leads me to propose the following characterization of acceptability, at any rate as a first approximation:

B is an acceptable alternative to A iff B is not worse than A
                                            or B (though worse than A) is not
                                            particularly bad,

with expected utility being the standard for judging courses good and bad. Now in order to apply the analysis, one has to make not only comparative judgments of courses of action but also ones which are absolute *in some sense* (I shall not try to specify it)—that is how I intend "particularly bad." If we were allowed only relative judgments we would risk concluding that whenever someone does what is unambiguously the best thing for him to do, he is forced to do that thing. But unflaggingly rational people are not perpetually constrained.

Some consequences of the definition are worth mentioning.

First, even if A is an extremely desirable course, one might be forced to take it, since all the alternatives to it are so bad. You could be forced to go to the superb restaurant because all the others are awful. It would then be unlikely that you are going to it (only) because you are forced to, but that is another matter. It is not true that you do everything you are forced to do because you are forced to do it.

Second, all the alternatives to A might be absolutely terrible and no better than A, and yet one still might not be forced to do A, since some of the alternatives might be no worse than A. To be sure, there would be constraint in such a situation. One would be forced to do A or B or C. But one would not be forced to do any one of them. One would not, that is, be forced to do A or forced to do B or forced to do C.

Third, the extreme difficulty of assessing probabilities and utilities in real life means that it will often be intractably moot whether or not someone is forced to do something. But that is not an objection to this account, since the matter often is intractably moot.

I assumed (see page 70) that the expected utility to John of trying to escape was less than that of taking the hazardous job. Then if my account

of acceptabililty in alternatives is sound, the substance of the risk objection
is saved if and only if that assumption is correct (since I am sure that taking
a hazardous job is bad enough to count as *particularly* bad).

Now I think it is not possible to say whether or not the disadvantaged
worker in hazardous employment has a superior alternative (in expected utility
terms). The relevant facts are too hard to get at, and hard to organize in
an informative way; they will, of course, vary with the varying situations of
workers. It follows that there is almost certainly no general answer to the
question which forms my title, and there is probably no definite answer to
it in a large number of individual cases either, since so many pertinent
assessments are contestable here. I shall comment shortly on the moral upshot
of this indeterminacy.

7

But first I must remark on an important simplification imposed on the
foregoing discussion. I took for granted that John *knew* what the hazards
were of the job he accepted. This was a simplification, since in fact much
hazard is revealed only after the contract has been signed, and a certain
amount of managerial effort is directed at preventing its revelation.[29] (If
workers controlled industry, there might be less head-long rush into new
products and processes with attention to hazard only after it has begun to
display itself vividly.)

When workers are unaware of hazards inherent in jobs they take, this has
implications, which I shall not try to trace here, for whether they take them
freely, for how free they are when they take them, and so forth. The following
is no doubt a valid argument, at any rate on one reading of its conclusion,
but only a fool would try to make ideological capital out of its conclusion—
which is not to say that there exist no fools:

> John chose to work in factory F.
> Factory F is hazardous. Therefore,
> John chose to work in a hazardous factory.

8

Whereas it is extremely unlikely that John contracted freely (see page 65),
it is hard to say whether or not he was forced to contract as he did, since
it is hard to say whether or not he had an acceptable alternative (pages
67–72). Philosophy cannot resolve the dispute between someone who says

that John was not forced to take a hazardous job since he had the acceptable alternative of leaving Hazelton and seeking unhazardous employment elsewhere, and someone who says that the stated alternative was not acceptable, since John would have had to break cherished ties of family, friendship, and community to take it, and he could not have been sure what he would have found elsewhere. But philosophy can display the conceptual background to disputes of that kind, and that is what I have tried to do.

Now participants in the seminar for which these remarks were prepared were asked, "What if anything follows ethically from our understanding of the facts about worker freedom and unfreedom?"[30] Since there is some obscurity as to what those facts are, one might think it is also obscure what follows ethically from them. And one might then think that the answer to the normative question, question III (Is it morally acceptable that people like John are situated as they are?) must remain uncertain. But that reasoning embodies two mistakes.

The first mistake is to suppose that the *precise* truth about John's freedom and lack of it is morally significant. John has no asset except labor power, and unskilled labor power at that. The *broad* truth of the matter is that this severely restricts his freedom, and that broad truth has moral implications. But I do not think we gain in morally relevant understanding by achieving a *precisely* correct description of John's situation from the point of view of freedom and constraint. A refined description of his condition in the language of force and freedom is irrelevant to the crucial moral question, which is whether it is *fair* that he is placed in his manifestly adverse circumstances.

And the second mistake in the reasoning described two paragraphs back is to suppose that the broad, and normatively *relevant*, truth about John and his freedom is normatively *decisive*. To think so is to misconstrue the relationship between freedom and justice. Questions of freedom do bear on questions of justice, but sometimes the bearing is highly indirect, and the particular question whether John is suffering from injustice is not setttled by a demonstration that he contracts unfreely and that he is forced to contract as he does.

The broad truth about John is that he is so placed that taking a job which ruins or threatens his health might be his best bet, while others are so placed that they can make money out of John's relative lack of freedom. This seems an injustice, but what if those others are morally legitimate owners of what they own? If capitalists are morally legitimate owners of means of production, then they have no obligation to offer workers jobs, and, *a fortiori*, no obligation to offer them salubrious jobs, whether or not those who take the unsalubrious ones actually offered are forced to do so. As far as I can see, their only relevant obligation would be to abstain from the fraud so many of them in fact practise when they fail to advise workers of the dangers of the jobs on offer. (Someone might object that even if capitalists are not morally obliged to offer jobs, they are obliged to offer unhazardous ones *if* they offer jobs. But while there is no conceptual incoherence in that view, I cannot see any reason for adopting it, once it has been provided that jobs known to be hazardous are labeled as such).

Someone who believes in the moral rights of capitalists could acknowledge that John was forced to take a hazardous job and add that, while his position was indeed unenviable, it is inevitable that some people's entitlements impose restrictions on other people's freedom.[31] That is a thoroughly consistent position, though the most prominent philosophical defender of capitalists' rights, Robert Nozick, seems not to think so. For he argues, absurdly, that a person's freedom is impaired only when his choices are restricted by actions of others which are unjust. As long as people do only what they are entitled to do, no one is unfree as a result.[32]

But you cannot *both* deny that justice restricts freedom *and* claim that private property is just, since the institution of private property, like any other set of rules for holding and using things, both grants freedom *and* restricts it; owners of private property are only free to do as they wish with what they own because nonowners are unfree to. A more consistent Nozickian would acknowledge the unfreedom inherent in private property and defend the justice of particular holdings of private property on the basis of their moral pedigree. Private property, he would say, is justly held, whatever may be its effect on nonowners' freedom, if it came into being justly and was transferred justly from person to person until it reached its present owner. That is what people like Nozick are really saying when the rhetoric of freedom, to which they are not entitled, is removed.

Let us focus on the claim that private property is justly held if (among other things) it came into being justly. Two questions must be answered about the initial formation of private property if a Nozick-like defense of existing private property is to stand and if, therefore, the currently dominant philosophical rationale for capitalism is to display John's adverse situation as free of moral taint. The first question is, by what means, if any, *could* private property be legitimately formed? And the second is, was *actual* private property formed by any such means?[33]

Note that all, or virtually all, physical private property either is, or is made of, something which was once no one's private property, since (virtually) all physical private property comes immediately or ultimately from the land, which was there before any people, hence before any private owners. Some of what was once no one's remains substantially no one's even now, and therefore accessible to everyone: The air people breathe is still public property. The rest has been removed from the public domain and turned into private property. If, then, someone claims a Nozick-like moral entitlement to something he legally owns, we may ask, apart from how he in particular got it, with what right it came to be anyone's private property in the first place; we may pose, in respect of his claim, the two questions raised at the end of the last paragraph.

We can be pretty confident that the answer to the second question will be "No". Imagine a typical property owner in confrontation with a trespasser who challenges the owner's property right, and imagine too, rather unrealistically, that the property owner is both thoroughly honest and exceptionally well informed. Then the dialogue between him and the trespasser might go as follows:

Owner: Get off my land!

Trepasser: What makes it yours?

O: I bought it from Smith.

T: Where did Smith get it?

O: His father willed it to him.

T: And how did Smith Senior come to have it?

O: It belonged to Alley Oop, who gave it to Smith Senior in payment for services rendered.

T: How did Alley Oop get it?

O: He seized it and successfully fought off all comers.

T: Well, I wasn't born soon enough to be one of those comers, so I'll fight you for it now.

To this O's only possible response is to apply, if he can, the same superior force which made the thing private property in the first place. Only readers with more intellectual restraint than I am able to muster will dissent from the view that if it was morally all right then for sheer force to make the land Oop's, it is morally all right now for sheer force to make it Trespasser's, so that even if the land is now legitimately Owner's, that does Owner limited good, since it may also be legitimately taken from him. If, on the other hand, Oop's original seizing was not morally right, then Owner's claim collapses. So either way Owner's claim is insecure, if it is historically based, given what the history was probably like.

Now Nozick does not say that sheer force, regardless of circumstance, legitimately makes public property private. His answer to the first question on page 73 is, roughly, that private property is formed legitimately if and when someone appropriates what no one privately owns without thereby making anyone else worse off than he would have been had the thing remained not privately owned.[34] But this condition is too weak, for reasons I am unable to develop here: It ignores what would have happened had the thing been privately appropriated by some other person, and also what would have happened had socialist rules been imposed on the use of the thing. The only different possibility Nozick considers is that in which the thing remains in unstructured common use, and there are other relevant possibilities to be considered.[35]

Philosophers of the political Right used to defend unrestricted private property against Left and liberal criticism in debate governed by a shared acceptance of principles of need, merit, and desert. Nozick's rejection of such "patterned" principles in favor of a focus on the history of holdings was supposed to make the philosophical defense of private property easier.[36] I do not think it does.[37]

Notes

1. I wish to thank the Earhart, Jon M. Olin, and Reason Foundations for making it possible, in part, for me to work on this project. I also wish to thank Bill Puka and Gertrude Ezorsky for their very valuable criticism of an earlier draft of this essay, despite their very likely disapproval of my views.

2. This observation rests, in part, on epistemological insights available, for example, in Hanna F. Pitkin, *Wittgenstin and Justice* (Berkeley, Calif.: University of California Press, 1972).

3. Tibor R. Machan, "A Reconsideration of Natural Rights Theory," *American Philosohical Quarterly* 19 (January 1980): 61–72.

4. Peter Huber, "Exorcists vs. Gatekeepers in Risk Regulation," *Regulation* (November/December 1983), 23.

5. But see Steven Kelman, "Regulation and Paternalism," *Rights and Regulation,* ed. T. R. Machan and M. B. Johnson (Cambridge, Mass.: Ballinger Publ. Co., 1983), 217–48.

6. David Braybrooke, *Ethics in the World of Business* (Totowa, N.J.: Rowman & Allanheld, 1983), 223.

7. Ibid., 224.

8. For an attempt to forge a collectivist theory of rights, see Tom Campbell, *The Left and Rights* (London and Boston: Routledge & Kegan Paul, 1983).

9. Huber, "Exorcists vs. Gatekeepers," 23.

10. Ibid. Huber observes that "Every insurance company knows that life is growing safer, but the public is firmly convinced that living is becoming ever more

hazardous" (p. 23). In general, capitalism's benefits to workers have simply not been acknowledged, especially by moral and political philosophers! It is hardly possible to avoid the simple fact that the workers of the world believe differently, judging by what system they prefer to emigrate to whenever possible.

11. The OSHA Act of 1970, Pub.L.No. 91–596, 84 Stat. 1590, is codified at 27 U.S.S. 651–78 (1976).

12. Cf. David Zimmerman's summary of the dispute, "Coercive Wage Offers," *Philosophy and Public Affairs* 10 (1981): 133–34.

13. Robert Nozick, "Coercion," *Philosophy, Politics and Society,* ed. P. Laslett, W. G. Runciman, and Q. Skinner (New York: Barnes & Noble Books, 1972), 450.

14. For example, Nozick considers the example of the drug supplier who proposes that he give an addict his usual dose for $20 only if the addict, in addition, performs a disagreeable task. Nozick suggests the proposal is a threat because here the addict's preference is for the normally expected baseline (the $20 dose), not the morally required baseline (no drug). We need to know why the addict's preference is here (always?) decisive. Cf. Nozick, "Coercion," 451 and Zimmerman, "Coercive Wage Offers," 129.

15. This objection is effectively argued by Zimmerman, "Coercive Wage Offers."

16. The elderly who have to eat dog food may be a case of quasi-coercion.

17. The theory is affirmed by some of those who call themselves Marxists, and a passage in *The German Ideology* of Marx and Engels might be thought to support it, but I would not read it that way. See Marx and Engels, *Collected Works,* vol. 5, (London, 1976): 231.

18. The normative questions addressed in section 8 do not lend themselves to the treatment appropriate to the conceptual questions discussed in sections 3 through 7.

19a. I obtained this datum from a Hastings Center document, *Occupational Health and the Concept of Responsibility* (January 1980), and hereafter referred to as Hastings (1980).

19b. Where "being able to do A" is taken in its narrow sense of "having the capacity to do A," being free to do A is not a necessary condition of being able to do A, but I intend "being able to do A" in a perfectly ordinary but broader sense.

20.   However, see pages 66–67, where I argue against this natural supposition.

21.   "Acting Freely", *Nous* 4 (1970): 381. I say "something like", since, to cater for a point made by Lawrence Davis, it would be better to say "A does X freely if and only if A does X and does not do X for reasons he minds acting from." See his *Philosohy of Action* (Englewood Cliffs, N.J.: Prentice-Hall, 1979), 123.

22.   Such as Ziyad Husami, if he is a Marxist, who says of the wage worker: "Deprived of the ownership of means of production and means of livelihood he is forced (not free) to sell his labour power to the capitalist." (Marx on Distributive Justice, *Philosophy and Public Affairs* [Fall 1978], 51–52). I contend that the phrase in parentheses introduces a falsehood into Husami's sentence, a falsehood that Karl Marx avoided when he said of the worker that "the time for which he is free to sell his labour power is the time for which he is forced to sell it." (*Capital* 1, [Moscow, 1961]: 302 and ibid., 766: "The wage-worker . . . is compelled to sell himself of his own free will.")

23.   The objection to this premiss which was raised on page 64 could also be raised here, but it can be dealt with as I dealt with it there.

24.   It would, I concede, be natural for him to say: "I was not free to stand fast, since I would have been shot had I done so." And it is in general natural to say of the unacceptable alternatives available when one is forced to do something that one is not free to take them, because of their costs. That is certainly a reason for denying T^1, but I think it is outweighed by the main reason for affirming it, which is the argument just given, and, in particular, its premise that one cannot do what one is not free to do.

   How might one who affirms T^1 contrive to explain the recalicitrant linguistic data? He might suggest that the person who says he was not free to stand fast is engaging in harmless hyperpole. The unhyperbolical truth is that he was much less than *entirely* free to stand fast. His freedom to stand fast was very restricted, and we understand him to mean that, and not that he was not at all free to stand fast, when he says what he does.

25.   Leftists are not, that is, questioning John's capacity to make decisions but emphasizing the limited scope he has for using that capacity. A tendency to confuse these importantly distinct issues is revealed in the following passage:

The very setting of a prison adds a coercive element which raises questions about the autonomous decision-making capacity of the prisoner. It is reasonable to assume that economic stress and the need for employment also represent a severe restriction of free choice. (Hastings 1980, p. 3)

Economically stringent circumstances restrict freedom regardless of the effect they have on agents' powers of decision. They can, indeed, have that further effect, but the Leftist claim about John does not entail that they do, and the claim is therefore not false if they do not.

26.   There is much more to be said about the relationship between individual freedom and collective unfreedom, and I have tried to say some of it in "The Structure of Proletarian Unfreedom," *Philosophy and Public Affairs*, 12 (Winter 1983) from which several pages of the present piece are drawn, by kind permission of the editor of *Philosophy and Public Affairs*.

27.   Hastings mentions working-class preoccupation with the present at the expense of the future, the cause of which is the greater urgency of present constraints, and one effect of which is a greater likelihood of remaining within those constraints. Since the situation of urgency that causes the psychological deficiency is imposed not by nature but by society, one might argue that this particular deficiency is an unfreedom. (See "The Structure of Proletarian Unfreedom," for further discussion of the difference between unfreedom and incapacity.)

28.   The expected utility of a course of action is the sum of the products of the utility and probability of each of its possible outcomes.

29.   See Nicholas Ashford, *Crisis in the Workplace* (Cambridge, Mass.: M.I.T. Press, 1976), 16, 19, 28–29.

30.   This essay was originally prepared for presentation at a seminar held at the Hastings Center in 1982. The question quoted above comes from a letter to its prospective participants by Thomas Murray.

31.   Compare the remarks of Mr. Justice Pitney quoted by Howard Lesnick on p. 6 of "The Consciousness of Work and the Consciousness of Freedom," which he presented at the Hastings seminar. Among the "inequalities of fortune that are the necessary result of the exercise of" the rights of private property are certain inequalities of freedom.

32.   See Robert Nozick, *Anarchy, State and Utopia,* (New York: 1974), 262. For criticism of Nozick's views on this matter, see my "Robert Nozick and Wilt Chamberlain," *Justice and Economic Distribution,* ed. John Arthur and William Shaw (Englewood Cliffs, N.J.: Prentice-Hall, 1978), 151; "Illusions about Private Property and Freedom," *Issues in Marxist Philosophy,* ed. John Mepham and David Ruben, 4, (Hassocks, Sussex: Harvester Press, 1981): 228–29; "Freedom, Justice and Capitalism," *New Left Review,* no. 126 (March/April 1981), 10–11.

33.   I ignore here the (surely unactualized) possibility that initial malinformation in the generation of private property was rectified later. See Nozick, *Justice and Economic Distribution,* 151–53, 230–31, on principles of rectification.

34.   See ibid., 178ff. If this is not Nozick's answer to that question, he has not, remarkably enough, publicly answered it.

35.   For an extended development of this point, see my "Nozick on Appropriation," *New Left Review,* no. 150 (March/April 1985), 80–107; "Self-Ownership, World-Ownership, and Equality: Part II," *Social Philosophy and Policy,* vol. 3, no. 2 (Spring 1986), 77–86.

36.   Nozick, *Justice and Economic Distribution,* 155ff.

37.   I thank John McMurtry, David Owen, and Steven Walt for their criticisms of a draft of this paper.

PART 3 _____

FREEDOM, COERCION, AND THE RIGHT TO PRIVACY

Whistle Blowing: The AMA and the Pharmaceutical Industry*

Report from the Conference on Professional Responsibility ____

> I reached a point where I could no longer live with myself.
>
> —Dale Console

In 1960, Dr. A. Dale Console, a former medical director at E. R. Squibb and Sons, gave the public and Congress their first detailed view of the way drug companies increase sales through exploitation of physicians and manipulation of improper prescription of drugs. In testimony before the Kefauver hearings on drug price competition, he described the "inroads the [drug] industry has made into the entire structure of medicine and medical care."[1]

"Unfortunately drugs are not always prescribed wisely," he told the committee, "and while the physician and patient among others must share the responsibility for this with the pharmaceutical industry, it is the industry that carefully nurtures and encourages the practice. . . .

"The pharmaceutical industry is unique in that it can make exploitation appear a noble purpose. It is the organized, carefully planned, and skillful execution of this exploitation which constitutes one of the costs of drugs, which must be measured not only in dollars but in terms of the inroads the industry has made into the entire structure of medicine and medical care. With the enormous resources at its command, it has usurped the place of the medical educator and has successfully substituted propaganda for education."[2]

---

* Reprinted from Ralph Nader, et al. eds., "The AMA and the Pharmaceutical Industry," *Whistleblowing* (New York: Grossman Publishers, 1972), 118–25, by permission of the editor. Copyright © 1972 by Ralph Nader.

Dr. Console went on to indict the industry—not Squibb alone—for promotional techniques that included:

1) a "barrage of irrelevant facts [the physician] has neither the time, the inclination, nor frequently the expert knowledge to examine critically,"[3]

2) the hard-sell tactics of detail men who follow the maxim "If you can't convince them, confuse them,"[4] and

3) the testimonials that "are used not only to give apparent substance to the advertising and promotion of relatively worthless products, but also to extend the indications of effective drugs beyond the range of their real utility."[5]

He was equally severe in his criticism of physicians and their organizations for the "unhealthy" and "in many ways corrupt" relationship with the drug companies they allowed and sometimes welcomed, frequently associated with the large grants and gifts the industry makes available to physicians.

It was a dramatic indictment, the more so because it came from the "inside," from someone who had been close to the drug industry as few critics had been before. For six and a half years, Dr. Console had worked as a drug company doctor, having resigned four years before the Kefauver hearings. Both then and in 1969, when he testified before Senator Gaylord Nelson's Monopoly Subcommittee of the Select Committee on Small Business, he gave the public a rare and vivid portrait of the individual who is forced to sacrifice his scruples to the will of the organization. His testimony was both a severe criticism of the industry and a comment on the manipulation of corporate employees to serve corporate aims.

As an example, Dr. Console described the company doctor's function of "reviewing" and "approving" advertising copy:

"Drug companies boast that all advertising copy is reviewed or approved by the medical staff. Most [ads] require 'approval' since review is pointless if the doctor has no voice in determining what is and what is not acceptable. This poses problems for the doctor. In the first place, *all* advertising copy makes a mountain of paper, some of which is difficult to digest. Overall, the task is dull and boring. In addition, the doctor who does not approve the majority of copy that reaches his desk is not likely to keep his job. Yet over and over again he is faced with advertising that is obviously misleading and which he cannot approve in good conscience. The dilemma is best resolved by a bizarre process of reasoning. . . .

"The doctor who reviews advertising copy must learn to ask himself not whether the advertisement is misleading, but rather whether it can pass. . . . Under [certain] conditions the advertisement can be defended against any attempt to prove it false or misleading. The doctor who wishes to keep his job in the drug industry will find it mandatory to use this kind of reasoning. In desperate situations what can pass can be stretched to almost infinite limits. The determining factors are the mental and verbal facility of the doctor or lawyer who must defend it."[6]

The list of what a drug company doctor must learn if he is to advance in the industry became so long, so personally and professionally obnoxious, that Console finally had enough.

He had found that the drug company doctor "must learn the many ways to deceive the Food and Drug Administration and, failing in this, to seduce, manipulate, or threaten the physician assigned to the New Drug Application into approving it even if it is incomplete.

"He must learn that anything that helps to sell a drug is valid even if it is supported by the crudest testimonial, while anything that decreases sales must be suppressed, distorted, and rejected because it is not absolutely conclusive proof.

"He must learn to word a warning statement so it will appear to be an inducement to use the drug rather than a warning of the dangers inherent in its use.

"He must learn, when a drug has been found too dangerous for use in this country, he can approve its use in other countries where the laws are less stringent and people have less protection. He must learn, when a drug has been found useless on one side of the Rio Grande, it can be sold as a panacea on the other side and that he is expected to approve claims made for it.

"He will find himself squeezed between businessmen who will sell anything and justify it on the basis that doctors ask for it and doctors who demand products they have been taught to want through the advertising and promotion schemes contrived by businessmen. If he can absorb all this, and more, and still maintain any sensibilities he will learn the true meaning of loneliness and alienation.

"During my tenure as medical director I learned the meaning of loneliness and alienation. I reached a point where I could no longer live with myself. I had compromised to the point where my back was against a wall and I had to choose between resigning myself to total capitulation or resigning as medical director. I chose the latter course."[7]

Dr. Console resigned from his position at Squibb in June, 1957. The next two years he spent on a psychiatric fellowship paid for by Squibb. When his relationship with the company was completely severed in 1959, and he began practicing psychiatry in Princeton, New Jersey, Console considered writing a book about the industry. His intention was not to pillory his former employer. On the contrary, he has defended Squibb as one of the "more ethical" pharmaceutical firms, and he destroyed the records in his private file when he resigned, records which might have been used as proof of specific abuses concerning specific drugs had Dr. Console chosen that route. He decided instead to offer "a distillate of my experience and the opinions I have formed as a result of that experience."[8]

But he was concerned about the possibility of a libel suit if he wrote the book. He was confident such a suit would not be successful, but it would mean heavy financial costs for him. Then the invitation to testify before the Kefauver committee offered him the platform he sought. It was an opportunity for whistle blowing that was certain to attract public attention and assured him immunity from "legal" harassment by the industry.

The fifty pages of testimony he subsequently produced for several congressional committees provided a strong witness for the need to strengthen government control over the testing and marketing of drugs. His evidence undermined notions that the industry was successfully policing itself or that physicians were providing a viable check to abuses. As a physician himself, Console was a unique critic of his own profession's willingness to turn over "postgraduate medical education" to the drug industry.[9] He reminded them that "we are still human in spite of being physicians. As humans, we are vulnerable to all forms of flattery, cajolery, and blandishments, subtle or otherwise." He then demonstrated how "the drug industry has learned to manipulate this vulnerability with techniques whose sophistication approaches perfection."[10]

Reflecting later on what motivated him to become a whistle blower, Console said, "While I am convinced that I am motivated by a deep sense of moral indignation, I am equally motivated by a deep personal feeling of resentment. The roots of that resentment run deep, and my contribution was an incredible degree of idealism and unrealistic expectations that set me up as a patsy for disillusionment and disappointment.

"I grew up with the concept that medicine is a noble profession. I spent some fourteen years, or one-quarter of my present life span, cloistered in an ivory tower. For four years I was a medical student. Eight years were spent in postdoctoral (or residency) training, and the remaining years I was a member of the faculty of the medical college. Throughout these years I was exposed to all the very best that medicine has to offer.

"I had been exposed to, and was appalled by, shabby practices I had observed when I served as a substitute intern in small hospitals during medical school vacations. These were brief stints and after each of them I returned to the cloistered life in the ivory tower. Naively I came to believe that the totality of my personal experience was a true and accurate representation of the reality of medical practice."[11]

What he discovered when he entered the drug industry was far different. He concluded that "in today's practice of medicine one of the simplest professional tasks a physician is required to perform is the writing of a prescription. Since it is simple and uncomplicated, many physicians would like to reduce the practice of medicine to the practice of writing prescriptions. . . . Since a drug company's profit is dependent on the number of prescriptions written for its products, its advertising and promotion practices carefully nurture the concept that the prescription pad is omnipotent. The end result is what I once labeled a *folie à deux*. The physician and the drug company each serves his own purposes. Both of them dance but the patient pays the piper."[12]

Console also observed the transition of Squibb, indeed of the entire drug industry, from a "family corporation" to the "modern corporation," huge, largely anonymous, concerned with profits and an ever-increasing market rather than with consumer interests. "When I joined it, twenty years ago, Squibb was still a family corporation, management was still guided by the philosophy and the policies of the company's founder, and the medical director was a physician's physician. In time, ownership of the company changed hands, management changed, and most important the entire drug industry changed. Having written some fifty pages of testimony on the nature, meaning, and consequences of those changes, I now find myself in the position of trying to say it all in one sentence. I heard the sentence frequently spoken by a vice-president who offered it as fatherly advice and as an unsubtle threat: 'It's easy to find a lawyer who will tell you that you can't do something; the trick is to find one who will show you how you can do it, even if he costs more.' To me this single sentence always has been, and still is, the epitome of shabbiness and all of its ramifications."[13]

To counter the new corporation's focusing of enormous resources on narrow interests, Console is convinced that people within the organization must speak out. "We could make no greater mistake than to be lulled into a sense of false security by believing that some disembodied force called the government will act like a beneficent big brother and make certain that the special interests will not predominate. If the general welfare is to be protected, it will be protected by the actions of people, not the government, and the actions of people are one of the primary concerns of this Whistle Blowers Conference."[14]

His view of whistle blowing (a term Console himself prefers not to use) is that it should ideally be a lifetime affair, carried on in the private as well as the public sphere. In addition to his public statements, he has criticized the medical profession through private correspondence for serving the interests of the drug industry and has tried to institute change through internal channels. Recently, for example, he wrote the editor of a state medical journal criticizing the journal's practice of blatantly endorsing the products of drug companies that bought advertisements. This journal scattered through its pages boxed notices urging its readers to "Patronize Our Advertisers. They Merit Your Support." Even worse, he found one issue to contain the notice: "Not everyone can advertise in this JOURNAL. When you see an advertisement here you know that the company or the service has been stamped 'approved.' As you read our advertising pages, you get a compact little course on what's new. And if you tell the company that you saw his notice in these pages you remind him that this is a happy medium for his services or his company. These pages deserve your consideration."

Console protested that "stamped as 'approved' " suggested the society or journal had actually tested the products. It was at least an unjustified endorsement of products based solely on the willingness of companies to purchase advertising space in the publication, he said. The medical society reviewed the practice, and it has since been discontinued.

Console has also made a study of the difference between claims made for drugs marketed in Italy, where restrictions on advertising and labeling are few, and claims for the same drugs in the United States. The comparison shows, he says, that "any notion of the morality of the drug industry is a hollow mockery." Drug companies blatantly omit warnings to physicians and consumers in markets where regulations do not require them, even though their products must carry such warnings by law elsewhere. His study was prepared for a congressional inquiry into drug company practices abroad.

Though he analyzed his own motivation to speak out, Console refused to do the same for the hundreds who fail to do so. "We are faced with the knotty problem of why a small handful of people do act while the vast majority remain passive even though its vital interests are at stake. A partial answer to this question is found in the simple fact that only a small handful of the people are ever exposed to a naked view of the operations, techniques, and methods used by the special interest groups. This is, at best, a partial answer since it is also obvious that only a small percentage of those who do gain access to this restricted information elect to 'speak out' while the majority elects to 'go along with it.' "[15]

One reason may be that there is not always a way out of the organization, such as Console found when he entered psychiatry as a private practitioner. For the drug company doctor who remains in the industry, there is little protection. What recourse does he have against losing his job if he refuses to "approve" a worthless drug or a misleading advertisement? The answer is, none. Console makes the point that policing of the industry cannot be done entirely through government regulation. Professional watchdogs within the organization, acting on a daily basis, have a far greater opportunity to assure that the public is not harmed and physicians are not gulled by unsafe drugs. But until the medical profession provides protection for the conscientious drug company doctor, he may, like Console, find his "back against a wall" with the untenable choice of "resigning himself to total capitulation" or resigning as medical director.

An Anatomy of Whistle Blowing*

Ralph Nader _____

Americans believe that they have set for themselves and for the rest of the world a high example of individual freedom. That example inevitably refers to the struggle by a minority of aggrieved citizens against the royal tyranny of King George III. Out of the struggle that established this nation some chains were struck off and royal fiats abolished. America became a nation with the conviction that arbitrary government action should not restrict the freedom of individuals to follow their own consciences.

Today arbitrary treatment of citizens by powerful institutions has assumed a new form, no less insidious than that which prevailed in an earlier time. The "organization" has emerged and spread its invisible chains. Within the structure of the organization there has taken place an erosion of both human values and the broader value of human beings as the possibility of dissent within the hierarchy has become so restricted that common candor requires uncommon courage. The large organization is lord and manor, and most of its employees have been desensitized much as were medieval peasants who never knew they were serfs. It is true that often the immediate physical deprivations are far fewer, but the price of this fragile shield has been the dulling of the senses and perceptions of new perils and pressures of a far more embracing consequence.

Some of these perils may be glimpsed when it is realized that our society now has the numbing capacity to destroy itself inadvertently by continuing the domestic chemical and biological warfare against its citizens and their environments. Our political economy has also developed an inverted genius that can combine an increase in the gross national product with an increase in the gross national misery. Increasingly, larger organizations—public and

* Reprinted from Ralph Nader et al. eds., *Whistleblowing* (New York: Grossman Publishers, 1972), 3–11, by permission of editor. Copyright © 1972 by Ralph Nader.

private—possess a Medea-like intensity to paralyze conscience, initiative, and proper concern for people outside the organization.

Until recently, all hopes for change in corporate and government behavior have been focused on external pressures on the organization, such as regulation, competition, litigation, and exposure to public opinion. There was little attention given to the simple truth that the adequacy of these external stimuli is very significantly dependent on the internal freedom of those within the organization.

Corporate employees are among the first to know about industrial dumping of mercury or fluoride sludge into waterways, defectively designed automobiles, or undisclosed adverse effects of prescription drugs and pesticides. They are the first to grasp the technical capabilities to prevent existing product or pollution hazards. But they are very often the last to speak out, much less to refuse to be recruited for acts of corporate or governmental negligence or predation. Staying silent in the face of a professional duty has direct impact on the level of consumer and environmental hazards. But this awareness has done little to upset the slavish adherence to "following company orders."

Silence in the face of abuses may also be evaluated in terms of the toll it takes on the individuals who in doing so subvert their own consciences. For example, the twenty-year collusion by the domestic automobile companies against development and marketing of exhaust control systems is a tragedy, among other things, for engineers who, minion-like, programmed the technical artifices of the industry's defiance. Settling the antitrust case brought by the Justice Department against such collusion did nothing to confront the question of subverted engineering integrity.

The key question is, at what point should an employee resolve that allegiance to society (e.g., the public safety) must supersede allegiance to the organization's policies (e.g., the corporate profit), and then act on that resolve by informing outsiders or legal authorities? It is a question that involves basic issues of individual freedom, concentration of power, and information flow to the public. These issues in turn involve daily choices such as the following:

To report or not to report:

1) defective vehicles in the process of being marketed to unsuspecting consumers;
2) vast waste of government funds by private contractors;
3) the industrial dumping of mercury in waterways;
4) the connection between companies and campaign contributions;
5) a pattern of discrimination by age, race, or sex in a labor union or company;
6) mishandling the operation of a workers' pension fund;
7) willful deception in advertising a worthless or harmful product;

8) the sale of putrid or adulterated meats, chemically camouflaged in supermarkets;
9) the use of government power for private, corporate, or industry gain;
10) the knowing nonenforcement of laws being seriously violated, such as pesticide laws;
11) rank corruption in an agency or company;
12) the suppression of serious occupational disease data.

It is clear that hundreds and often thousands of people are privy to such information but choose to remain silent within their organizations. Some are conscience-stricken in so doing and want guidance. Actually, the general responsibility is made clear for the professional by codes of ethics. These codes invariably etch the primary allegiance to the public interest, while the Code of Ethics for United States Government Service does the same: "Put loyalty to the highest moral principles and to country above loyalty to persons, party, or Government department." The difficulty rests in the judgment to be exercised by the individual and its implementation. Any potential whistle blower has to ask and try to answer a number of questions:

1) Is my knowledge of the matter complete and accurate?
2) What are the objectionable practices and what public interests do they harm?
3) How far should I and can I go inside the organization with my concern or objection?
4) Will I be violating any rules by contacting outside parties and, if so, is whistle blowing nevertheless justified?
5) Will I be violating any laws or ethical duties by *not* contacting external parties?
6) Once I have decided to act, what is the best way to blow the whistle—anonymously, overtly, by resignation prior to speaking out, or in some other way?
7) What will be likely responses from various sources—inside and outside the organization—to the whistle blowing action?
8) What is expected to be achieved by whistle blowing in the particular situation? . . .

There is a great need to develop an ethic of whistle blowing which can be practically applied in many contexts, especially within corporate and governmental bureaucracies. For this to occur, people must be permitted to cultivate their own form of allegiance to their fellow citizens and exercise it without having their professional careers or employment opportunities destroyed. This new ethic will develop if employees have the right to due process within their organizations and if they have at least some of the rights—such as the right to speak freely—that now protect them from state power. In the past, as the balance of this book documents, whistle blowing has illuminated dark corners of our society, saved lives, prevented injuries and disease, and stopped corruption, economic waste, and material exploitation. Conversely, the absence of such professional and individual responsibility has perpetuated these conditions. In this context, whistle blowing, if carefully defined and protected by law, can become another of those adaptive, self-implementing mechanisms which mark the relative difference between a free society that relies on free institutions and a closed society that depends on authoritarian institutions.

Indeed, the basic status of a citizen in a democracy underscores the themes implicit in a form of professional and individual responsibility that places responsibility to society over that to an illegal or negligent or unjust organizational policy or activity. These themes touch the right of free speech, the right to information, the citizen's right to participate in important public decisions, and the individual's obligation to avoid complicity in harmful, fraudulent, or corrupt activities. Obviously, as in the exercise of constitutional rights, abuses may occur, but this has long been considered an acceptable risk of free speech within very broad limits. . . .

Still, the willingness and ability of insiders to blow the whistle is the last line of defense ordinary citizens have against the denial of their rights and the destruction of their interests by secretive and powerful institutions. As organizations penetrate deeper and deeper into the lives of people—from pollution to poverty to income erosion to privacy invasion—more of their rights and interests are adversely affected. This fact of contemporary life has generated an ever greater moral imperative for employees to be reasonably protected in upholding such rights regardless of their employers' policies. The corporation, the labor unions and professional societies to which its employees belong, the government in its capacity as employer, and the law must all change or be changed to make protection of the responsible whistle blower possible.

Each corporation should have a bill of rights for its employees and a system of internal appeals to guarantee these rights. As a condition of employment, workers at every level in the corporate hierarchy should have the right to express their reservations about the company's activities and policies, and their views should be accorded a fair hearing. They should have the right to "go public," and the corporation should expect them to do so when internal channels of communication are exhausted and the problem remains uncorrected.

Unions and professional societies should strengthen their ethical codes— and adopt such codes if they do not already have them. They should put teeth into mechanisms for implementing their codes and require that they be observed not only by members but also by organizations that employ their members. Unions should move beyond the traditional "bread and butter" issues, the societies should escape their preoccupation with abstract professionalism, and both should apply their significant potential power to protecting members who refuse to be automatons. Whistle blowers who belong to labor unions have fared only slightly better than their unorganized counterparts, except when public opinion and the whistle blower's fellow workers are sufficiently aroused. This is partly a result of the bureaucratized cooptation of many labor leaders by management and the suppression of rank and file dissent within the union or local.

Government employees should be treated like public servants if they are to be expected to behave like them. Today, civil service laws and regulations serve two primary functions, each the exact opposite of those intended by Congress. First, they tend to reward or at least shield incompetence and sloth. Second, they discourage creativity and diligence and undermine the professional and individual responsibility of those who serve. You might say that the speed of exit of a public servant is almost directly proportional to his commitment to serve the public. The Civil Service Commission itself is in need of major reform. Its clients are the personnel managers of the various agencies, not the individual employees. Like other regulatory agencies it has been captured by the very group whose conduct it was created to regulate. A new administrative court should be created and invested with all the employee protection functions now given to the commission. Civil servants should be guaranteed the right to bring agency dereliction to public attention as a last resort. And they should have the right to go to court to protect themselves from harassment and discharge for doing their duty. To reduce the high cost of pursuing their lawful remedies, employees who challenge agency action against them should continue to receive their pay until all of their appeals are exhausted, and they should be permitted to recover the costs of their appeals from the government if they ultimately win.

All areas of the law touching upon the employee-employer relationship should be reexamined with an eye to modifying substantially the old rule that an employer can discharge an employee for acts of conscience without regard to the damage done to the employee. Existing laws that regulate industry should be amended to include provisions protecting employees who cooperate with authorities. The concept of trade secrecy is now used by business and government alike to suppress information that the public has a substantial need to know. A sharp distinction must be drawn between individual privacy and corporate secrecy, and the law of trade secrecy is a good place to begin. The Freedom of Information Act, which purports to establish public access to all but the most sensitive information in the hands of the federal government, can become a toothless perversion because civil servants who release information in the spirit of the act are punished while those who suppress it are rewarded.

Whistle blowing is encouraged actively by some laws and government administrators to assist in law enforcement. Under the recently rediscovered Refuse Act of 1899, for example, anyone who reports a polluter is entitled to one-half of any fine collected—even if the person making the report is an employee of the polluting company. And corporations constantly probe government agencies to locate whistle blowers on their behalf. Consumers need routine mechanisms to encourage the increased flow of information that deals with health, safety, environmental hazards, corruption, and waste inside corporate and governmental institutions. Whistle blowing can show the need for such systemic affirmations of the public's right to know.

The Clearinghouse for Professional Responsibility, P. O. Box 486, Washington, D.C. 20044, will assist in the endeavor to establish such mechanisms and will suggest alternative actions to sincere persons considering blowing the whistle. Organization dissenters on matters of important public interest should feel free to contact the Clearinghouse with any information they believe will help citizens protect themselves from the depredations of large organizations.

The rise in public consciousness among the young and among minority groups has generated a sharper concept of duty among many citizens, recalling Alfred North Whitehead's dictum, "Duty arises from our potential control over the course of events." But loyalties do not end at the boundaries of an organization. "Just following orders" was an attitude that the United States military tribunals rejected in judging others after World War II at Nuremberg. And for those who set their behavior by the ethics of the great religions, with their universal golden rule, the right to appeal to a higher authority is the holiest of rights.

The whistle blowing ethic is not new; it simply has to begin flowering responsibly in new fields where its harvests will benefit people as citizens and consumers. Once developed and defended as recommended by the other participants in the Conference on Professional Responsibility and by the final chapters of this book, a most powerful lever for organizational responsibility and accountability will be available. The realistic tendency of such an internal check within General Motors or the Department of the Interior will be to assist traditional external checks to work more effectively in their statutory or market-defined missions in the public interest. . . .

. . . The exercise of ethical whistle blowing requires a broader, enabling environment for it to be effective. There must be those who listen and those whose potential or realized power can utilize the information for advancing justice. Thus, as with any democratic institutions, other links are necessary to secure the objective changes beyond the mere exposure of the abuses. the courts, professional and citizen groups, the media, the Congress, and honorable segments throughout our society are part of this enabling environment. They must comprehend that the tyranny of organizations, with their excessive security against accountability, must be prevented from trammeling a fortified conscience within their midst. Organizational power must be insecure to some degree if it is to be more responsible. A greater freedom of individual conviction within the organization can provide the needed deterrent—the creative insecurity which generates a more suitable climate of responsiveness to the public interest and public rights.

Freedom of Contract*

Included in the right of personal liberty and the right of private property—partaking of the nature of each—is the right to make contracts for the acquisition of property. Chief among such contracts is that of personal employment, by which labor and other services are exchanged for money or other forms of property. If this right be struck down or arbitrarily interfered with, there is a substantial impairment of liberty in the long-established constitutional sense. The right is as essential to the laborer as to the capitalist, to the poor as to the rich; for the vast majority of persons have no other honest way to begin to acquire property, save by working for money. . . .

No doubt, wherever the right of private property exists, there must and will be inequalities of fortune; and thus it naturally happens that parties negotiating about a contract are not equally unhampered by circumstances. This applies to all contracts, and not merely to that between employer and employee. Indeed a little reflection will show that wherever the right of private property and the right of free contract co-exist, each party when contracting is inevitably more or less influenced by the question whether he has much property, or little, or none; for the contract is made to the very end that each may gain something that he needs or desires more urgently than that which he proposed to give in exchange. And, since it is self-evident that, unless all things are held in common, some persons must have more property than others, it is from the nature of things impossible to uphold freedom of contract and the right of private property without at the same time recognizing as legitimate those inequalities of fortune that are the necessary result of the exercise of those rights.

---

* *Coppage* v. *Kansas,* 236 U.S. (1914), 14–17.

Work and Freedom in Capitalism

Kurt Nutting _____

Defenders of capitalist social and economic institutions sometimes claim these institutions allow more individual freedom than any other feasible system. For example, the economist Milton Friedman says that "a society dedicated to freedom" must rely "primarily on the market to organize economic activity," and this, he says, involves a system of "competitive capitalism."[16]

Traditionally, defenders of laissez-faire capitalism define "freedom" negatively, as a lack of coercion, interference, or obstruction by others of one person's actions.[17] And a capitalist economy is characterized by the ownership of the means of production, distribution, and exchange (for example, land, buildings, and machinery) by private individuals. But it is not necessary in a capitalist economy for everyone to own enough of these things (capital) on which to live. Typically, in fact, in such economies ownership of capital is quite unequal. The claim I criticize here is that in the absence of state regulation, capitalist economies involve only minimal coercion. Or, to put it another way, capitalist economies allow a maximum of individual freedom.

It is my contention here that this claim—that laissez-faire, capitalist economic institutions maximize individual freedom—is mistaken. Economic systems in which capital is not controlled by all of the actual laborers will involve coercion and, therefore, a lessening of individual freedom.

Part of what is involved in owning something is that the owner has a right to manage it. This means that the owner has the "right to decide how and by whom the thing owned shall be used.[18] For example, if the thing owned is a factory, the right to manage includes the powers to decide what shall be produced, where, and in what manner, and the power to contract with others to provide raw materials, to hire and fire labor, and so forth.

Owners are, therefore, legally empowered to regulate the working conditions of others. When the law allows unrestricted management rights for owners, the owners may decide what time of day workers will work, and what goods and services will be produced in what quantity. They may fix the pace of work, the manner of work, and decide who will work and who will not. They may decide how much people are paid, who gets promoted or disciplined, and who receives a pension on retiring.

Under the common law in the United States, the employer-employee relationship is governed by the doctrine of "employment at will." Employment continues only so long as both parties agree to it; unless there is a contract specifying otherwise, an employer may discharge an employee at any time without notice and without cause. The courts have held that the meaning of "employment at will" is that an employee may be discharged for good reasons, for bad reasons, or for no reasons at all, without giving the employee any legal grounds to sue for reinstatement or damages.[19] This is Friedman's system of "competitive capitalism." Although over the last fifty years or so it has been modified by legislation and court decisions (which forbid, for example, discharges for race or sex, or for organizing a union), for the most part it continues to be the legal basis for employment contracts in the United States.

Having singled out the right to manage one's own capital as a basic characteristic of capitalist economic institutions, I can now proceed to the core of my discussion.

In a very straightforward and recognizable sense, what is involved in the owner's exercise of management rights in disciplining and discharging employees is the exercise of coercive power. Since a legal system with private ownership of capital includes these management rights, the capitalist workplace is one of legally protected coercion. The libertarian economist F.A. Hayek defines "coercion" as

such control of the environment or circumstances of a person by another that, in order to avoid greater evil, he is forced to act not according to a coherent plan of his own but to serve the ends of another.[20]

This describes precisely the relation between the owner and the employee. The employee at work is acting not according to a coherent plan of his or her own—surely a coherent plan of one's own includes, at a minimum, the ability to refuse to discuss one's political beliefs, drinking habits, money problems, or sex life while strapped to an (unreliable) polygraph; to refuse to obey immoral or illegal directives; or, for that matter, to visit the restroom as nature demands and not as the break schedule allows, without risking discipline or discharge. But employers may demand any of these actions from their employees under the doctrine of employment at will. The employee is, then, serving the ends of another. The employee is being coerced.

Let us imagine a more-or-less typical example of the exercise of management rights. Smith, the office manager, acting as the agent for the firm's owners (the stockholders), tells an at-will employee, Jones, a typist in the pool, to type some letters. Jones does so, though she prefers to do something else. Has the typist been coerced into doing this (or coerced into not refusing to do this)? Is the typist free to refuse to do the work? Let us suppose that the work is covered by the typist's job description and that on Jones' very first day at work Smith told her, "Failure to perform assigned work within this job description is grounds for discharge."

The case might readily be described with more precision, as follows:

(1) Smith (knowingly) threatens to fire Jones if Jones doesn't type the letters.
(2) Not typing the letters and being fired is "substantially less eligible" as a course of conduct for Jones than is failing to type the letters without being fired.
(3) Part of Smith's reason for making this threat is that Smith thinks firing Jones, or making Jones believe she'll be fired, worsens her alternative of not typing the letters.
(4) Jones types the letters.
(5) Part of Jones's reasons for typing the letters is to avoid or lessen the likelihood of being fired.
(6) Jones knows that Smith has threatened to fire her if she doesn't type the letters.
(7) Jones believes that being fired would leave her worse off than if she types the letters and doesn't get fired, and Smith also believes Jones thinks she'll be worse off if she's fired.

If statements 1–7 are true, then this case satisfies the seven central conditions for coercion offered by the libertarian philosopher Robert Nozick.[21] According to the definitions of coercion suggested by two leading defenders of laissez-faire capitalism, Hayek and Nozick, the ordinary exercise of management rights in the workplace is a case of coercion.

The defender of capitalism can, I take it, respond to this challenge in one of three ways. (I ignore here the responses arguing that the coercion could be justified by its contribution to the production of *another* value, such as economic efficiency. My discussion here focuses on maximization-of-freedom arguments.)

First, the defender of capitalism might claim that while technically capital owners do have this coercive power, they don't exercise it very often or very extensively.

Second, the defender of capitalism might claim that while the exercise of ownership rights does permit coercion of employees by employers, the net effect of allowing coercion in the workplace is less coercion in society overall. A little coercion here allows a lot of freedom someplace else.

Finally, the defender of capitalism might say that the exercise of management rights is not really coercive, but only apparently so. I'll discuss these three responses in turn.

The first imagined response, that employer coercion is empirically unimportant, is implausible for several reasons. The history of the capitalist workplace in the United States is riddled with racial, ethnic, and sexual discrimination: yellow-dog contracts, blacklists, unsafe working conditions, Pinkerton goon squads, and spying. The exercise of management rights has clearly led people to act contrary to their wills; it has often, therefore, led to a (prima facie) lessening of individual freedom. One writer estimates that several hundred thousand American workers are disciplined or discharged every year.[22] Some of the ways employers exercise their right to discharge employees are vividly demonstrated by court decisions from the past few years. For example:

(1) A research doctor could legally be fired by a drug company for refusing, on grounds of safety, to conduct saccharine experiments on human subjects.

(2) An employee could be dismissed, legally, after other employees complained that he was living with a woman employee to whom he was not married.

(3) A nurse could be fired, legally, for refusing to falsify hospital records.

(4) An employee could be dismissed for uncovering evidence of criminal activities within the firm.

(5) A fifty-nine-year-old employee with forty-three years seniority could be legally dismissed a year before becoming eligible for retirement with a pension.[23]

Furthermore, this first way of rejecting my argument is a particularly unlikely one for the libertarian defender of capitalism, since as a matter of historical fact the exercise of employer management rights has been restricted more and more by the laws of the state and the legally protected actions of labor unions in the United States, and even more so in other capitalist countries; therefore, the libertarian cannot claim that voluntary decisions alone have sufficed to guard against employer excesses. The excesses have begun to fade only with the use of state power directly and indirectly forbidding them.

The second imagined response is more difficult to assess. It concedes that people are coerced by owners exercising their rights of management, but contends that forbidding such employer coercion would lead to an even greater loss of freedom. This is because a ban on employer coercion would severely

rtail large-scale private ownership of the means of production, and pre-
mably such private ownership is an important element of individual freedom.
Unfortunately we don't have very exact methods for comparing the overall
els of freedom in two situations. Two rules of thumb come to mind,
wever.

(A) State 1 has a higher level of freedom overall than State 2, other
things being equal, if (absolutely or proportionally) more people
are coerced in State 2 than in State 1.

(B) State 1 has a higher level of freedom overall than State 2, other
things being equal, if the activities people are coercively prevented
from doing in State 2 are more important (however this is determined) than the activities people are coercively prevented from doing
in State 1.

We also need to say a bit more about some possible alternatives to the
ideal of unrestricted capitalism.[24] Here are two:

(X) A democratic state regulates, directly and through its legal protection
of labor unions, certain workplace conditions and thus restricts
certain rights of management. This might include a comprehensive
"employee bill of rights," allowing discipline or discharge only for
just cause and enforceable in the courts. Call this "welfare-state
capitalism."

(Y) A democratic state limits the rights of owners to hire employees.
This might result in a system of employee ownership of business
enterprises within a market economy. Call this "worker-control
socialism."

How does a system of unregulated capitalism, allowing *some* people to
own *all* the available capital (and, therefore, allowing them to hire and fire
employees at will) fare on these two tests, *(A)* and *(B)*, at least as compared
to the two alternatives I mentioned?

In regard to the first, quantitiative, test, it seems that alternatives X and
Y both allow freedom to more individuals than does laissez-faire capitalism,
at least in those circumstances where there are more workers than owners of
capital; that is, fewer people are coerced, and coerced less often, under
alternatives X and Y than under laissez-faire. All industrialized capitalistic
economies we know about have had more workers than owners or managers—
in the United States today, the ratio of workers to managers seems to be
better than four-to-one.

As for the second, qualitative, test for comparing levels of overall freedom, once again it seems likely that the two alternatives allow a more important sort of freedom and restrict a less important kind of freedom.

True, both welfare-state capitalism and worker-control socialism restrict or eliminate the freedom of individuals to manage the activities of employees. But is this freedom of owners more important than the freedoms of employees to control larger areas of their own lives, including their lives at work? If we take seriously, as the liberal tradition does, the value of individual autonomy, then it's hard to see how the freedom to control the lives of others at work (and off work, too, in some cases) can be counted as more important than the freedom to control one's own life at work (and off work).

This leads us to the third imagined response: that the owner's exercise of management rights over workers is not coercive. What features of this situation, a situation in which one party issues orders or directives and the other parties follow them (on pain of unpleasant consequences), make it uncoercive despite appearances? The defender of laissez-faire capitalism is apt to respond that the worker is not coerced because the rules are part of a contractual agreement to which the worker consented, or that the worker is not coerced because the worker is free to leave the owner's employ.

The mere existence of expressed consent, or of alternatives, does not, of course, suffice to show that there is no coercion. If the highwayman says, "Your money or your life," and I hand over my money, the existence of the alternative does not show that I have not been coerced into handing over my money. In general, to know if an agreement was reached noncoercively, we need to know if the agreement was between parties relatively equal in bargaining power—and this means that neither side faced a significantly "greater evil" than the other if the agreement could not be reached. Are defenders of laissez-faire capitalism ready to rest their case, in this dispute, on the (rather implausible) claim that owners and workers in such economics bargain as equals? Probably not.

This is the point at which the debate between critics and defenders of capitalism tends to break down, over whether the employment contract is genuinely voluntary in a modern (or in laissez-faire) capitalist economy. This question is an interesting one, but the discussion so far seems inconclusive. As a result, I'd like to try another tack.

What both sides to this dispute miss, I think, is this: *Whatever* the available alternatives elsewhere, the fact that workers can leave the workplace doesn't make it any the less coercive for those who stay, given that discipline and discharge are bad in themselves. Libertarians and businessmen who complain about oppressive environmental regulations or high income taxes in the United States aren't mollified by learning that there is no EPA in Mali or that Switzerland has no income tax, even though they are free to emigrate to these places. Likewise, the workplace remains an environment in which some people give orders to others, who face sanctions if they disobey, and this is coercive even if "emigration" is allowed.

Compare this situation to that of volunteers in the military or merchant marine, or that of members of certain religious orders—we agree that these people have less individual freedom than the rest of us, even if they *chose,* voluntarily, to have less freedom. Most of us believe, also, that voluntary personal relationships can be coercive, even though either party is in some sense free to end the relationship at any time. For example, an old-fashioned husband may use his superior economic position and the threat of divorce to keep his wife from returning to school or taking a part-time job. Or a male teacher may be able to use his control over grades and academic recommendations to demand sexual favors from female students.

In consistency, libertarians at least should agree that the workplace is frequently coercive. They object to the exercise of state power, beyond enforcing contracts and preventing force and fraud, as coercive, even when emigration is allowed. Why object to *state* power over individual lives, but not to *employer* power over individual lives?

Why don't libertarians see the owner of capital as a threat to individual freedom just as the state can be? I offer two possibilities. The first is that the libertarian or other defender of traditional capitalist property relations has made a conceptual mistake. The question of whether something exists is confused with the question of whether its existence can be justified morally. The libertarian thinks the coercive exercise of management rights can be morally *justified,* perhaps because this is seen as a natural result of a private ownership justified on other grounds, or perhaps because it is thought to be necessary for economic efficiency. The libertarian then comes to believe that since the coercion is morally justified, it is not really coercion at all. This is a mistake. Morally justified coercion is still coercion.

The second possibility is that the libertarian myopia about coercion in the workplace stems from a earlier view of capital ownership as occurring within a *private* household, whose head exercised great authority over his wife, servants, and children. Since this authority was exercised in private, in the household, it didn't need to meet the public standards appropriate to the exercise of state power. The libertarian fails to see that economic power is also, in modern circumstances, a kind of public or political power as well.

The efficiency of a capitalist market economy has often been thought to be the direct result of the greater freedom allowed in such an economy. Insofar as this efficiency amounts to the ability to rapidly allocate labor as a factor of production among competing uses, the argument in this paper shows that efficiency actually depends upon the ability to coerce people. Rather than *equality* and liberty existing in an uneasy tension, as is often suggested, I have argued that the real tension is between *efficiency* and liberty.

Is Motivation Management Manipulative?

Raymond S. Pfeiffer _____

One of the great challenges confronting managers in contemporary workplaces is to find and effect ways of increasing the productive efficiency of their subordinates. Most industrial and management psychologists assume that this goal is laudable and clearly to the advantage of the workers. They write in terms of increasing workers' "satisfaction" in what they do; "maximizing task involvement" and "responsibility"; improving worker "achievement," "recognition of achievement," "participation," "growth," and "advancement." In the language of the human potential movement, they affirm that good management is good for people.

Others have, however, referred to the various psychological approaches to management as if there were something sinister about them. Management consultant, Peter Drucker, states: "Most of the recent writers on industrial psychology . . . use terms like 'self-fulfillment,' 'creativity' and 'the whole person.' But what they mean is control through psychological manipulation." Again, he says: "Under this new psychological approach, persuasion replaces command. . . . Psychological manipulation replaces the carrot of financial rewards."[25] The critic of capitalism, Harry Braverman, has stated that "industrial psychology and sociology . . . from their confident beginnings as 'sciences' were devoted to discovering the springs of human behavior the better to manipulate them in the interest of management." He refers to personnel administration as representing "a manipulation to habituate the worker" to the job as it has been set up in advance.[26] Such writers view the psychological approach to management as a less than forthright means of promoting productive efficiency.

It is, I take it, of significance that both Drucker and Braverman describe the effects of industrial psychology using the word 'manipulation.' My task is to explicate their claims. There is no attempt here to determine whether or not any actual management practices of individual managers are in fact manipulative. The present concern is with the prior questions: first, what significance is attached to the claim that a practice is manipulative; second, the extent to which recent industrial psychologists prescribe manipulative management practices; and third, the degree to which such manipulative element is objectionable.

The concept of manipulation has been invoked with increasing frequency since the Second World War among writers on psychology, social criticism, sociology, and social and political philosophy.[27] To manipulate someone, such writers broadly agree, involves a subtle influence on that person's actions, beliefs, desires, feelings, or values, which in turn inhibits rational deliberation. It may involve the falsification or omission of information, or it may involve a play on one's nonrational impulses. But it is widely characterized by an element of subtle and often deceptive persuasiveness.

We can clarify and summarize the content of the various views on the subject in the form of a set of conditions necessary and sufficient for manipulation to occur.

(1) There is an action of commission or omission performed by a party, A.

(2) The action is intended by A to influence in a certain way the feelings, thoughts, desires, values, inclinations or actions of another party, B.

(3) The action consists of at least one of the following:
   (a) providing B with false information intended to influence B's feelings, thoughts, desires, values, inclinations or actions, where A has access to the truth; or
   (b) withholding from B information which would influence B's feelings, thoughts, desires, values, inclinations or actions, where A has access to the truth; or
   (c) inhibiting B's informed, deliberate use of his or her rational or deliberative capacities.

(4) The action is subtle and its effects irresistible.[28]

The first condition covers acts of omission because one can be responsible for manipulating another or be an accomplice in the manipulation by purposefully refraining from action. One can, as the second condition accounts for, influence a person merely by withholding information. The third condition depends on a broad construal of information, such as empirical data, impressions, value judgments, opinions, and even hints, which if B knew of them could serve as evidence as to whether B ought to have the feelings, thoughts, desires, values, inclinations, or perform the acitons that he or she subsequently does. Subtle cues, innuendo, tone of voice, or even body language could count as potentially relevant evidence under the appropriate circumstances. Condition 3c allows the manipulation to be a kind of influence based on powerful emotional appeals instead of distortion or withholding of evidence. This would permit some advertising to count as manipulative, as well as certain appeals by political leaders. The subtlety as required by the fourth condition is relevant to B's perspective, not necessarily that of anyone else. The means of persuasion in question may be blatant to some observers, but subtle in its actual effect on B. It may even be obvious to B, but have an effect of which he or she is quite unaware. It may be subtle to the exent that B may not be fully aware of having missed a chance to proceed deliberately and rationally. We can, following Stanley Benn, say that the action is irresistible if a person in B's position "could not reasonably be expected to resist it.[29]

The conditions cited serve to demarcate cases of manipulation from lying and other types of deception. Not all cases of manipulation involve lying, as one can mislead without lying. Nor need they involve clear cases of deception if they are based on strong emotional appeals. Moreover, it is possible to lie to or deceive a person without manipulating him or her if, for example, the deceiver does not intend to influence the other party's life by doing so. Thus, one who was a compulsive, pathological liar might not necessarily be a manipulator.

The conditions allow us to distinguish between persuasion that is manipulative and that which is not. A persuader who constructs rational arguments, freely offers all his or her knowledge and beliefs on the subject, and encourages the other to think critically is not manipulative. A salesperson who is trying to sell a product need not be manipulative. The customer knows the salesperson's goals, and the salesperson need neither falsify nor withhold relevant information, and may well contribute to the customer's rational assessment of the situation.

Bribery is to be distinguished from manipulation by the absence of subtlety and the failure to subvert rational thought. The party to be bribed may be openly encouraged to think and decide immorally, not necessarily irrationally. And there may be no information withheld or distorted. A threat can be distinguished from manipulation on nearly the same grounds, and so can other uses of force.

To manipulate someone is morally objectionable on two main grounds. First, it consists in a violation of the person's capacity to live autonomously, and second, it may, depending on the circumstances, produce results inimical to the interests of that party. The four criteria do not entail that all acts of manipulation are necessarily morally unjustifiable. Such final verdicts depend upon an assessment of the particulars of each individual case. But cases of manipulation are usually identified for evaluative purposes and most frequently singled out as objects of blame.

When critics such as Drucker or Braverman charge that management practices based on the use of industrial psychology are manipulative, they can be interpreted in the following way: Such management involves a subtle and irresistable influence on employees through some inhibition of their rational, deliberative capacities. To determine the plausibility of such a charge, it is helpful to consider briefly some of the historical developments of industrial psychology.

Current management trends have developed largely as a reaction to the theory and practices developed from the end of the nineteenth century until the Second World War. These began with and embellished upon the ideas of Frederick W. Taylor, who developed in the 1880s the principles of Scientific Management. Taylor's goal was to increase the efficiency of each worker by management's redesigning, dictating, and simplifying work patterns. Taylor's approach led to the widespread simplification of the tasks of factory workers and a significant increase in productivity per worker.[30]

The simplification of work came under considerable criticism after the Second World War. "Most modern writers regard nearly all division of labor, with the resulting job simplification and specialization, as leading almost inevitably to monotony, boredom, job dissatisfaction, and inappropriate (from the point of view of management) behavior patterns."[31] Douglas McGregor described the basis of this approach as "Theory X," according to which the purpose of management is above all to promote worker efficiency. It is based, he held, on the view that workers are lazy and will work only in response to rewards and threats. It has led to a self-defeating management psychology resulting in alienation and ultimately a decline in productivity.[32]

The solution, argued McGregor, is to adopt what he called "Theory Y," by which management helps employees develop their potential in working at their jobs, and promotes efficiency as a by-product. The theory assumes that people want to achieve and will do so given the opportunity. This opportunity requires the worker to shoulder increased responsibility. To implement the theory, McGregor recommended strategies to enlarge jobs and make them more varied and challenging: to invite workers to participate in decisions regarding their work; for managers to act in the capacities of consultants to their workers; and for workers' progress and achievements to be appraised on a regular basis, and they counseled regularly on the results.[33]

The revision in management psychology after World War II included a call for increased worker satisfaction and motivation resulting from the enlargement of job tasks, the return of decision making to the workers, and an increase in worker responsibility, and potential for job satisfaction. The change appeared healthy and humane and promised a real improvement in the quality of worker life, not merely in productive output.

To what extent such improvement has in fact occurred is debatable. But the focus here is not with this question. The question at issue is whether the new psychology of worker management through the promotion of job motivation and satisfaction is, in principle, as laudable as it appears, or whether it contains a deletory manipulative element. I shall argue that it does contain such an element, and that the charges of Drucker and Braverman are not merely hollow rhetoric.

The intent of management, according to the proponents of motivation management, should be to promote employee motivation on the job. Motivated behavior has been described as that which (1) contains a deep commitment to attaining an objective, (2) displays a high degree of effort; and (3) is to a significant extent free of inner psychological conflict.[34] In a work environment, the objective referred to in (1) would presumably be completion of the assigned tasks in an efficient manner. And management can only afford to encourage worker stimulation, satisfaction, and fulfillment to the extent that it promotes worker efficiency. Both the worker's effort and the freedom from conflict he or she feels are necessarily at the service of work efficiency. This reveals that the first two conditions of an act's being manipulatory are fulfilled. According to motivation management, the manager acts in order to influence the performance of the employee.

The third condition of manipulatory action is also fulfilled by motivation management. Such management involves the use of strategies designed to foster certain attitudes in the employee. The attitudes are promoted by the manager's projecting a positive approach toward the work. Moreover, the manager can hardly afford to express doubts or reservations about the work to the worker. Such expression would be viewed as indecisive, uninspiring, and poor leadership.

It is not a part of the doctrine of motivation management that the manager assists the workers to arrive at a motivated state as the result of a wholly free, fully informed, open, rational, analytic, or critical approach to the issues. The proponents of motivation management have shown no interest in promoting open discussion between manager and subordinate of such important issues as the following: whether or not the employee is in the best job given his or her abilities; the degree of commitment the manager has to helping the subordinate in his or her career; the degree to which the manager communicates honestly and openly to the subordinate; the question of to what extent the job and the organization makes a positive contribution to the well-being of the community; the advantages and disadvantages of collective bargaining; the pros and cons of the subordinate participating to a greater extent in decision making. A manager's deliberate and calculated avoidance of or pat responses to such issues represents an effort to limit the worker's informed use of his or her rational, deliberative decision-making capacities.

The point here is not merely that the worker does not, during working hours, contemplate such issues as mentioned above. If it were, then any situation in which one sought to direct the activities and attentions of others would begin to look manipulative. A professor's giving an exam to students might serve as a case in point. Notice that the situation in the workplace is fundamentally different from that in the examination room on three relevant counts. They differ first in the relative brevity of the examination period. It lasts only an hour or two, in contrast with the many hours of class comprising the remainder of the course. During those classes, the professor encourages the students to question any relevant topic, to read widely, to talk amongst themselves about issues, and even to see him or her during office hours for further discussion. Motivation managers are not eager to engage in such encouragement.

A second relevant difference between the workplace and the academic environment is that many workers are tired after work, having little opportunity to consider in an informed, intelligent way such issues as mentioned above. They lack the resources of other people who are capable and inclined to discuss such issues; they lack the energy with which to do so, the encouragement which might arouse such energy, and often the knowledge of how to begin and the intellectual capacity to do so. Students are in quite a different situation.

A third relevant difference between the context of education and the motivation managed workplace is that the professor does not seek to convert the students to any one set of beliefs or ways of living in regard to the issues. The student is expected to learn, and the professor's goal is not to establish opinions, attitudes or value judgments. The motivation manager, on the other hand, has a strong interest in the worker's developing and enacting certain attitudes toward the work. Rational discussion is risky, and the motivation manager may seek to avoid that risk by holding back any topics or information that would require lengthy, subtle, or tenuous explanations. The third condition of manipulatory action is fulfilled in motivation management in the motivation manager's efforts to avoid the occurrence of an ongoing, shared rational discussion about many issues of importance to workers.

The fourth condition is that an action, to be manipulatory, must achieve its effects in a way that is subtle from the perspective of the person manipulated, and also irresistible to that person. From the outset of a new job, even the dullest employee hopes, however unrealistically, to find the work interesting, stimulating, challenging, and rewarding. Indeed, McGregor explicitly bases his case for Theory Y on this assumption.[35] Thus, the worker wants to be motivated in his or her work, and the motivation manager plays right to this desire. The effectiveness of motivation management is thus based in part upon its irresistibility.

The subtlety of motivation management is part and parcel with its irresistibility. It is subtle in the sense that the manager seeks to help and in many ways promote what appear to be the interests of the subordinate worker. The manager strives to gain the confidence of the worker, to appear not as a task master holding the carrot or stick, but instead as an ally of the worker, one who can assist the worker to meet his or her needs. Ideally both manager and employee come to view productivity as merely a function of other factors, as if it will naturally increase as other needs are met. Thus, the manager's primary job, which is to improve productivity, is masked by his or her role as assistant to the employee, and the workplace loses an air of conflict.

The subtlety of motivation management is due in large part to the exploitation by the manager of the worker's very deep and pressing needs. The worker is under great pressure to accept the relationship offered by the manager. The failure to do so may well mark the worker as noncooperative, whereas the acceptance of this relationship is viewed as a healthy attitude characteristic of "teamwork."

We can summarize the charge that motivation management is manipulative as the thesis that the motivation manager seeks to create in the workers, through a subtle, irresistible strategy, a certain set of attitudes and ways of thinking about the workplace; this strategy is designed to reduce the likelihood of workers discussing or thinking through certain issues in a rational, informed, independent manner. Now even if true, the charge can be meaningful or significant only if there really is something wrong with this manipulation. I shall examine the question of what is objectionable about it by first noting two main ways in which one might object to cases of manipulation.

One might argue first that manipulation is objectionable when and to the extent that it interferes with the interests of the parties manipulated. However, such interference might be justified by other considerations, such as the well-being of the larger society. Although employees under motivation management are prevented from acting in fully autonomous ways, this sacrifice might be outweighed by the greater social good of increased happiness and productivity. But even a forcefully established case to this effect might not justify manipulatory practices, for another objection could be brought to the fore.

The second objection is that manipulation is intrinsically objectionable to the extent that it violates a basic human right. This is the right to act in a fully self-determining, rational, or autonomous manner unless one forfeits this right by a well-informed, rationally made decision to do so. Commitment to the right to autonomous action together with acceptance of the argument that motivation management is manipulative are the elements of a strong ethical objection to motivation management.

One might defend motivation management in three main ways at this point. First, one might argue that the sacrifice of worker autonomy by motivation management is warranted by the advantageous consequences for both the worker and society. The increase in productivity raises wages, lowers consumer costs, promotes commerce and industry and the material well-being of the society at large. Moreover, it makes workers happier and more fulfilled, and meets more of their needs.

Second, one might press the claim that worker sacrifice of autonomy in motivation management is so slight as to be negligible. Far from being warped by such working environments, employees are instead encouraged to become productive, proud, and fulfilled, thus realizing their best potential in contributing to the well-being of society. Moreover, their abilities to exercise judgment and live in autonomous ways outside of the workplace are not compromised. They are free to think things through on their own: they are merely encouraged to take a positive attitude toward their work.

Third is the case that some manipulation is unavoidable in human relationships and that the degree of it promoted by motivation management is no more objectionable than that promoted by governments, religions, and even marriages or friendships. Thus, the manipulatory dimension at issue is slight, overshadowed by the benefits of motivation management, and would probably be replaced by some other form of manipulation in the absence of it.

One might bolster each argument by appeal to the principle of free employment, by which workers are free to find new employers without opposition such as blacklists. Such appeal is, however, of no consequence. If employees are in fact manipulated, then such manipulation is objectionable for violating their autonomy and possibly damaging their interests. To wrong one who is unaware under the supposed disclaimer that the person was free to go elsewhere is to give no defense at all.

Each of the three arguments rests on the judgment that greater human well-being results from motivation management rather than from any other management strategy. Such claims are broad and merit a lengthy discussion that is inappropriate here. It is helpful, however, to note in outline one answer that merits attention.

The thrust of the arguments could be thwarted by a management strategy that would effectively promote productivity in a nonmanipulative way. Two such strategies are worth noting here. One is known variously as workplace democracy or participatory management. Under such an arrangement, the employees themselves determine democratically what institutional policy is to be, and how managers are to do their jobs.[36] This reduces significantly the opportunity for manipulative management, and such workplaces are characterized by a high degree of worker motivation and high productivity.[37] There is, however, a practical and ideological question as to whether these present a viable alternative to motivation management.

The question is whether such democratic organizations are viable in a capitalist economy. Since the employees at large determine institutional policy, it appears they they in effect own the institution. In any case, the role and power of management in such organizations is different from what it is in most capitalist institutions. Thus, democratic management may be fundamentally unacceptable to capitalist managers who wish to retain the capitalist power structure. However, it is worth noting that a considerable number of capitalist firms have conducted experiments with such democratic apaproaches in recent years. Although many have been temporary, with limited lasting impact, this may indicate that the ideological conflict is not insurmountable.

A different approach has been developed by D. McClelland and his students. Their courses in achievement motivation training have sought to promote employee dispositions to seek challenge, responsibility, and evaluation of performance in the fulfillment of work goals. Their work represents an effort to promote motivation through the development of personal autonomy. They help the apparently unmotivated indivual to understand the implications of the negative attitudes toward achievement he or she holds, and then offer the support and opportunity to make some personal changes of attitude. McClelland's achievement motivation training course involves four main parts:

(1) Participants are trained to examine themselves carefully—their behavior, their needs, and their feelings.
(2) Participants are trained to be aware of the thoughts and actions of "motivated" individuals and are helped to learn how to think and behave like those individuals.
(3) Participants are trained to set realistic goals they can responsibly achieve.
(4) Participants, in group setting, are supported in their attempt at personal change.[38]

The achievement motivation training course provides an open forum for addressing any real concerns of the participants. Their awareness and understanding of themselves is nourished, and their motivation to be achievers is promoted solely to the extent that this motivation is of real personal benefit; that is, the courses are not designed specifically as means to promote increased productivity of a worker in a certain job slot, as are the strategies of motivation management. Whether or not graduates of their courses return to their jobs to perform more effectively in the eyes of management is immaterial to the success of the courses. This success is determined by the extent to which they promote in subjects the increased desire and effort to take on more responsibility, more risks, and seek more evaluation of their own performance. If graduates sought better positions elsewhere and improved their performance in the new positions, these would count as successes for the course. They would, on the other hand, count as failure from the perspective of motivation management.[39]

A capitalistic system of production includes two factors that exacerbate the conflict between worker well-being and productive efficiency. These are the power of management on the one hand and the pressure upon it to maximize productivity on the other. The magnitude of both this power and the pressure to produce, together with social pressures to promote worker well-being, naturally incline management toward a subtly effective and thus manipulative approach. Any replacement of this approach would, it seems, have to bring either high levels of productivity or limitation of the power of management. Achievement motivation training courses appear to produce the former results, and democratic work arrangements the latter. To grant both that such options merit further inquiry and development and that motivation management does contain a manipulative element as argued here is further support for the thesis that this element may in fact be eliminated from management practice and that objections to its presence warrant serious consideration.

Is Sexual Harassment Coercive?

Larry May and John C. Hughes _____

A number of recent lawsuits filed under Title VII of the 1964 Civil Rights Act have brought the problem of sexual harassment into the footlights of contemporary political and moral discussion.[40] Is sexual harassment a purely private matter between two individuals, or is it a social problem? If sexual harassment is to be treated as something more than a purely personal dispute, how do we distinguish the social problem from benevolent forms of social interaction between members of a work hierarchy? We will argue here that sexual harassment of women workers is a public issue because it is inherently coercive, regardless of whether it takes the form of a threat for noncompliance, or of a reward for compliance. We will further argue that the harm of harassment is felt beyond the individuals immediately involved because it contributes to a pervasive pattern of discrimination and exploitation based on sex.

The term *sexual harassment* refers to the intimidation of persons in subordinate positions by those holding power and authority over them in order to exact sexual favors that would ordinarily not have been granted. Sexual harassment of male subordinates by female superiors is conceivable, and probably occurs, albeit infrequently. Positions of authority are more likely to be occupied by males, while women are predominantly relegated to positions of subservience and dependency. Furthermore, strong cultural patterns induce female sexual passivity and acquiescence to male initiative.[41] These factors combine to produce a dominant pattern of male harassment of females. However, it might bear reflecting that the poisoning of the work environment that may result from sexual intimidation may affect members of both sexes, so that sexual harassment should be viewed as more than merely a women's issue.

Truly systematic empirical studies of the incidence of sexual harassment are yet to be done. Most of the studies by social scientists to date suffer from severe methodological flaws. Nevertheless, they reveal a pattern of sexual harassment of working women that is too strong to ignore. Perhaps the most telling study is that conducted by Peggy Crull.[42] Working with a self-selected sample, Crull sought to discern the nature, extent, and effects of sexual harassment on women, as well as the predominant relationship between harasser and victim. Her data show the victims of harassment to be likely to occupy low-status and low-paying positions of economic vulnerability. Fifty-three percent of the victims on her survey were clerical workers (including secretaries, typists, and general office help), with another 15 percent occupying service positions (waitresses, hospital aids, and the like). The most frequent pattern involved verbal harassment, but over half of Crull's respondents also reported incidents of physical harassment that persisted over time despite their protestations, with 39 percent reporting fondling. Twelve percent claimed to have been physically restrained during incidents of sexual harassment.

What is perhaps most significant in Crull's finding is that 79 percent of the men involved held power to fire or promote the victim, while only 16 percent threatened an explicit employment sanction. Seventy-nine percent of the victims complained about the incident to the harasser or to someone in authority (often though not always the same person), but in only 9 percent of the cases did the behavior stop. Forty-nine percent of the women who complained felt their claims were not taken seriously, while 26 percent experienced retaliation for their complaints. Crull also discovered that whether the victim complained or not, her experience of harassment placed her job in jeopardy. A full 24 percent of Crull's respondents were soon fired, while another 42 percent were pressured into resigning by the intolerable working conditions that resulted from the behavior of their supervisors. If this figure is not striking enough, 83 percent claimed the harassment interfered in some way with their job performance. Indeed, 96 percent reported symptoms of emotional stress, with 63 percent reporting symptoms of physical stress. Twelve percent sought some form of therapeutic help in dealing with these symptoms. Faced with such results, it seems fair to say that sexual harassment is a problem that must be taken seriously.

I

Like most interpersonal transactions, sexual advances may take many forms. There is of course the sincere proposal, motivated by genuine feeling for another, made in a context of mutual respect for the other's autonomy and dignity. Such offers are possible between members of a work hierarchy, but are of no concern here. Rather, we are interested in advances that take the following forms: (1) Sexual threat: "If you don't provide a sexual benefit, I will punish you by withholding a promotion or a raise that would otherwise be due, or ultimately fire you." (2) Sexual offer: "If you provide a sexual benefit, I will reward you with a promotion or a raise that would otherwise not be due." There are also sexual harassment situations that are merely annoying, but without demonstrable sanction or reward. It is worth noting at the outset that all three forms of sexual harassment have been proscribed under recently promulgated Equal Employment Opportunity Commission guidelines implementing Title VII.[43]

Sexual harassment in the form of threats is coercive behavior that forces the employee to accept a course of conduct she wouldn't otherwise accept. What is wrong with this? Why can't she simply resist the threats and remain as before? Viewed in the abstract, one can seemingly resist threats, for unlike physical restraint, threatening does not completely deny individual choice over her alternatives. A person who is physically restrained is literally no longer in control of her own life. The victim is no longer reaching decisions of her own and autonomously carrying them out. Threats do not have this dramatic effect on a person's autonomy. Rather, the effect of the threat is that the recipient of a threat is much less inclined to act as she would have absent the threat—generally out of fear. Fear is the calculation of expected harm and the decision to avoid it. Reasonably prudent individuals will not, without a sufficiently expected possibility of gain, risk harm. The first thing wrong with sexual threats then is that, for the reasonable person, it now takes a very good reason to resist the threat, whereas no such strength of reasoning was required before to resist a sexual advance.

Sexual threats are coercive because they worsen the objective situation the employee finds herself in. To examine this claim, consider her situation before and after the threat has been made (preproposition stage and postproposition stage).[44] In the preproposition stage, a secretary, for example, is judged by standards of efficiency to determine whether she should be allowed to retain her job. She would naturally view her employer as having power over her, but only in the rather limited domain concerning the job-related functions she performs. Her personal life would be her own. She could choose her own social relationships, without fear that these decisions might adversely affect her job. In the postproposition stage, she can no longer remain employed under the same conditions while not choosing to have relations with her employer. Further, the efficient performance of job-related functions is no longer sufficient for the retention of her job. She can no longer look to her supervisor as one who exercises power merely over the performance of her office duties. He now wields power over a part of her personal life. This may help to explain Crull's finding that many women leave their jobs after such a proposition has been tendered. They cannot simply go on as before, for their new situation is correctly perceived as worse than the old situation.

It is the worsening of the woman's situation after the threat has been made that contributes to the likelihood of her acquiescence to the threat. The perception of job insecurity created by the threat can only be alleviated by her acceptance of the sexual proposition. But what of the woman who prefers to have a sexual relationship with her employer than not to do so? Has this woman also been made objectively worse off than she was before the threat occurred? We contend that she has, for before the threat was made she could pursue her preference without feeling forced to do so. If the liaison developed and then turned sour, she could quit the relationship and not so clearly risk a worsening of her employment situation. Now, however, her continued job success might be held ransom to the continued sexual demands of her employer. This also may adversely affect other women in the business organization. What the employer has done is to establish a precedent for employment decisions based upon the stereotype that values women for their sexuality rather than for their job skills. This has a discriminatory impact on women individually and as a group. Focusing on this effect will shed some light on the harm of both sexual threats and sexual offers.

II

Consider the following case.[45] Barnes was hired as an administrative assistant by the director of a federal agency. In a preemployment interview, the director, a male, promised to promote Barnes, a female, within ninety days. Shortly after beginning her job, (1) the director repeatedly asked her for a date after work hours, even though she consistently refused; (2) made repeated remarks to her that were sexual in nature; and (3) repeatedly told her that if she did not cooperate with him by engaging in sexual relations, her employment status would be affected. After consistently rebuffing him, she finally told him she wished for their relationship to remain a strictly professional one. Thereafter the director, sometimes in concert with others, began a campaign to belittle and demean her within the office. Subsequently she was stripped of most of her job duties, culminating in the eventual abolition of her job. Barnes filed suit, claiming that these actions would not have occurred but for the fact that she was a woman.

Under Title VII, it is now widely accepted that the kind of sexual threat illustrated by this case is an instance of sex discrimination in employment.[46] Such threats treat women differently than men in employment contexts even though gender is not a relevantly applicable category for making employment-related decisions. The underlying principle here is that like persons should be treated alike. Unless there are relevant differences among persons, it is harmful to disadvantage one particular class of persons. In the normal course of events, male employees are not threatened sexually by employers or supervisors. The threats disadvantage a woman in that an additional requirement is placed in her path for successful job retention, one not placed in the path of male employees. When persons who are otherwise similarly situated are distinguished on the basis of their sex, and rewards or burdens are apportioned according to these gender-based classifications, illegal sex discrimination has occurred. Applying this theory of discrimination to Barnes' complaint, the federal appellate court ruled:

So it was, by her version, that retention of her job was conditioned upon submission to sexual relations—an exaction which the supervisor would not have made of any male. It is much too late in the day to contend that Title VII does not outlaw terms of employment for women which differ appreciably from those set for men and which are not genuinely and reasonably related to the performance on the job. . . .Put another way, she became the target of her superior's sexual desires because she was a woman and was asked to bow to demands as the price for holding her job.[47]

There is a second way in which this behavior might be viewed as discriminatory. Sexual threats also contribute to a pervasive pattern of disadvantaged treatment of women as a group. Under this approach, the harm is not viewed as resulting from the arbitrary and unfair use of gender as a criterion for employment decisions. Rather, emphasis is on the effect the classification has of continuing the subordination of women as a group. The harm results regardless of whether the specific incident could be given an employment rationale or not. Sexual harassment perpetuates sex discrimination, and illustrates the harm that occurs for members of a group that have historically been disadvantaged. This theory was applied to sexual harrassment in another federal lawsuit, *Tomkins* v. *Public Service Gas and Electric Co.*[48] The plaintiff's lawyers argued that employer tolerance of sexual harassment and its pattern of reprisals had a disparate impact upon women as an already disadvantaged group and was inherently degrading to all women.

Sexual threats are harmful to the individual woman because she is coerced and treated unfairly by her employer, disadvantaging her for no good reason. Beyond this, such practices further contribute to a pervasive pattern of disadvantaged status for her and all women in society. The sexual stereotyping makes it less likely, and sometimes impossible, that women will be treated on the basis of job efficiency, intelligence, or administrative skill. These women must now compete on a very different level, and in the case where sexual threats are common or at least accepted, this level is clearly inferior to that occupied by men. The few male employees who are harassed in the workplace suffer the first harm but not the second. We shall next show that there are also two harms of sexual offers in employment, only one of which can also be said to befall men.

III

The harm of sexual offers is much more difficult to identify and analyze. Indeed, some may even see sexual offers as contributing to a differentiation based on sex that advantages rather than disadvantages women, individually and as a group. After all, males cannot normally gain promotions by engaging in sexual relations with their employers. We shall argue, on the contrary, that a sexual offer disadvantages the woman employee by changing the work environment so that she is viewed by others, and may come to view herself, less in terms of her work productivity and more in terms of her sexual allure. This change, like the threat, makes it unlikely that she can return to the preproposition stage even though she might prefer to do so. Furthermore, to offset her diminished status and to protect against later retaliation, a prudent woman would feel that she must accept the offer. Here, sexual offers resemble the coercive threat. The specific harm to women becomes clearer when one looks at the group impact of sexual offers in employment. Women are already more economically vulnerable and socially passive than men. When sexual offers are tendered, exploitation of a woman employee is accomplished by taking advantage of a preexisting vulnerability males generally do not share.

Seduction accomplished through sexual offers and coercive threats blend together most clearly in the mixed case of the sexual offer of a promotion with the lurking threat of retaliation if the offer is turned down. Both combine together to compel the woman to engage in sexual relations with her employer. Gifts are so rare in economic matters that it is best to be suspicious of all offers and to look for their hidden costs. As Crull's study showed, only 16 percent of those harassed were explicitly threatened. Yet 24 percent were fired, and another 42 percent reported that they were forced to resign. This evidence leads us to surmise that sexual offers often contain veiled threats and are for that reason coercive.

Why are the clearly mixed cases, where there is both an offer and a (sometimes only implied) threat, coercive rather than noncoercive? To return to our initial discussion, why is it that one is made worse off by the existence of these proposals? In one sense they enable women to do things they couldn't otherwise do, namely, get a promotion that they did not deserve, thus seeming to be noncoercive. On the other hand, if the woman prefers not having sexual relations with her employer (while retaining her job) to having sexual relations with him (with ensuing promotion), then it is predominantly a threat and more clearly coercive. The best reason for not preferring the postposition stage is that she is then made worse off if she rejects the proposition, and if she accepts, she nonetheless risks future harm or retaliation. This latter condition is also true for more straightforward offers, as we shall now show.

A number of contemporary philosophers have argued that offers place people in truly advantageous positons, for they can always be turned down with the ensuing return to the preoffer stage.[49] In the case of sexual offers, however, the mere proposal of a promotion in exchange for sexual relations changes the work environment. Once sexual relations are seriously proposed as a sufficient condition for employment success, the woman realizes that this male employer sees her (and will probably continue to see her) as a sex object as well as an employee. A prudent woman will henceforth worry that she is not being regarded as an employee who simply happens to be a woman, but rather as a woman made more vulnerable by the fact that she happens to be an employee. If she accepts the offer, she lends credence to the stereotype, and because of this, it is more likely that she may experience future offers or even threats. She would thus worry about her ability to achieve on the basis of her work-related merits. If she rejects the offer, she would still worry about her employer's attitude toward her status as a worker. Furthermore, because of the volatility of sexual feelings, these offers cannot be turned down without the risk of offending or alienating one's employer, something any employee would wish to avoid. She may reasonably conclude from these two considerations that neither postoffer alternative is desirable. This is one of the hidden costs of sexual offers in the workplace.

It may be claimed that such environmental changes are no different for men who can also be the objects of sexual offers in the workplace. One needs to show that the changed environment is worse for those who are women. Sexual employment offers take advantage of unequal power relations that exist between employer and employee so as to force a particular outcome further benefitting those who are already in advantageous positons. But beyond this, sexual offers are doubly exploitative for female employees, because women already enter the employment arena from a position of vulnerability. As we have indicated, this is true because of the history of their economic powerlessness and because of their culturally ingrained passivity and acquiescence in the face of male initiatives. Women enter the employment arena much more ripe for coercion than their male colleagues. Thus, women are more likely to be harmed by these offers.

This may partially explain Crull's finding that women frequently experience extreme stress and sometimes even require professional therapy when harassed in this way. Men are not similarly harmed by sexual offers because they do not have the same history of sexual exploitation. Men are likely to regard such seductive offers either humorously or as insults to be aggressively combatted, while women have been socialized to be passive rather than combative in such situations. The woman to whom the offer is made becomes less sure of her real abilities by virtue of the proposal itself. This self-denigrating response to an unwelcomed proposal is a vestige of women's history of subordination. Even without the veiled threat, sexual offers can cause women to act in ways they would not choose to act otherwise. To this extent, these sexual offers are coercive.

Most offers are not coercive because one would prefer to have the offer made. This is because one of the postoffer alternatives (rejecting the offer) is equivalent to the preoffer alternative (having no offer at all). Sexual offers made by male employers to female employees are different, however, because they more closely resemble threats than ordinary offers.[50] As we have shown, the preoffer alternative—being employed, unpromoted, yet able to obtain promotion according to one's merits—is different from, and preferable to, either of the postoffer alternatives—accepting the promotion, and having sexual relations with her employer, with all of its negative consequences, or rejecting the offer of promotion, but with the risk that the promotion may now prove unobtainable on the basis of merit. By blocking a return to the more preferable preoffer alternative, the male employer has acted similarly to the employer who uses sexual threats. The woman is forced to choose between two undesirable alternatives because she cannot have what she would have chosen before the proposal was made. Stressing these hidden costs, which are much greater for women than for men, exposes the coercive element inherent in sexual offers as well as in sexual threats. We are thus led to conclude that both of these employment practices are harmful to women and recently were properly proscribed by the U.S. Equal Employment Opportunity Commission.

On Sexual Offers and Threats

Laurence Thomas _____

Sexual threats in the workplace, where the person making the threat is in a position of authority over the person threatened, are inarguably wrong morally. Such threats involve an abuse of the legitimate authority that the superior has over the subordinate, which is hardly true of all sexual threats. For example, suppose A, a mere acquaintance of B, happens across some revealing information about B and makes one of the following threats to B:

(1) If you don't have sex with me, then I shall tell certain others (family or professional colleagues) that you are a lesbian/homosexual.
(2) If you don't have sex with me, then I shall tell your spouse about your sordid past.

A knows that there is nothing that B wants more than for the relevant persons not to know these things about her/him. So, A has threatened B in order to obtain sex from B; however, there is no abuse of authority here, since A has no authority over B.

Now not all threats are morally wrong. If A threatens to pull out of a partnership unless B and C do such-and-such, it does not thereby follow that A is doing what is morally wrong. And it is not clear to me that we, ipso facto, have a moral wrong when the threat is a sexual one.

Now a threat of any kind, not just a sexual one, made by a superior to a subordinate, alters the nature of their working relationship for the worse, from the subordinate's point of view. This is because (1) the superior thereby invokes non-job-related criteria, criteria that the superior is not entitled to invoke, in order to determine whether or not the person will keep her or his job or be promoted; and (2) the subordinate strongly prefers not to be evaluated by the non-job-related criteria. If superior A threatens to dismiss or not to promote subordinate B unless B cleans A's house at least once a week, their working relationship has been no less altered for the worse than

123

if A had threatened B in this way for the purpose of obtaining sex from B. Of course, one is inclined to say that sexual threats, especially those where the woman is threatened by her male superior, are objectionable morally. But why is that?

My theory is that the reason why such threats are especially objectionable morally is that they embody the sexist view that if a man has authority over a woman then he has access to her sexually. For it should be remembered that until recently, a husband was deemed to have almost complete authority over his wife—so much so in fact a husband could not be accused of raping his wife. Sexual access to his wife was thought to be something that the husband was entitled to by virtue of his satisfactorily fulfilling what I call the provider role. The husband was, therefore, thought to have a right to threaten his wife with the withdrawal of his support as provider if she failed to grant him access to her sexually. *There can be legitimate threats.* And in such a case, it was supposed that the husband's threat to withdraw his support as provider was a legitimate threat. To a sexist-minded male, the situation in the workplace where the male is the superior and the woman the subordinate may be seen as just a variation on this theme; thus, to him the threat has an air of legitimacy to it. Other kinds of threats do not embody an analogous view. In particular, sexual threats by women toward men do not do so. They do not have an air of legitimacy to them—at least not in virtue of being threats of that kind.

As I have said, it is not clear to me that all sexual threats are morally wrong. Suppose a wife threatens to take a job out of state unless her husband becomes more sexually active. It is not at all obvious that she does what is morally wrong here. In any case, I assume that the view that persons have sexual access to others by virtue of their authority over them is a morally indefensible view. *Such a practice constitutes an abuse of authority.* That sexual threats (by men) toward women in the workplace embodies this view is, I believe, the reason why such threats are especially objectionable morally.

I should note that there is one important difference between women who acquiesce to sexual threats in the workplace and women who acquiesce to sexual threats from their spouses. The former have little or no recourse should their superior dismiss them or fail to promote them; whereas the latter can often pursue some legal channels if their spouse should fail to provide for them. The claim here is that we have a difference—not that married women are at some tremendous advantage.

Let me turn now to sexual offers (by men) to women in the workplace. According to Larry May and John C. Hughes,* sexual offers often contain veiled threats. This is surely true. And for that very reason such offers are

---

* "Is Sexual Harassment Coercive?" Larry May and John C. Hughes, p. 115.

no less morally wrong than sexual threats. But what about sexual offers that do not? Are they morally wrong, too? As far as I can tell the authors think that while such nonthreatening sexual offers (by men) to women in the work place may be possible in principle, they rarely occur in practice. This move, however, evades rather than answers the question.

Let us consider four cases:

Case 1: John offers to pay Sheila so many dollars per week if she would be his exclusive sexual partner.

Case 2: Deborah is Peter's secretary. Peter offers to pay Deborah so many dollars per week, in addition to her present salary, if she would be his exclusive sexual partner. The money would come out of his own pocket.

Case 3: Mable is Paul's secretary. Paul is a corporate executive. Paul offers to pay Mable so many dollars per week, in addition to her present salary, if she would be his exclusive sexual partner. The corporation would foot the bill. Given Paul's discretionary powers, this can be done with no difficulty, for executives in Paul's company have virtually complete say over the salary of their secretaries.

Case 4: Gail and Bessie, who are equally qualified, both apply for the same job. Mark says to Bessie that he will offer her the job if she would be willing to be his exclusive sexual partner.

These are offers pure and simple. They contain no veiled threats whatsoever. Sheila, Deborah, Mable, Gail, and Bessie each firmly believe this; that is, they each see themselves as being made an offer that they can freely refuse. No one is under psychological duress due to life's circumstances. Finally, I assume that there is nothing about the nature of sex that a person ipso facto does what is morally wrong in selling or trading sex. Obviously enough, without this assumption, there would not be much to discuss concerning the differences between the above cases.

I maintain that we do not have a moral wrong in case 1 and that we do in cases 3 and 4. We have an abuse of authority in both cases 3 and 4. It can be wrong to make someone an offer even if that offer contains no veiled threats. After all, some things are a matter of moral propriety, let us say. For example, given my views on marital fidelity, it would be an act of great moral impropriety for my brother to offer himself to my wife, since he knows of my views on the subject, though the offer contains no veiled threats. As far as I can see, May and Hughes were so busy trying to get a threat out of every offer in the workplace, that they failed to notice that pure offers can be morally objectionable.

As for case 2, I am not inclined to think that we have a moral wrong here. (Recall the qualifications given after the four cases.) That we might have a conflict of interest here seems clear, but not all such conflicts constitute a moral wrong. If you and I both want the one and only job available in our speciality, then we have an acute conflict of interest, and there is nothing morally objectionable about it. Given the very strong possibility that a conflict of interest might arise, prudence would seem to dictate that Peter not make Deborah such an offer. I cannot see that Peter has a stronger, that is, moral, reason for not doing so. Of course, there is always the possibility that something may go wrong: The relationship between Peter and Deborah may sour and, as a result, Peter may treat Deborah in morally objectionable ways. This is a consideration, not part of the scenario, that should not be taken lightly. However, I would not think it necessarily decisive. Any number of morally innocent interactions can become morally explosive. This is true of, for example, love relationships between teachers and students, but it hardly seems to follow that there should be no such relationships. It simply cannot be the case that we should not enter into any interaction if there is the possibility that it might become morally explosive. To so conduct our lives would be to make the mistake of treating possibilities as if they were in fact actualities. A reason to proceed with caution is just that—a reason to proceed with caution. It is not a reason not to proceed at all.

Let me conclude with the reminder that throughout this essay I have assumed, for the sake of discussion, that selling or trading sex is not morally wrong in and of itself.

Privacy in Employment

Joseph R. Des Jardins _____

It would be convenient if we could begin a paper on privacy rights in employment by citing a commonly accepted definition of privacy and proceeding to develop the paper by applying that definition to employment situations. Unfortunately, there is little consensus regarding the definition, nature, and justification of privacy rights in general. Statutory protection of privacy is a relatively recent development in American legal history. The U.S. Constitution, for example, makes no explicit reference to a general right of privacy. It is not found among the numerous political rights mentioned in the Bill of Rights. The legal discussion of privacy typically is traced to the 1890 *Harvard Law Review* article by Samuel Warren and Louis Brandeis and the 1965 Supreme Court decision in *Griswold* v. *Connecticut*. Indeed, it was not until this 1965 decision that the Supreme Court recognized any Constitutional basis for privacy. Further, the very meaning of privacy is so confused that in 1977 the congressionally established Privacy Protection Study Commission reported that after two years of study its members could reach no consensus on a definition of privacy.

Fortunately, we do not need to settle upon one precise definition of the general civil right of privacy before considering the range of privacy rights in employment. In fact, one good way to sharpen a definition is to fix its context and reflect upon the use of the word within that particular situation. With this in mind, this paper considers the extent and justification of an employee's claim to privacy in the workplace.

There tend to be three general meanings to "privacy" used in the legal and philosophical literature on this topic: (1) the proprietary relationship that a person has to his/her own name or likeness; (2) the right to be "let alone" within one's own zone of solitude; and (3) the right to control information about oneself. There may be other ways to understand privacy, but these seem to cover the most obvious cases.

The origin of the first meaning of privacy is in tort law and often is traced to a New York statute passed after a well-publicized case involving the unauthorized use of a woman's likeness in a commercial endorsement. This use of a person's likeness or name without consent was said to involve an invasion of personal privacy.

I will not be concerned with this sense of privacy here. It is unlikely that employees need to be much concerned with privacy in this sense. Further, it seems clear that what really is at issue in this definition would be more a matter of ownership or property rights and not specifically a matter of privacy. The confusion with privacy arises because of the special nature of what is claimed as property (i.e., one's own name or likeness). But the unauthorized use of a person's name or likeness is neither a necessary nor sufficient condition for a violation of privacy. For example, monitoring an employee's phone conversation would violate her privacy although no unauthorized use of her name or likeness was involved. On the other hand, we would not say that an employee's privacy was violated when, for example, her identification photograph was used in a personnel file or when her name was used in conversations among other employees without consent. Employment is an essentially social activity and as such it requires the relatively unrestricted use of a person's name among coworkers. Granting employees a right to privacy in this first sense would make most work activities terribly difficult if not altogether impossible.

A more common understanding of privacy centers around the notion of being "let alone." Beginning with the Warren and Brandeis article in 1890 and the 1965 decision in *Griswold* v. *Connecticut,* this sense of privacy has dominated the legal discussions. Privacy as a right "to be let alone" is also the understanding typically found in ordinary linguistic usage. Since this is such a common understanding of privacy and since I will suggest that it is inadequate for employment contexts, it will be useful to consider this view in some detail.

In their article, Warren and Brandeis were concerned that certain technological advances and business practices, notably the practice among some newspapers of printing stories and photographs of private parties, were causing an increasing threat to the solitude of individual citizens. They defended the right of privacy as "the next step which must be taken for the protection of the person, and for securing to the individual . . . the right 'to be let alone.' "[51]

It was not until 1965, however, that the Supreme Court recognized Constitutional protection of this right to privacy. In *Griswold* v. *Connecticut,* the Court ruled that the Constitution guaranteed citizens a "zone of privacy" around their person that could not be violated by government. The Court found privacy within the "penumbra" of rights established by the First,

Third, Fourth, and Fifth Amendments. By doing so, the Court found privacy implicit in the liberty-based rights established by the Bill of Rights.

Much of the discussion concerning the right of privacy in employment begins with this definition of privacy. The aim of some employee-rights advocates is to preserve the integrity of this zone within the workplace. According to this view, a citizen's right "to be let alone" should not be lost when he or she enters into an employment agreement. Some defenders of employee rights use this definition in developing extensive lists of privacy rights in the workplace. These lists include not only such issues as privacy of personnel records and freedom from polygraph and psychological testing, but also surveillance at work, restrictions upon afterhours activities, peace and quiet at work, employee lounges, privacy of personal property at work, and employee grooming, dress, and manners.[52]

Unfortunately there are problems with this definition of privacy. Phrases like *right to be let alone* and *zone of privacy* are quite vague, and their application tends to be much broader than is appropriate. It is difficult to see how a legitimate claim to be let alone can be consistently maintained at the same time in which one wishes to participate in an essentially social and cooperative activity like work. The difficulty with this second definition is that it confuses privacy with the more general right of liberty. Liberty, understood as the freedom from interference, can be used to generate a variety of specific rights. Free speech, freedom of religious worship, freedom of press, and private property have all been thought of as liberty-based rights. It seems that both Warren and Brandeis and the Griswold decision assume that privacy is simply another liberty-based right. It is understandable that they do so. In the *Griswold* case, the Court stated that the Connecticut law might require police searches of the bedrooms of married couples. Certainly this would be an unjustified interference with personal liberty. Being free from interference is virtually synonymous with Warren and Brandeis' definition of privacy as the right to be "let alone." Certainly privacy can be closely related to liberty. Indeed, in many cases a right to privacy can be justified by appeal to liberty. Nevertheless, the justification of a right claim is independent of the definition of that right. It seems a confusion between justification and definition may underlie much of the problem with this second definition of privacy.

Violating someone's liberty is neither necessary nor sufficient for violating privacy. We can imagine a situation in which a "peeping tom" monitors someone's activities from a distance. While this would violate privacy it would not be an interference with their liberty, in any straightforward sense. Further, some coercive activities could well violate liberty without affecting the privacy of the person coerced. For example, subliminal advertising would, if effective, violate liberty without necessarily violating privacy. These examples show not only that privacy cannot be identified with liberty, but also that not all privacy claims can be justified by appeal to liberty.[53]

This brings us to the third understanding of privacy, privacy as involving information about oneself and the right to privacy as the right to control that information. To understand this view, let us return to the concerns of Warren and Brandeis. It seems that Mrs. Warren was troubled by the publicity that inevitably followed her social gatherings and parties. No doubt Mrs. Warren wanted to be "let alone," and Warren and Brandeis certainly were correct in identifying her concern as involving privacy. But surely Mrs. Warren's objections were to the publication of personal information and not simply with the violation of her liberty. No one was, after all, directly interfering with her parties. Her privacy was violated not by an interference with her actions, but when she lost control over information that was essentially private. More precisely, her privacy was violated when people who had no legitimate claim to this information (i.e., newspaper reporters and their readers) came to know the details of her parties. Her privacy was not violated when invited guests, for example, came to know about the party.

Despite the centrality of the Court's concern with the "fundamental liberties of citizens," it is also true that this informational sense of privacy played a crucial role in the *Griswold* case. Justice Douglas' majority opinion abhorred the violation of marital intimacy that would occur if government agents came to know the details of the sexual lives of married citizens.

These examples suggest that the right to privacy does not involve, as some have argued, merely the control that a person has over information about herself.[54] Rather, the relationship that exists between the persons involved also plays a crucial role. Because they were invited guests, some people could claim that they were entitled to know certain things about Mrs. Warren's party. Since no such relationship existed between Mrs. Warren and the general public, the public was not entitled to that information. In the *Griswold* case, the relationship that exists between a citizen and a liberal-democratic state makes it illegitimate for that state to come to possess intimate information about its citizens' married lives.

In an insightful article, George Brenkert recently has developed this view.[55] Brenkert claims that the right to privacy involved a three place relation between person, A, some information, X, and another person, Z. The right of privacy is violated only when Z comes to possess information X, *and* no relationship exists between A and Z that would justify Z's coming to know X. Following Brenkert, I shall say that the right to privacy is the "right of individuals, groups, or institutions that [have] access to and information about themselves is limited in certain ways by the relationships in which they exist to others."[56]

Note that this definition will help resolve some of the difficulties associated with the liberty-based understanding of privacy. If privacy receives its value simply by being derived from the more general right of liberty, then it would seem that privacy could be seriously restricted in the workplace. After all, one of the things one gives up when entering an employment agreement is the freedom to do as one chooses. The cooperative nature of work will require, at least, some restrictions on employee liberties. If privacy were justified solely by its derivation from liberty, privacy in employment would be similarly limited. But a good case can be made for protecting employee privacy even though the employee has voluntarily accepted a general restriction upon her liberty. Brenkert's definition allows the employee to retain various privacy rights while relinquishing the general claim to liberty. It does this by recognizing that specific relationships between people can justify limiting access to information in certain ways. Consequently, even if an appeal to liberty cannot justify an employee's privacy claims, the nature of the employment relationship itself can.

Accordingly, the nature and extent of privacy rights in the workplace can be determined by identifying the relationship that exists between employer and employee. On one traditional view, the relationship that exists is that of an agent-principal. The employee is the agent of the employer and as such must comply with any legal request of the employer. On this view the only right that an employee can claim is the right to quit her job. At the same time, the employee has the obligations of obedience, loyalty, and confidentiality.[57] However, there are good reasons to reject this view. This model of the employer-employee relationship developed out of a common law tradition that viewed labor merely as one type of capital and the employee as merely one type of property. But surely this outdated model cannot be justified from a moral point of view since it does not treat both parties as autonomous moral agents. Consequently, the agent-principal model has come under increasing attack and is being replaced by a contractual model of the employer-employee relationship.[58]

The existence of a contractual relationship between employer and employee, whether the contract is implicit or explicit, will entail certain ground rules. These ground rules, in turn, can be used to generate the privacy rights that should exist within the workplace. Among these ground rules are, first, that contracts presuppose a legal framework to guarantee their enforcement. An unenforceable contract is an empty contract. Contracts also must be noncoercive, voluntary agreements between rational and free agents. Contracts involving children or mentally handicapped adults, or those involving a threat of force are invalid. Finally, contracts must be free from fraud and deception. This initial sketch can help us to begin to identify the nature of privacy rights in employment.

First, since the contract presupposes the existence of a legal framework, it must conform to the requirements of that legal system. In particular, obedience to tax, social security, equal opportunity, and health and safety laws would require an employer to collect and store certain information about all employees. Providing, of course, that this information is used only in the proper legal manner, an employer coming to know an employee's age, number of dependents, sex, race, social security number, and so on would not violate the employee's privacy.

There is much other information that an employer can come to know about employees without violating employee privacy. Certainly information needed to insure that the contract is voluntary and free from fraud or deception can be required. Accordingly, prior to the employment agreement, an employer can require, under the threat of not hiring the potential employee, information about job qualifications, work experience, educational background, and other information relevant to the hiring decision. However, this relevancy test should be taken seriously. There is no reason to require information concerning marital status, arrest records (as opposed to conviction records), credit or other financial data, military records (unless required by law), or such things as religious convictions and sexual or political preferences. This information is irrelevant for deciding whether or not the employee is capable of fulfilling her part of the employment contract. Further, as Brenkert argues, the use of polygraph tests prior to employment is also suspect since it seeks information in ways that bypass the employee's consent.[59]

Only after the employment agreement has been reached does other information about employees become relevant. Health and insurance plans, for example, may require information about the employee. However, since the contract is already in force, since, in other words, the relationship is grounded upon mutual consent, such information can only be requested with the consent of the employee. Thus, if an employee can choose not to participate in health or insurance packages, the medical examination required for such participation cannot be required (although, of course, there may be other reasons to require a medical examination). After the employment agreement has been reached, and the employer is satisfied with the employee's qualifications for the job, there is a prima facie prohibition against collecting or verifying evaluative information without the employee's consent. This would rule out such things as electronic or other covert surveillance, polygraph or psychological tests, background checks by third parties, and unconsented searches of an employee's desk, files, or locker.

Finally, since the contract does require the voluntary agreement of both parties, the use of third parties to gather or verify information about employees should be limited only to those cases in which the employee has given her uncoerced consent and in which the information sought is relevant to the employment relationship. Thus, checks with an employee's school to verify educational background can be justified, while credit agencies, private investigators, and police agencies are highly suspect as sources of information.

Two further issues need to be considered before this preliminary examination of privacy in employment will be complete. First, we need to consider how employers can use information about employees that has been legitimately collected, and second, we need to discuss employee access to and control over that information once the employer has come to know it.

Given the important function consent plays in the employment contract, we can say that, in general, employers should use personal information about employees only in those instances for which consent was granted. For example, social security numbers given to comply with legal requirements should not be used as employee identification numbers. Medical information released for insurance purposes should not be used during an evaluation for promotion. Information relevant for evaluations should not become the object of office gossip.

More importantly, the information an employer collects about an employee is not a commodity that can be exchanged, sold, or released in the marketplace. Accordingly, the release of information to a landlord, credit grantor, or any other third party without the employee's consent is a violation of that employee's privacy. Release of information to law enforcement agencies without either the employee's consent or a warrant also violates employee privacy. Releasing information about an employee to a credit agency, either in response to a credit check or in exchange for information about other present or potential employees, is another clear violation of employee privacy. In short, there is a prima facie prohibition against the release of any information about an employee to a third party without the employee's explicit consent.

Finally, the number of people within a company who have access to employee files should be strictly limited. Immediate supervisors ought not to have access to an employee's medical file, for example. Consent granted by employees should restrict not only the use to which personal information is put, but also the parties to whom that information is available. If an employee has not consented to release information to a particular person, release of that information again represents a prima facia violation of that employee's privacy.

The last issue to consider involves an employee's access to, and control over, information already released to an employer. In general, the rule here should be that employees ought to have access to all personal information within an employer's possession. A separate but equally important rule is that employees ought to be informed about the exact extent of the information an employer has. Access rights to personal information will prove empty unless employees know what files exist. Of course, third parties who come to possess information about an employee while providing services to the employer have similar obligations to make available the information they possess.

A morally legitimate contract must involve parties who are free and equal. An agreement between radically unequal parties easily can become coercive. To insure that this not occur in the employment agreement, it is important that neither party occupy a significantly superior position. When one party possesses a great deal more information about the other party, the relationship can become unequal and the agreement unfair. This needs special protection in employment relationships where employers typically have significant resources available for collecting and storing information about employees. Without knowledge of and access to their own personnel files, employees will be at an unfair "competitive disadvantage." As a result, this will undermine the legitimacy of the employment contract.

Of course, there can be exceptions to this rule. In some cases a third party (e.g., a physician or evaluating supervisor) may receive a pledge of confidentiality as a condition for providing information about an employee. In some cases, this pledge of confidentiality might restrict an employee's access. We should consider exactly why and when such restrictions are justified.

It may be the case that some information necessary to fulfill the employment contract can only be acquired with a promise of confidentiality to a third party. Its necessity to the contract would justify an employer coming to know this information, but does the promise of confidentiality justify restricting an employee's access? Consider two examples: In order to provide medical insurance, a medical examination might be required. The physician may request that the medical records be kept confidential. (Perhaps she thinks it unwise for the employee to have access without her being present to explain and interpret the report.) Or a supervisor is requested to evaluate an employee. The supervisor expects the evaluation to be kept confidential. Should the employee have access to such records? It seems to me that if the information is essential to the employment contract (as a medical exam might be necessary for insurance or an evaluation necessary for promotion), then access can be limited. However, if it is essential, then employee consent would be an appropriate precondition. Similar to standard practice with student recommendations, employees should be asked to sign a waiver of access rights. Employees who desire the medical insurance or promotion, for example, would waive their access rights. Those who choose not to waive their rights must acknowledge that they are jeapordizing these other goods. In general, there ought to be a presumption of access, but with employee consent confidential information can be excluded.

Before moving on, two caveats are in order. First, we should distinguish between evaluations made for promotion purposes from those made to determine satisfactory performance levels. Since the employee likely will desire the benefits of promotion, consent to limit access will be to everyone's advantage. However, we can imagine some workers who would rather not be evaluated on job performance at all. Unsatisfactory workers could hinder legitimate evaluations somewhat by refusing to waive their access rights. To overcome this potential problem, a time limit could be established, perhaps six months or a year, in which all evaluations could be kept confidential. After that time, we could assume that the employer is satisfied with job performance and make future evaluations open to employee inspection. (This latter issue may be more a concern of an employee's right to due process than a privacy concern.)

Second, some evaluations involve comparisons of employees. Since access here may involve violating another employee's privacy, some limitation may be in order. However, it would seem that if all parties consented, the same conditions should apply to these files that apply to single employee evaluation files.

Nevertheless, an employee's right to see, copy, challenge, respond to, and know about personal information held by an employer is very strong. Since numerous decisions involving an employee's life prospects are made on the basis of this information, simple justice requires that the information be accurate, complete, and relevant. To guarantee this, employees must have access to this information; they must be able to correct it when it is mistaken, and they must be allowed to challenge it when it is in question. To do otherwise would make the employment relationship radically unequal and unfair, and thereby make the contract fundamentally coercive.

More needs to be done to specify the exact extent of privacy rights in employment. Different employment situations will no doubt require different privacy rights. IBM employees, for example, likely will have different specific privacy rights than employees of the CIA. Government employees might have more extensive rights than employees in the private sector. This paper has attempted to sketch a framework into which the details of particular employment situations can be fit.

Notes

1. "Competitive Problems in the Drug Industry," Hearings of the U.S. Senate Monopoly Subcommittee of the Select Committee on Small Business, 14 March 1969, 4501.

2. Ibid., 4501.

3.   Ibid., 4503.

4.   Ibid., 4501.

5.   Ibid., 4503.

6.   Ibid., 4493–4.

7.   Ibid., 4496.

8.   Ibid., 4501.

9.   Ibid., 4479.

10. Ibid., 4480.

11. Whistle Blowers Conference, 30 January 1971.

12. Conference.

13. Conference.

14. Conference.

15. Conference.

16. Milton Friedman, *Capitalism and Freedom* (Chicago: The University of Chicago Press, 1962), 4.

17. Isaiah Berlin, "Two Concepts of Liberty," *Four Essays on Liberty* (New York: Oxford University Press, 1970), 122.

18. A.M. Honoré, "Ownership," *Oxford Essays in Jurisprudence,* ed. A.G. Guest (London: Oxford University Press, 1961), 116.

19. Herbert B. Chemside and John E. Keefe, "Master and Servant," *American Jurisprudence,* ed. Oscar C. Sattinger, 2d ed., vol. 53 (Rochester, N.Y.: Lawyers Cooperative Publishing Co., 1970).

20. F.A. Hayek, *The Constitution of Liberty* (London: Routledge & Kegan Paul, 1960), 20–21.

21. Robert Nozick, "Coercion," *Philosophy, Politics and Society,* ed. P. Laslett, W.G. Runciman, and Q. Skinner (New York: Barnes & Noble Books, 1972), 100–135, especially 102–6.

22.   Cornelius J. Peck, "Unjust Discharges From Employment: A Necessary Change in the Law," *Ohio State Law Journal* 40 (1979):9–10.

23.   (1)*Pierce* v. *Ortho Pharmaceutical Corp.*, 84 N.J. 58, 417 A.2d 505 (1980); (2) *Ward* v. *Frito-Lay, Inc.*, 95 Wis.2d 372, 290 N.W.2d 536 (App. 1980); (3) *Hinrichs v. Tranquilaire Hosp.*, 352 So.2d 1130 (Ala. 1977); (4) *Goodroe* v. Georgia Power Co., 148 Ga. App. 193, 251 S.E. 2d 51 (1978); (5) *Hablas* v. *Armour & Co.*, 270 F.2d 71 (8th Cir. 1959).

24.   See A.F. Westin and S. Salisbury, eds., *Individual Rights in the Corporation: A Reader on Employee Rights* (New York: Pantheon Books, 1980).

25.   Peter F. Drucker, *Management* (London: Pan Books, 1979), 229–30.

26.   Harry Braverman, *Labor and Monopoly Capital* (New York: Monthly Review Press, 1974), 145.

27.   Cf. Robert K. Merton, *Mass Persuasion* (New York: Harper & Row, 1946), 86; Robert Dahl, *Modern Political Analysis,* 3d ed. (Englewood Cliffs, N.J.: Prentice-Hall, 1976), 46; Peter Abel, "The Many Faces of Power and Liberty," *Sociology* 11 (1977): 20; C.E. Moustakas, "Honesty, Idiocy and Manipulation," *Journal of Humanistic Psychology* 2 (1962): 1–15; Lawrence Stern, "Freedom, Blame and Moral Community," *Journal of Philosophy* 71 (1974): 74; Stanley Benn, "Freedom and Persuasion," *Ethical Theory and Business,* ed. T.L. Beauchamp and N.E. Bowie (Englewood Cliffs, N.J.: Prentice-Hall, 1979), 512–21.

28.   Raymond S. Pfeiffer, "The Concept of Interpersonal Manipulation in Social Critique and Psychological Research," *Philosophy and Social Criticism* 8 (1981): 211–15.

29.   Cf. Benn, "Freedom and Persuasion," 515.

30.   Curt Tauksy, *Work Organizations: Major Theoretical Perspectives* (Itasca, Ill.: F.E. Peacock, 1970), 24–68; cf. Braverman, *Labor and Monopoly Capital* and Drucker, *Management.*

31.   Charles L. Hulin and Milton R. Blood, "Job Enlargement, Individual Differences, and Worker Responses," *Concepts and Controversy,* 2d ed., ed. W.R. Nord (Santa Monica, Calif.: Goodyear, 1976), 104.

32.   Douglas Murray McGregor, "The Human Side of Enterprise," *Concepts and Controversy,* ed. Nord, 56–61.

33.   McGregor, "The Human Side," 61–64. Another important proponent of this view is Frederick Herzberg, "One More Time: How Do You Motivate Employees?" *Concepts and Controversy,* ed. Nord, 69.

34. Karl W. Jackson and Dennis J. Shea, "Motivation Training in Perspective," *Concepts and Controversy,* ed. Nord, 81–82.

35. McGregor, "The Human Side," 61–62.

36. A wide variety of arrangements are covered by this term; cf. Daniel Zwerdling, *Workplace Democracy* (New York: Harper & Row, 1980) and Gerry Hunnius, G. David Garson, and John Case, *Worker's Control* (New York: Vintage Books, 1973).

37. Paul Blumberg, *Industrial Democracy* (New York: Schocken Books, 1968), 123; Karl Frieden, *Workplace Democracy and Productivity* (Washington, D.C.: National Center for Economic Alternatives, 1980).

38. Jackson and Shea, "Motivation Training," 89.

39. Jackson and Shea, "Motivation Training," 92–93.

40. For a careful analysis of these cases we recommend Catherine MacKinnon's book, *Sexual Harassment of Working Women* (New Haven, Conn.: Yale University Press, 1979).

41. For the historical evidence, see William Chaffe, *Women and Equality* (New York: Oxford University Press, 1977). For the sociological evidence, see J.R. Feagin and C.B. Feagin, *Discrimination American Style* (Englewood Cliffs, N.J.: Prentice-Hall, 1978).

42. Peggy Crull, "The Impact of Sexual Harassment on the Job: a Profile of the Experiences of 92 Women," *Sexuality in Organizations,* ed. D.A. Neugarten and J.M. Shafritz (Oak Park, Ill.: Moore Publishing Co., 1980), 67–72.

43. 45 Fed. Reg. 74, 677 (1980); 29 C.F.R. 1604.11 (a).

44. We proceed from the general analysis developed by Robert Nozick, "Coercion," *Philosophy, Science and Method,* ed. Morgenbesser, Suppes, and White (New York: St. Martin's Press, 1969). A very large literature has grown out of this analysis. We recommend the essays by Bernard Gert, Michael Bayles, and especially Virginia Held, collected in *NOMOS XIV: Coercion* (New York: Lieber Atherton, 1973).

45. Summary of the facts for *Barnes* v. *Costel,* 561 F.2d 984 (D.C. Cir. 1977).

46. For more elaboration, see Section II of our essay, "Sexual Harassment," *Social Theory and Practice* (1980), 256–68.

47. 561 F.2d 989, 990, 992 n. 68 (D.C. Cir. 1977).

48.   568 F.2d 1044 (3rd Cir. 1977).

49.   See Michael Bayles, "Coercive Offers and Public Benefits," *The Personalist,* vol. 55 (1974); Donald Vandeveer, "Coercion, Seduction and Rights," *The Personalist,* vol. 58 (1977); and Nozick, "Coercion," among others.

50.   Some other employment offers have been seen as coercive also. See David Zimmerman, "Coercive Wage Offers," *Philosophy and Public Affairs,* vol. 10 (1981).

51.   Louis D. Brandeis and Samuel Warren, "The Right to Privacy," *Harvard Law Review* 4 (1890): 193.

52.   See, for example, the chapter on "Privacy in Employment" in Robert Ellis Smith, *Privacy* (New York: Anchor, Doubleday 1979).

53.   For more developed analyses of the relationship between privacy and liberty, see Hyman Gross, "Privacy and Autonomy," *Privacy: Nomos XIII,* ed. J.R. Pennock and J.W. Chapman (New York: Lieber Atherton, 1971) and H.J. McCloskcy, "Privacy and the Right to Privacy," *Philosophy,* vol. 55, no. 211 (1980).

54.   For example, see Alan Westin, *Privacy and Freedom* (New York: Atheneum Publishers, 1976), 7.

55.   George Brenkert, "Privacy, Polygraphs, and Work," *Business and Professional Ethics Journal,* vol. 1, no. 1 (1982), 19–35.

56.   Ibid., 23.

57.   For a good discussion of this model, see Phillip Blumberg, "Corporate Responsibility and the Employee's Duty of Loyalty and Obedience: A Preliminary Inquiry," *Oklahoma Law Review,* vol. 24, no. 3 (August 1971).

58.   Besides the Blumberg article, also see David Ewing, "Your Right to Fire," *Harvard Business Review,* vol. 61, no. 2 (March-April 1983), 32–42 and Norm Bowie, "The Moral Contract Between Employer and Employee," *The Work Ethic in Business,* ed. W.M. Hoffman and T.J. Wyly (Cambridge, Mass.: Oelgeschlager, Gunn, and Hair, 1981), 195–202.

59.   Brenkert, "Privacy, Polygraphs, and Work."

PART 4

THE RIGHT
TO ORGANIZE

Trade Unions: Past and Future

Michael Harrington _____

Historically, the greatest single example of masses of people organizing themselves for economic and social action is the trade union movement. And it is precisely the exercise of that right to organize that is under the most severe attack in the United States today.

There is a legal assault on unions being led by the National Labor Relations Board (NLRB), an institution set up under the Wagner Act to facilitate collective bargaining. In many ways, it is now the most effective center of antiunionism in the United States. But the NLRB cannot make law on its own. The U.S. Supreme Court has declared many assaults upon traditional labor rights constitutional.

At the same time, employers have intervened militantly to break strikes and even crush unions. In 1981 the president of the United States fired thousands of flight controllers who belonged to the Professional Air Traffic Controllers Union (PATCO). Even more problematic, the very evolution—or revolution—of the economy has tended to reduce union power in those smokestack industries and regions where it was once most powerful. And some serious analysts suggested that the transformation of work and technology may do more to undermine the workers' right to organize than the antiunion employers, the NLRB, and the courts.

I propose to begin with a brief historical survey focused on the relationship between economic and social power on the one hand and legal rights on the other. Then I will look at the current situation, one which the *London Economist* describes as the "deunionization of America." Finally, I want to look at some problems related to union organizing and the future of American technology.

I

Historically, capital in the United States and Europe has resisted unionization at every point in the past two centuries. They have used the law and the courts wherever possible, and they have violated the law when necessary for their purposes. There was a brief, and partial, exception to this historic rule in the post-World War II years, 1945–1975, but the current trend, particularly within the United States, is toward an intensification of the historic, and even illegal, hostile acts of employers against workers.

As far back as 1791, when the French Revolution was still moving toward the Jacobin "Left," one can find a classic case of bourgeois opposition to the right to organize.

The spring of 1791 saw workers' coalitions which alarmed the bourgeoisie of the constituent assembly. In particular, they were frightened by the carpenters who attempted to get the municipality of Paris to impose a charge *(tarif)* upon the employers. In this climate of workers' demands, the *loi Le Chapelier* was voted on June 14th, 1791.

It forbade the citizens who belonged to the same profession, whether workers or masters, the right to name presidents, secretaries, syndics or to "deliberate or make decisions on their supposed common rights." In short it prohibited organization and strikes, an interdiction which went in the opposite direction to the right of association and assembly. The liberty of labor prevailed over the liberty of association. . . . The interdiction lasted up until 1894 for the right to strike and until 1888 for the right to unionization. It was a key to free enterprise capitalism: liberalism, based upon the abstration of a social egalitarian individualism, profited the most strong.

The notion behind the *loi Le Chapelier* that "coalitions" of workers were a conspiracy against the common good of the society, while the collusion of the rich was to the benefit of all is to be found among some antiunionists to this day. It merely abstracts from the fact of social inequality; it is the egalitarianism beloved of the wealthy, for it treats everyone in the same way even though everyone is not, from the point of view of economic and social power, the same. Once again, the quintessential capitalistic notion that the organization of the lower orders is a violation of the freedom of capital was invoked. Punishment for violation of the Combination Acts included public whippings as well as imprisonment and financial ruin.

Not the slightest feeling was manifested by anyone for them unfortunate sufferers. Justice was entirely out of the question; they could seldom obtain a hearing before a magistrate, never without impatience or insult.

In the United States, the early period did not see such legal measures against the unions. Indeed, the first labor parties organized anywhere in the world emerged in Philadelphia and New York in the 1820s (one of the important figures in them was the early American feminist and interracialist, Frances Wright). In part the United States lagged well behind Britain and France at the turn of the nineteenth century; in part the democratic traditions in this country were stronger so that, for instance, the right of white males to vote was achieved earlier here than in any European country. But these factors were, ironically, to prove a hindrance to the development of the American labor and socialist movements.

In Britain and on the Continent, the struggle for the right to vote was the emotionally powerful impulse for workers' organization in the early years of the labor movement. The struggles of the Chartists come to mind, of course. Indeed, it is fair to say that the British and European socialist movements began as civil rights movements and only turned to economic demands later on. In the United States, the "free gift of the ballot"—free, that is, to white men, not to women and slaves—was one of the factors that robbed the labor movement of a certain dynamism.[3]

One should not, however, paint the American exception in a rosey color. There were, in the early factory towns like Lowell, "moral police" to discipline the largely female and transient labor force.[4] My point is that, in this country, the repressive legal action against the workers' right to organize came not at the turn of the nineteenth century, but in the period of tremendous capitalist, and working class advance after the Civil War. It was then that America became, in law and in fact, a "yellow-dog" nation (the yellow-dog contract required that a worker agree not to join a union as a condition of being hired).

During the 1890s, for instance, there was the bitter struggle of the steelworkers at Homestead, Pennsylvania, and the strike of the American Railway Union led by Eugene Victor Debs, the greatest socialist leader America ever produced. Injunctions, Pinkertons, the National Guard, and the Federal troops were used. In the Ludlow strike against a Rockefeller controlled company, a primitive tank was used against workers and their families in a "massacre."

So it was that when the great surge of unionization came during the 1930s, the New Deal, the American labor movement had been reduced to a thin stratum of mainly American born, skilled tradespeople. And, a fact that bears significantly upon the argument of the next section, that lack of unionization, and the subsequent depressed wage structure, was one of the reasons for the Great Depression.

During the 1920s, American employers, exploiting the fears of revolution provoked by events in Russia, pushed hard for the "American plan" (i.e., deunionization of the country). John Edgerton, the president of the National Association of Manufacturers, put it plainly enought in 1923:

I can't conceive of any principle that is more purely American, that comes nearer representing the very essence of all those traditions and institutions that are dearest to us than the open-shop principle.[5]

So it was that the values of the *loi Le Chapelier,* heritage of the French Revolution, were translated into reactionary English within the United States.

One can find *that statement* appalling on democratic and moral grounds, as I do. It also made no sense in terms of practical economics, for the antiunionism of the American employers was one of the sources of the Crash of 1929. During the 1920s, productivity rose by 43 percent, but wages, salaries, and prices remained relatively stable. There was, therefore, a large increase in investment outlays, but little or no rise in consumption power. In considerable measure, that last fact was the consequence of the attack on the unions, which kept the wages of all workers quite low. Profits, however, were high. John Kenneth Galbraith summarized the situation:

This highly unequal income distribution meant that the economy was dependent on a high level of investment or a high level of luxury consumer spending or both. The rich cannot buy great quantities of bread. If they are to dispose of what they receive it must be on luxuries or by way of investment in new plants and new projects. . . . This high-bracket spending and investment was especially susceptible, we may assume, to the crushing news from the stock market in October of 1929.[6]

The Depression did not, of course, bring an immediate surge of unionization. In general the first impact of economic catastrophes is not to radicalize but to demoralize workers. Alcoholism, family breakdown, spouse and child abuse are the realistic indices of that phase of crisis, not radicalism. But when Roosevelt was inaugurated in 1933, a mood of hope spread among the working people. And with the passage of the National Industrial Recovery Act (NIRA) and the creation of the National Recovery Administration (NRA), it seemed that optimism was indeed justified. The NIRA's section 7 gave workers the legal right to organize—there had to be some symmetry in a law that gave employers the right to fix prices.

Workers poured into unions—and poured out almost as fast when they discovered that their bosses did not believe in such laws. Even when the Wagner Act made it U.S. public policy in 1935 to encourage collective bargaining, there was a similar response. The counsel for the Wierton Steel

Company and chairman of the American Liberty League said, "I feel perfectly free to advise a client not to be bound by a law that I consider unconstitutional."[7]

So it was that most of the class struggles of the 1930s took place *after* the passage of the Wagner Act and pitted civilly (and uncivilly) disobedient employers against workers backed by the law. The point is that unions' right to organize is almost always realized by economic power, not by legislation. This interpretative principle, we will see in the third section of this paper, is extremely important to the future of the right to organize in the United States.

During World War II, unionization proceeded apace, in part because of the full employment generated by war production, and in part because patriotic businessmen working for the government discovered that a New Deal staffed by corporate executives was not their foe but their friend. Right after the Second World War, there were bitter clashes, such as the 1946 General Motors strike, but then a number of developments changed the industrial landscape.

The Cold War tended to move the mood of the nation to the right; the Eisenhower presidency of 1952–1960 showed that the conservatives had come to terms with the welfare state; the shift in American technology from the goods-producing, mass production sector to service and "high tech," began to reduce the "social weight" of the blue-collar working class in society and to cause union power to stagnate. Some of those trends were moderated by the Kennedy-Johnson years. A relatively prolabor administration in Washington facilitated the growth of unionism among federal employees; the Great Society programs and, perhaps even more important, the spirit of social experimentation allowed the public employee unions (most notably the American Federation of State, County, and Municipal Employees and the Service Employees International Union) to expand.

At the same time, many Americans—including the more sophisticated executives—concluded that high wages were a positive good, permitting an economy of mass consumption and big profits. Sociologists like Daniel Bell and magazines like *Fortune* proclaimed the "end of ideology" and the "zero sum" game of the class struggle. If only labor and management behaved rationally, there could be a "positive sum" game in which all would win. During these years, it seemed that unionism had come to be accepted by all social forces in America. Thus, in the 1964 election, the American *haute bourgeoisie,* led by Henry Ford, joined with Martin Luther King, Jr., and Walter Reuther to back the New Dealer, Lyndon Johnson, against the classic conservative, Barry Goldwater.

The workers' right to organize, it seemed, was secure.

II

Beginning with the 1969 recession, the drastically changed economic situation had a profound impact upon the workers' right to organize.

From 1969 to 1983 there were four major downturns in the economy, culminating in the recession of 1982–1983, the most severe since the Great Depression of the 1930s. This may well have refracted a secular transition in the world capitalistic economy from a "long wave" of growth (1945–1970) to a "long wave" of stagnation and decline (1970–?), to use Kondratlev's terms; there certainly were shifts within the advanced economies as stagflation—chronic and high unemployment accompanied by rising prices—took over. This subverted the traditional Keynesian wisdom of the post-war period in which unemployment and inflation were "traded off" against each other. Now they move in tandem.

At the same time, three major trends were further transforming the Western economies in ways that affected the position of the unions. First, there was a shift in the international division of labor as the South Koreans became able to produce steel, not simply more cheaply than the Americans with their often obsolete mills, but as cheaply as the technologically advanced Japanese. Second, multi-national corporations emerged as a dominant form of corporate organization, and capital thereby acquired unprecedented mobility. Third, a technological revolution, still very much in progress, began to transform the nature of work.

Because of poor performance in the 1970s and early 1980s, profits were down for American corporations, and some of these core industries, most notably steel and auto, were in deep trouble. Management tried to blame its lack of competitiveness on their unionized workers' high wages. This was done despite abundant evidence that managerial incompetence and short-run profit taking were both major, perhaps even dominant, factors in the crisis. Steel, for instance, had refused to modernize and had invested much of its cash flow in other sectors of the economy, Auto, which had lost much of the small car market to foreign competitors because management preferred the high profits from large, inefficient vehicles, continued this emphasis in the recovery of 1983–1984, and thus made itself even more dependent on Japanese suppliers for its parts.[8]

Faced with enormous problems and dedicated to scapegoating workers, many American companies managed to convince the public that antiunion efforts promoted the common good. A new industry of consultant firms, tutored employers in how to decertify existing unions, break strikes, and avoid new unionization. Workers were threatened with the loss of their jobs if they refused to make concessions. At the same time, the shift in technology away from "smokestack" industries, the geographical move of American manufacturing toward non- and antiunion areas in the South and the Southwest, and the double-digit unemployment of the 1982–1983 recession meant a loss in union membership, dues income, and therefore the capacity to fight against the management offensive.

The assault on unions in the marketplace was accompanied by new antilabor theories. A book by Morgan O. Reynolds called *Power and Privilege* revived the argument about the dangers of a labor "monopoly" in a capitalist economy. (The monopoly agreement is developed in this book by Charles Landesman. But a study by Richard Freeman and James Medoff demonstrated that the gains in labor stability achieved by unionization offset any monopolistic wage effects. And Lester Thurow showed that the market model does not apply in the labor market, not the least because older workers must be persuaded to help train young workers—something they will only do in an efficient way if there are guarantees that they are not educating their own replacements.[9]

Even more to the present point, Wassily Leontiev, the Nobel laureate in economics, has noted that two basic trends, automation and multinationalization, have severely restricted whatever "monopoly" unions ever held. Both make capital much more mobile than labor and thus provide alternatives that did not exist before (robots, foreign workers).

The fact is, then, that "big labor" is not nearly as powerful as big business (it never was, but that is another issue). *The London Economist* was right to say in 1983 that

the retreat of American labor unions has become a rout. Between 1950 and 1980, union membership dropped from about a third of the labor force to 18%. Since then, it has tumbled to about 15%. Membership of the big blue-collar union has fallen most sharply since 1983. The memberships of the steel, carmaking and building and transport unions have all declined by a third.[10]

The recovery of 1983–1984 somewhat reversed that trend as auto and other corporations recalled laidoff workers. But it is clear that, even in good times, American unions will never, in the goods-producing sector, reach the strength they once attained.

III

Finally, will the system of work now emerging change the workers themselves to the point that they will not see the need for union organization: The point is subtle and problematic and I can do little here except to introduce it.

Capitalist technology, Harry Braverman showed in his study *Labor and Monopoly Capital,* is *capitalist* technology; "that is, it is not simply designed to carry out a technical function in the system of production, but to do so in a certain way. The ideal, Braverman documented, was to find alternatives to autonomous workers actually controlling their own work environment, and to get, as far as possible, human robots who would do simple, repetitive tasks in an obedient manner. Therefore, he concluded, the notion of worker's control (or, in the French phrase, *socialisme autogestioinaire*) makes the unwarranted assumption that one can easily impose humane working relationships on a technology that is inhumane on principle.

More recently, that idea has been generalized by Andre Gorz in *Farewell to the Working Class.*[12] Writing much as Braverman did, but taking the point to extremely radical conclusions, Gorz argues that management has

organized the work force in such a way as to make it impossible for the worker to experience work as a potentially creative activity. The fragmentation of work, taylorism, scientific management and, finally, automation, have succeeded in abolishing the trades and the skilled workers whose 'pride in a job well done' was indicative of a certain consciousness of their practical sovereignty. The idea of a subject class of united producers capable of seizing power has been specific to those skilled workers proud of their trade. [p. 46]

I do not want to deal here with Gorz's long range theories and his own alternative to classical Marxism—I should note, however, that I have serious disagreements with him on these matters. How does his analysis relate to the practical exercise of the right to organize? Semiskilled U.S. workers did not even join unions in large numbers until the rise of the CIO in the 1930s. And even then, there is no question that the more skilled, and better paid, workers have historicaly been the most militant. There are exceptions—coal miners and seamen because of their isolation in extremely cohesive class communities are an obvious case in point—but the trend in terms of union organization has been to rely upon those skilled, self-confident workers.

Are such workers disappearing? Yes and no. On the one hand, there is clearly a tendency in the direction of a "bi-modal" labor force. There has been significant job generation in the upper reaches of the economy, creating new posts for educated employees in high technology. At the same time, employment has grown at the bottom of the occupational structure (health aides, orderlies, fast-food workers, untrained security personnel, and so forth). It is the "middle," where unionism had the strongest roots, where membership is declining.

But it would be a mistake to exaggerate this trend. Workers, Charles Sabel has shown in an excellent study, are anything but a homogeneous mass.[13] There are "peasant workers" (in the United States, rural workers who split their time between farm and factory), who think of themselves as passing through the factory and are not open to unionization; ghetto workers who suffer from the special indignaties of racism and marginalization; downgraded skilled workers and workers who have managed to defend their skills; and so forth.

The trend, Sabel documents, currently destroys some skilled jobs, but creates others. It has even seen the return of the sweatshop and, in Italy, the appearance of small, worker-owned units. Therefore, Gorz's sweeping theories are, I think, much too abstract.

And yet, the right to organize—subverted by the French left and British right, thwarted by the "American Plan," and expanded by the 1930s crisis and the post-World War II prosperity—may be even more precarious now than ever before. It is not just a matter of the recessions since 1969. Perhaps it has to do with the very evolution of work and workers. One thing is certain: To the degree that the right to organize is weakened, the power of the genuine monopolists—multinational capital—will be strengthened to the detriment of democracy.

The Union Movement and the Right to Organize

Charles Landesman _____

In his Nobel Peace Prize acceptance speech, Lech Whalesa, the head of the outlawed Polish union Solidarity, said: "We are fighting for the right of the working people to organize and for the dignity of the human labor."[14] The suppression of the union by the military-dominated regime was generally perceived as a blow to attempts to introduce democratic practices and civil liberties into Poland. An association of working people that is not a pawn of those in power is seen, quite rightly, as a way of ameliorating the harshness of the regime by functioning as a countervailing power responsive to the needs and preferences of the vast majority of the Polish people.

In the United States, the rights that Walesa is fighting for in Poland have been recognized by the legal system since Roosevelt's New Deal. Workers have the legal right to organize and to form unions for the purpose of raising their wages and improving their working conditions. Once organized, unions generally have the right to engage in collective bargaining with employers. Should bargaining be unsuccessful, unions have the right to strike and thus impose severe economic costs upon employers. In addition, unions are permitted to engage in lobbying to influence the legislative process. Unions are also permitted to support political candidates and thus have become a major influence in American politics. To protect union members against unresponsive and corrupt leaders, unions are required to be democratically organized and to hold periodic elections of officers. American unions have everything that Solidarity would want in the way of legal rights.

Most western observers, noting the absence of independent unions in the Soviet block countries, believe that the development of independent unions would be favorable to the democratic values they uphold. However, many U.S. students of the union movement do not look with similar favor on American independent unions. By and large, they do not challenge the right of workers to form voluntary and peaceful associations, a right that can be given strong moral backing and has been recognized as a legal right by the First Amendment. An acceptable voluntary association is one whose members are not required to join by force or by the threat of force, whose members are able to leave at will, and which pursues legitimate goals by morally acceptable means. There would be no problem if unions were simply voluntary associations of this sort, engaged in self-help and philanthropic activities. The right to organize would then just be a special case of the more general right of voluntary association. But as unions have evolved in the past half century, they have lost their character as voluntary associations and have acquired quite special legal rights that place their activities in a problematic light. The legitimacy of much of current union activity cannot be based simply on the right of association. But then how shall union activity be evaluated? We cannot answer this question by appealing to the legal system as it now exists, for the question is intended to raise doubts as to whether the *legal* rights unions have been granted in American law should be continued. In this paper, I shall survey several major criticisms directed against the union movement in order to achieve some clarity on what sort of basis the right of workers to organize unions can be founded.

One major point of difference between unions and ordinary, voluntary self-help associations is derived from the fact that unions, unlike business firms, are exempt from the Sherman Antitrust Act. Thus, unions are able to exercise monopoly power. In general, "monopoly exists when a specific individual or enterprise has sufficient control over a particular product or service to determine significantly the terms on which other individuals shall have access to it."[15] In contrast to the monopolist, "the participant in a competitive market has no appreciable power to alter the terms of exchange."[16] Unions exercise monopoly power when they attempt, by a strike or by means of the threat of a strike, to set the price of labor higher than what the competitive market would provide. Instead of just accepting the wage rates that are the outcome of countless agreements between individual workers and firms, unions attempt to fix the rates at a level that their leader and members find acceptable.

Economists committed to an economic system based upon competitive markets invariably oppose the exercise of monopoly power on the part of both firms and unions. Thus, Frank Knight has argued that unions

quite certainly should not exercise monopoly power, and the state should as far as possible prevent their having it—especially the right to strike (in concert, collusively)—as it should do with respect to enterprise. Monopolistic action by labor unions inevitably interferes with the performance by entrepreneurs of their necessary functions—the anticipation of changes and adaptation to change, especially the selection and introduction of innovations on which growth depends.[17]

According to Knight, by exercising monopoly power, unions introduce distortions into the economic system that reduce the wealth it would produce under more competitive conditions. Unions retard economic growth, it is claimed; they make the economic system less *efficient*. The value of competitive markets is their efficiency and their capacity to produce and distribute large quantities of consumable goods. What interferes with efficiency is, to that extent, undesirable.

Of course, efficiency is not the only thing that is desirable, and defenders of union activity may very well reply to this argument by pointing to various good things that unions accomplish—such as protecting the worker against arbitrary, unfair, and harsh treatment by the employer—that compensate for a slight reduction in efficiency. It is just because a variety of values are at stake with various possibilities of trade-offs among them that the case for or against unions is complex.

A second major criticism frequently leveled against union power is that it suppresses or tends to suppress certain freedoms that are so valuable that society ought to protect them. Once the wages and other employment terms have been fixed by a collective bargaining agreement or as a result of a strike, no worker is free to accept any other terms, even if he should find it to his advantage to accept lower wages or longer hours than the contract stipulates. Union power, it is said, prevents workers and firms from forming mutually advantageous bargains.[18] Moreover, unions frequently attempt to force workers to become members, whether they want to or not and whether they find it advantageous to themselves or not. Many labor contracts require all employees to join the union or lose their jobs. Even when membership is not compulsory, employees are frequently required to pay union dues. Not only do unions attempt to coerce firms to accept terms of employment that they would not accept but for the threat of a strike, they also significantly limit the freedoms of their members and of other workers who would like the jobs.

According to Mancur Olson, the tendency to make membership compulsory is not an unimportant feature of American unions.

By far the most important single factor enabling large, national unions to survive was that membership in those unions, and support of the strikes they called, was to a great degree compulsory. . . .Compulsory unionism, far from being a modern innovation, goes back to the earliest days of organized labor.[19]

The explanation for compulsory membership, thinks Olsen, "centers around the need for coercion implicit in attempts to provide collective goods to large groups."[20] Because any benefit that the union gains must be provided to all the workers in the bargaining unit, any individual worker will gain by being a free rider, that is, will receive the benefit without incurring the costs of membership. Since the union will only have the power and authority to win advantages for its members if a significant majority become members, the only way to prevent free riders is to force membership on the workers. Of course many if not most workers in a firm may be willing to lose this freedom because union benefits outweigh the loss of liberty. For the same reason, citizens may be willing to be forced to pay taxes because of the overall benefits they receive from government expenditure. Frequently collective action by large groups of individuals entails coercion just in order to produce the benefits that flow from the action. There is an argument that justifies such coercion when the value of the benefits is greater than the evil of the loss of liberty.

A third criticism of union power is that it is *unfair* because it tends to magnify *unjustified inequalities* among members of the working class taken as a whole. Milton Friedman explains:

If unions raise wage rates in a particular occupation or industry, they necessarily make the amount of employment available in that occupation or industry less than it otherwise would be—just as any higher price cuts down the amount purchased. The effect is an increased number of persons seeking other jobs, which forces down wages in other occupations. Since unions have generally been strongest among groups that would have been high paid anyway, their effect has been to make high-paid workers higher paid at the expense of lower paid workers. Unions have therefore not only harmed the public at large and workers as a whole by distorting the use of labor; they have also made the incomes of the working class more unequal by reducing the opportunities available to the most disadvantaged workers.[21]

There are two steps in the argument. The first concludes on the basis of economic analysis that unions have contributed to increasing inequality of income. The second concludes on the basis of ethical analysis that the increase of inequality is unfair or unjust because it is produced by monopoly power rather than by competition of the marketplace. But why should wage rates set by competitive markets be judged to be fair, whereas rates set by other methods—monopoly power or government price fixing—be condemned as unfair? How is fairness judged? This is a large question that cannot be settled here. I will suggest an answer that appeals to me. The institutions of society are needed because of the *functions* they perform and the needs that they satisfy. For example, an army is wanted for defense and a factory for the goods it produces. An institution can perform its function well or poorly. The army may repel the invader, or it may be defeated. The factory may produce well-made goods inexpensively, or it may produce shoddy goods at a high price. A rule of institutional performance is a good rule just to the extent that by conformity to it the institution is enabled to perform its function well. Such a rule possesses *functional utility*. If a rule possesses functional utility and if the institution and its goals are accepted as legitimate, violation of the rule will be perceived as wrong or unfair or unjust. Justice in the workings of institutions is a type of functional utility.

Suppose that the free market economists are correct about the superior efficiency of competition over other methods of setting prices. Then the rules that stipulate that prices are to be set as a result of free competition have functional utility. Inequalities that result from conformity to such rules will not be perceived to be unfair. But inequalities that result from the exercise of monopoly power whether of firms or of unions will be deemed unfair because they result from a poorly functioning institution, one that fails to satisfy society's needs as well as it could.

Historically, the union movement began by organizing manual laborers and only recently has it attempted to organize clerical, white-collar, and professional employees. One should not conclude, however, that the claim that union power has led to an unfair distribution of wealth necessarily favors professionals over manual laborers, or the rich over the poor. There are professional organizations that, while not technically classified as unions, function to some extent like unions. Some of these organizations are in a posititition to exercise monopoly power to sustain the income of their members at a level considerably higher than it would be under a more competitive system. For example, for many years the American Medical Association was able to restrict entry into the medical profession and thus keep up the income of physicians by keeping down the number of those who practice medicine.[22] By the same argument, we may judge that the difference in income between physicians and others due to the monopoly power that physicians are able to exercise is unfair. This argument assumes, of course, that the exercise of monopoly power does not have functional utility, an assumption that many physicians would be quick to reject.

A fourth criticism is that even within its own terms, the union movement as a whole is unsuccessful. the main goal of the typical American labor union is to raise the total compensation of its members. While it is quite difficult to determine what the rate of compenstion would have been if there were no union, a standard economic conjecture is that more successful unions cause wages to be about 15 percent higher.[23] Of course, not all unions are successful, and only a fraction of the working class is organized. Thus, Friedman estimates:

Because of unions something like 10 to 15 percent of the working population has had its wages raised by something like 10 to 15 percent. This means that something like 85 or 90 percent of working population has had its wage rates reduced by some 4 percent.[24]

However, although it is likely that some unions have been successful in raising wages, there is no evidence that the union movement as a whole has increased labor's share at the expense of profits.[25] The share of the total earnings of industry that goes to compensate the worker has not increased, as far as we can tell, as a result of the union movement.If union gains are not made at the expense of capital, they are likely to be made at the expense of nonunion labor. According to Rees, unions redistribute income by holding down the wages of nonunion workers. In addition, nonunion workers, in their role as consumers, have to pay more for the products of union labor.[26]

Moreover, according to Friedman, not only have unions been unsuccessful in reducing the share that goes to profits, it is not possible for them to be successful because profits are not big enough. The Friedmans estimate that corporate profits represent about 10 percent of the national income before taxes and 6 percent after taxes. Even if all these profits were to be distributed to the workers, "that would kill the goose that lays the golden eggs. The small margin of profit provides the incentive for investment in factories and machines, and for developing new products and methods."[27] Thus, although certain workers benefit as a result of belonging to a strong union, the working class as a whole is not that much better off, at least with respect to wages.

These criticisms of the exercise of union power have been based on the standpoint of those who favor a free market competitive system. With this system as the ideal, they claim that unions have introduced inefficiency, coercion, and unfairness into the economic system and done so without benefiting the working class as a whole or without benefiting it sufficiently to compensate for these disadvantages. There is another type of criticism that is frequently formulated by socialists who reject private ownership of the means of production and the competitive system based upon it. To understand this criticism, it is necessary to distinguish between two conceptions of the proper function of union activity: political and business unionism.[28] A political union is one that is primarily concerned with improving the lot of the working class by activities intended to change the capitalist system into a socialist system. Union activity provides an opportunity for workers to develop class consciousness as well as to become aware of the (alleged) evils of capitalism. Unions can use their political and economic power no only to ameliorate these evils, but to move society in a different direction. Workers' control, public ownership of the means of production, centralized planning, and market socialism are some of the methods that have been proposed by socialists to replace capitalist organization.

Business unionism, on the other hand, does not challenge the capitalist system, but works within its framework to improve working class conditions. Business unions engage in collective bargaining, file grievances on behalf of their members, employ legal forms of coercion, such as the strike, and restrict jobs to union members; all this is done for the purpose of raising the wages of members, improving their working conditions, and, not least of all, maintaining and expanding their own power. Such unions are part of the system, and union leaders turn into bureaucrats who administer large organizations, try to keep themselves in office, and find themselves with as great a stake in the smooth operation of the economy as do representatives of capital. The socialist criticism of business unionism is that it tends to preserve a system of production and distribution that ought not to be preserved; business unionism, it is said, stands in the way of ending exploitation and inhibits the radical reform needed to transform capitalism into a morally acceptable economic system. Of course, one will find this criticism acceptable only if one buys the socialist evaluation of capitalism together with the belief that the working class will be better off under socialism.

Upon the basis of this survey of criticisms of union power, we are now in a position to understand that the right of workers to organize, a right derived from the more general right of association, cannot be used to justify the particular legal rights that unions have been granted. For these legal rights allow unions to apply coercion against and limit the liberties of the firms with which they bargain their own members, and nonunion workers. In this respect, unions do not operate like typical fraternal or philanthropic associations.

Some critics of union practices have supported their negative evaluations by appealing to certain moral rights that these practices are alleged to infringe. For example, compulsory union membership has frequently been challenged by a so-called right to work. It is said that requiring a worker to join a union in order to keep his job violates this right by laying down a morally illegitimate condition for keeping his job. No one's livelihood, it is said, should depend on joining an organization with whose philosophy and practices he may be in deep disagreement. Even if the worker is benefited by the union, society should not force him to join an organization for his own good. Paternalism may be acceptable for children, but not for mature people who are capable of planning their own lives and acting so as to realize their goals.

One response to this appeal to a right to work asserts that "the enforcement of 'right-to-work' laws would bring about the death of trade unions. A rational worker will not voluntarily contribute to a (large) union providing a collective benefit since he alone would not perceptibly strengthen the union, and since he would get the benefits of any union achievements whether or not he supported the union."[29] Thus, right-to-work laws that make union membership voluntary could be interpreted as themselves violating the right of workers to organize, to bargain with their employers, to engage in work stoppages, and so forth. We seem to have arrived at a collision among rights.

Each side of the dispute appeals to the right that it finds suitable in justifying what it wants. Is there any way of resolving such conflicting appeals?

Olson thinks the trouble arises from our appealing to rights in the first place. Such appeals are "unhelpful." The argument over the right to work is typical of many situations in which an organization tries to extract a contribution from its constituency, some members of which are unwilling to make the contribution. For example, a citizen may claim that compulsory taxation violates his right to use his own income as he wishes, whereas society may insist that compulsion is necessary to gain the benefit that most people want anyway. Since the appeal to rights tends to leave us with unresolved conflicts, perhaps we should reject speaking of rights altogether. "The debate on the 'right-to-work' laws should center, not around the 'rights' involved, but on whether or not a country would be better off if its unions were stronger or weaker."[30]

Olson implicitly distinguishes between two styles of argument concerning economic policy. One style attempts to justify or criticize a practice or a policy by appealing to the rights of the individuals concerned. The other style bases its evaluations on the overall utility of a policy, on what makes people better or worse off. Whereas the rights approach tends to leave the debate hanging in the air amidst a plethora of conflicting rights, the utility approach at least has the advantage that we can actually observe how a policy works out in practice, how it affects people for better or for worse; therefore, we have something concrete and specific on which to base our judgments. However, one need not be forced into a position of having to choose between these approaches, for rights themselves can be based upon utility. The contrast between something's being a moral right and its being merely desirable is based on its importance for the pursuit of a life worth living. What we consider to be basic human rights are conditions, opportunites, and resources that are generally required under most circumstances to sustain life and to live a good life. Freedom of expression, association, religion, access to the means of subsistence, and so forth can be classified as moral rights in that they are among the things society ought to guarantee the citizen because of their overall importance in sustaining human welfare. Conditions of lesser importance are not classified as rights, but as items that are merely desirable. Disagreements between conflicting rights claims can be resolved in principle by examining the overall utility of the competing policies. Thus, the question of whether the right of a union to exist is or is not superior to the right of an individual to work without joining an organization he opposes depends upon whether and to what extent union activity makes everyone affected better off. However, although the reduction of arguments about rights to arguments about utility does at least clarify what we have to observe in order to settle the issue, it does not necessarily make such issues easy to resolve. Many factors fall under the class of items that affect human welfare; their prediction is not easy; their comparison is controversial; disagreements about them abound. But at least we know what we are disagreeing about.

Collective Bargaining and Workers' Liberty

Burton Hall _____

Employment At Will

Most adult Americans are dependent for their livelihoods upon wages and salaries. As a condition of survival, they offer their labor power for sale on the labor market. If they lose their jobs and can find no others, they lose all means of support save for the relief provided by public assistance. The power of an employer to terminate an employment relationship, therefore, is in most instances the power to inflict serious economic hardship upon the employee.

Such power is coercive. A threat of termination in the event that the employee incurs his employer's dislike is implicit in virtually every employment relationship. By such threat, even where merely implied, employees are coerced in the exercise of personal rights and liberties—and are often coerced into committing acts, sometimes illegal ones, against their will. The evidence recorded in myriad court files, arbitration transcripts, labor board decisions, EEOC records, and congressional hearings suggests that such coercion is neither rare nor occasional but, rather, the general rule. It indicates, for example, that employees are commonly subjected to threat of discharge, or to actual discharge, for exercising their rights to express controversial ideas (at home, on the job, or elsewhere), organize unions, oppose corrupt union leaders, complain about unsafe or unhealthy conditions, or complain about racial or sexual discrimination. Off and on the job, it is demanded that they be "team players," and "playing" with the "team" requires that they adopt the manners and habits favored by their employers and espouse only those ideas that are favored by their employers.

Can anyone in such a status of dependency be a free person? In regard to governmental power, personal liberty is protected by constitutional and other restraints upon the government's exercise of its powers over individuals. In private employment, however, employees (unless represented by a labor union) have no such protection, for there are no comparable restraints upon the employer's exercise of his power over them. In legal language, they are employees "at will," meaning that their employer is free, at any time, to discharge or discipline them for any reason not specifically forbidden by law, or for *no* reason at all. His power over them is *arbitrary*. Its arbitrariness is the measure of the employees' lack of freedom. Eugene Deb's classic characterization states, "[s]o long as one man depends upon the will of another or more often the whim and caprice of another for employment, he is a slave."

A century ago, a Tennessee court stated the law simply: Employers "may dismiss their employees at will . . . for good cause, for no cause, or even for cause morally wrong, without being thereby guilty of legal wrong." More recently, a California court, dealing with a secretary who had been discharged because she refused her supervisor's order to evade jury duty, ruled that "her employer could discharge her . . . with or without cause[;] . . . [i]t makes no difference if the employer had a bad motive in so doing." And that, in substance, remains the law. Courts have repeated the litany in cases where employees were fired for such reasons as refusing to assist in smuggling aliens into the country, refusing to smuggle liquor into the country, refusing to assist a supervisor in seducing the employee's spouse, and giving truthful testimony in court proceedings that was unfavorable to the employer. Similarly, employees were discharged for expressing views the employer disliked on public issues and for refusing to support candidates favored by the employer in public elections. Though the First Amendment bars Congress from infringing freedom of speech, it does not bar private employers from doing so.

In recent years, the courts of some states have found exceptions to the doctrine. In some states a "public policy" exception has been developed, permitting the courts to provide relief for employees discharged for "whistle blowing" or for refusing to commit illegal acts. In rare instances, courts have found employees protected against arbitrary discharge by individual contracts of employment. But the exceptions are narrow. They are only slight emendations upon the traditional rule of employment at will.

Lawrence Blades, after surveying the cases, has commented that "[t]his traditional rule . . . tends to make [the nonunion employee] a docile follower of his employer's every wish . . . It is the fear of being discharged which above all else renders the great majority of employees vulnerable to employer coercion.[31]

Legislative Restrictions Upon Employment-At-Will

Legislators take the existence of such coercion for granted when enacting social legislation. Antidiscrimination statutes regularly provide that it shall be unlawful for employers to retaliate against an employee for filing a complaint. Similarly, an Occupational Safety and Health Act, or a Pension Reform Act, or even workers compensation laws so protect employees. The ubiquitous provisions protecting claimants demonstrate the legislators' awareness that, if no such protection were provided, employees would be intimidated and would not file complaints; such legislation would then become a dead letter.

The most important example of such social legislation is the Wagner Act, or National Labor Relations Act of 1935, which guarantees to employees covered by it the rights to form, join, assist, and bargain through labor unions of their own choosing, and to "engage in other concerted activities for the purpose of collective bargaining or other mutual aid or protection." Under the act, it is an "unfair labor practice" for an employer to coerce employees in the exercise of those rights or to discharge them for exercising them. Among the protected rights, is of course, the right to file a charge of an unfair labor practice.

The Wagner Act's protections are invaluable. Without them, union efforts to organize the mass production industries in the late 1930s and early 1940s would have been far less successful than they were. Thus, Joseph Rosenfarb, writing in 1945, has acutely remarked:

The workers' paralysing fear that they would lose their jobs if they joined a union was removed by the Wagner Act. Now, when American workers foregather in a meeting to determine matters which vitally concern their livelihood and whether to form or join a union, they really can enjoy their constitutional liberties.[32]

But the act's protection is limited to the rights of self-organization and collective bargaining. As the Supreme Court noted in 1937 (while upholding the act's constitutionality), the act "does not interfere with the normal exercise of the right of the employer to select its employees or to discharge them." The act permits the National Labor Relations Board to protect employees only against coercion with respect to the rights specified in the act; in other respects, "the Board is not entitled to make its authority a pretext for interference with the right of discharge.[33]

The act does not protect employees against discharge for expressing controversial views, off or on the job, or for the employer's suspicion regarding their personal views. Nor does it protect employees against discharge for exercise of any other right, or refusal to commit any act, unless such exercise or refusal is part of a concerted activity involving more than one employee, for the purpose of collective bargaining or other mutual aid or protection.

Federal law thus protects employees only against discharge for specifically forbidden reasons. The employer remains free to discharge any employee for any *other* reason not specifically forbidden, or for no reason at all. The Michigan Department of Labor has described the situation cogently. It receives hundreds of inquiries each month from discharged employees, asking what recourse is available. It answers, "Probably nothing, because the reasons why most people are fired are not against the law.[34] Efforts to remedy the situation by state legislation have so far been unsuccessful. In 1972 a bill was introduced in the Connecticut legislature to provide protection to employees against unjust discharge; though supported by organized labor, however, it was killed by opposition from organized employers. In the early 1980s, a similar bill, providing for arbitration of claims of unjust discharge (the employee splitting the arbitration bill with the employer), was introduced in the Michigan legislature. It is still awaiting a vote at the time of this writing.

The power that American employers possess over their (nonunion) employees is inessential to (and probably dysfunctional to) the functioning of any modern economic system. Virtually every industrialized, Western country *other than* the United States—including those whose businesses are outcompeting American businesses—provides by law at least some protection to employees against unjust discharge. Some, like France and Italy, provide money damages to the unjustly discharged employee. West German law provides the employee with reinstatement as well, and places the burden upon the employer of proving to a labor court that the discharge was "based on reasons connected with the person or conduct of the employee or on urgent service need." Britain requires the employer to satisfy an industrial tribunal that the discharge was reasonable. Japanese law requires "just cause" for discharge and compliance with preestablished procedural rules. Roughly similar protection is provided employees by Canada, the Netherlands, Belgium, Luxemburg, Sweden, Denmark, and Norway.

These countries, along with almost all others, have invited the United States to join them. At a conference convened in June 1982 by the International Labor Organization (ILO), representatives of 126 countries, including the United States, considered for approval a convention (or multilateral treaty) proposing that "[the] employment of a worker shall not be terminated unless there is a valid reason for such termination connected with the capacity or conduct of the worker or based on the operational requirements of the undertaking." The governmental representatives from 124 of the 126 countries voted in favor; Australia abstained and only the United States voted "no." Of the separate employers' representatives, only those from Brazil, Chile, Fiji, Grenada, Swaziland, Switzerland, and the United States voted "no." The principal spokesman for the American employers' group explained that the employers opposed the convention "basically because its very concept . . . erodes the principle of termination at will."[35]

Although the ILO's constitution requires each member nation to submit any convention approved by an ILO conference to its national legislature within one year for implementation, there is no sign that the United States will take any action to adopt it.

Liberation Through Collective Bargaining

A labor union, in at least a part of its essence, is a civil liberties defense organization. Its purpose is to protect the individual freedom of employees against arbitrary employer power. Nearly seventy years ago, the Commission on Industrial Relations described that purpose eloquently: "The struggle of labor for organization," it said, "is not merely an attempt to secure an increased measure of the material comforts of life, but is part of the age-long struggle for liberty; . . . even if men were well fed they would still struggle to be free." Unions have expressed that purpose in terms of the dignity of workers and, most familiarly, in the slogan that an injury to one is the concern of, or an injury to, all. As D.C. Coates put the matter, "[A]s long as we are in this class struggle, the injury of one is an injury of every one of that class."[36]

The fact that "we are in this class struggle" is obvious to any employee who intelligently contemplates the power of employers over him and over other members of his class. So is the necessity for organized resistance to that power. Oliver Wendell Holmes, Jr., long ago rejected the suggestion that the struggle of unions against employer power was not legitimate "competition," by commenting that "[i]f the policy on which our law is founded is too narrowly expressed in the term *free competition*, we may substitute *free struggle for life*." Four years later, he argued that a strike for a closed shop was within the policy of the law as a means to strengthen the union and "to enable it to make a better fight on questions of wages or other matters of clashing interests," because "unity of organization is necessary to make the contest of labor effectual."[37]

Throughout the fifty years of Holmes' judicial career, however, the courts permitted such freedom of struggle only to employers. Employees were routinely enjoined by the courts from striking and from other concerted action. By enforcing yellow-dog contracts, the courts enjoined employees even from joining or assisting unions. Employers, meanwhile, remained free to combine. The general corporation laws aided them in doing so and allowed each combining employer to escape individual liability for their collective, corporate actions.

By 1935 the law's onesidedness was a national scandal. In adopting the Wagner Act, Congress found that "[t]he inequality of bargaining power between employees who do not possess full freedom of association . . . and employers who are organized in the corporate or other forms of ownership association" had become a burden to commerce and an aggravating cause of recurrent business depressions.[38]

The Wagner Act's protection of employees' rights to organize and be represented by unions of their own choosing was the heart of New Deal labor policy. Since the New Deal, however, the persons who administer our national affairs have revamped the nature of union-employer relations by creating an elaborate, juridical-ideological structure, based in part upon legislative enactments and labor board decisions, but deriving most of all from the Supreme Court's enunciation of federal labor policy. The new structure is designed to curb the Holmesian implications of the Wagner Act's protections.

It is federal policy, the Court said in 1960, "to promote industrial stabilization through the collective bargaining agreement." Such an agreement is entered into between a union, as exclusive bargaining representative for all employees; in a bargaining "unit," and their employers. It is, said the Court, "more than a contract"; it is "a generalized code to govern a myriad of cases which the draftsman cannot wholly anticipate." It is "an effort to erect a system of industrial self-government," and "[it] calls into being a new common law—the common law of a particular industry or a particular plant."

Its keystone is arbitration of grievances. "A major factor in achieving industrial peace," the Court said, "is the inclusion of a provision for arbitration of grievances in the collective bargaining agreement." And "[c]omplete effectuation of the federal policy is achieved when the agreement contains both an arbitration provision for all unresolved grievances and an absolute prohibition of strikes. . . ." Indeed, as the Court subsequently held, federal policy implies a no-strike provision, even where none exists, by the presence of an arbitration clause.

Under this structure, the arbitrator is "part of the system of self-government"; he "solve[s] the unforeseeable by molding a system of private law for all the problems which may arise."[39]

As far as the freedom of employees from employer power is concerned, the essential part of that "system of private law" is the provision, explicit in most bargaining agreements and implicit in others, that no employee shall be discharged or disciplined except for "just cause." *That provision is fundamental.* As one arbitrator has held, a failure to deem it implied where not explicitly stated "would reduce to a nullity the fundamental provision of a labor-management agreement—the security of a worker in his job." The "just cause" requirement means in practice that an employer, in discharging or disciplining an employee, must have acted for a legitimate reason, sufficient to justify the discipline, and used a fair procedure. In slightly more than one-half the reported discharge-arbitration decisions, the arbitrator has found that the employer failed to establish "just cause."[40]

Perfect justice is rarely achieved since arbitrators must please employers in order to be selected by them. The decisions often involve "splitting the baby": giving the employee reinstatement without back pay, or without full back pay—even where the employer's action is found to be utterly unjustified. And far worse are the *un*reported decisions. For there is a seamy side to arbitration, and underworld in which employers, in collusion with corrupt union officials, rig arbitration awards and select "rascals in arbitration" to sign them as arbitrators. In that underworld, employees' rights are literally sold out. Judge Paul R. Hays described the process in his 1966 Storrs Lectures, and anyone who has ever counseled employees represented by corrupt union officials recognizes the picture he draws as accurate.[41] Where the union's officials are open to employer bribery or where the union has become, in Daniel Bell's phrase, "part of the control system of management," there is obvious danger of such collusion. Fair arbitration, even more than fair litigation, requires *adversarial* representation, for in arbitration, the representatives jointly select and pay the decision maker.

It is nevertheless the opinion of many authorities that "[employees] in the United States protected by arbitration under collective agreements probably have more complete and sensitive protection against unjust discipline, more efficient procedures, and more effective remedies than employees in any other country.[42] Obviously, that judgment is not applicable to the seamy side of arbitration. But even at its almost worst, arbitration under a collective bargaining agreement provides at least some check upon the arbitrariness of the employer's power. To the extent it does, it provides a needed defense of individual liberty.

Oppression Through Collective Bargaining?

Is collective bargaining also an oppressor of individual liberty? That question is raised by critics of the "union shop" clauses in bargaining agreements, which (in those states where they are not forbidden by law) require all employees covered by the agreement to apply for union membership and pay dues.

Attacks upon "union shop" provisions are traditional on the part of employers. Benjamin Fairless says he used to say to John L. Lewis, "John, it's just as wrong to make a man join a union if he doesn't want to as it is to dictate what church he should belong to."[49] The analogy to a church, however, is strained. Unlike a church, a union imposes no belief system upon its members. If the union were to spend any dues money for any ideological purpose unconnected with its proper functions, any member disagreeing would be entitled to a refund of so much of his dues money as was expended. Every union member retains the right, protected by federal law, to express any views, inside or outside the union hall, and the union (unlike the employer) is forbidden to infringe on that right or discipline him for exercising it.

More to the point, the union is legally obligated to represent all employees in the bargaining unit fairly and nondiscriminatorily, whether members or nonmembers, and every employee in the union is governed by the bargaining agreement that the union negotiates. But *only as union members* can employees participate in shaping the policies and bargaining demands that will govern them, and in electing the union officials who will represent them.

A requirement that employees join the union thus follows logically from the union's status as exclusive bargaining representative for all employees in the bargaining unit. It would seem that anyone seriously challenging the former must challenge the latter as well—*Wer A sagt muss auch B sagen*— but few do. To challenge exclusivity of representation would be to challenge the entire structure.

Protection of working conditions is necessarily based upon what the Webbs termed the "Device of the Common Rule." For such protection to be effective, the common rule must govern all workers in the craft or plant or industry. One traditional way of accomplishing this was by refusal of union members to work with nonunion workers—or with anyone undermining established trade rules. The obviously preferable method is collective bargaining. But for collective bargaining to achieve that purpose, it must cover all employees; there is hence no practical alternative to exclusivity.

Nor do recalcitrant employees have a practical alternative even if they are allowed to bargain separately. It is common knowledge that the strength of one employee out of many is no match for the employer's bargaining power. The same applies to grievance bargaining. Though the 1947 Taft-Hartley amendments to the Wagner Act guarantee to individual employees and groups of employees the right to present grievances to the employer independently of their bargaining representative, that right has proved ineffectual. The employee who seeks effective protection against his employer's power must seek it through the union. The inevitable compulsion implied by exclusive representation thus becomes, as the Webbs prophesied it would, "so irresistible as to cease to be noticed," and "[i]n the most perfected form of Collective Bargaining, compulsory membership becomes as much a matter of course as compulsory citizenship."[44]

It is obviously desirable that the minority who may have opposed the majority's choice of bargaining representative nevertheless remain part of the voting constituency that decides upon the representative's leadership and policies. Individual freedom would be far more seriously infringed by denying opponents the rights to participate in membership meetings, to vote, to nominate candidates, and to be candidates for union leadership, than it would by requiring them to obtain such rights by joining the union. Where individual freedom can only be the product of group action—for it must be wrested from the employer—liberty *within* the group is far more important than the liberty not to join it. The desirability of a compulsory membership requirement would appear to follow from the practical necessity for exclusivity in bargaining representation.

But What of the Nonrepresented?

There are many things wrong with the unions and with collective bargaining as currently practiced. What is "wrongest," however, from the standpoint of personal liberty, is that collective bargaining has failed as yet to embrace the bulk of employees in private employment, and shows no sign of extending beyond the roughly 22 percent presently covered. More than 70 million employees on private payrolls in the United States remain unprotected by bargaining agreements. As employees at will, they are defenseless against their employers' power to discharge them at any time, for any reason not specifically forbidden by law, or for no reason at all.

Who are these millions of people? Many are employees in those trades and industries that are difficult for structural reasons to organize and that union organization has touched but not penetrated deeply: clerical workers, service workers, bank clerks, garage mechanics, insurance employees to name a few. Several million more are unprotected by federal law: agricultural employees, domestic servants, supervisory employees, college faculty, "managerial" employees, and persons employed as "independent contractors." Still others, in industries otherwise organized, are employees of "rogue employers—that is, flagrant law violators (most notoriously, J.P. Stevens & Co., Litton Industries, Inc., Dow Chemical Corporation, and Monroe Auto Equipment Company, but including many others as well) who have staved off union organization by the device of repeated and multitudinous violations of law.

A substantial reason why many of these employees remain unorganized is that, since the 1940s, the labor board has severely narrowed its interpretation of the rights guaranteed to employees by the Wagner Act and of what acts by employers constitute an "unfair labor practice." Even worse, the boards procedures—for employees, not for employers (for the charges principally filed by employers have statutory priority)—have become increasingly tortuous and slow. Even where the board takes action to protect an employee, that protection is rarely accomplished in time to offset the coercive and intimidating effect that his discharge or discipline has had upon other employees.

Had the board provided as little protection to employees in the late 1930s and early 1940s as it has since 1970, there is reason to doubt that the United Automobile Workers would ever have succeeded at Ford Motor Company, or the Packinghouse Workers at Wilson & Co., or the Steelworkers at Republic Steel. These antiunion bastions of yesteryear were the forerunners of the modern "rogue employers." The latter's antiunion tactics have been successful because of the board's failure to provide employees with effective and early protection of the rights guaranteed by the Wagner Act. And the problem is likely to grow worse. Recent events, especially defeat of the Labor Reform Bill of 1978, suggest that the trend toward lessened and more delayed protection of employee rights will continue.

It, therefore, appears that this anomaly will remain; one-fifth of private employees in the United States will continue to enjoy better protection against unjust discharge than employees in any other country—while the remaining four-fifths, unlike employees in any other modern, Western nation, enjoy *no* protection at all. In four-fifths measure, America will remain the land of the coerced and unfree employee.

The Public Worker's Right to Strike*

Mary Gibson _____

Let us now consider the main arguments advanced against the right of public employees to strike. (In view of the clarification above, I should say that I shall understand arguments against the right to strike as supporting specific legislative prohibition, and arguments for the right as supporting specific legislative recognition.)

Perhaps the oldest argument—if it can be called an argument—is based on the doctrine of sovereignty. . . .

As originally conceived, this doctrine was appealed to as justification for denying public employees not only the right to strike, but the right to bargain as well:

What this position comes down to is that governmental power includes the power, through law, to fix the terms and conditions of government employment, that this power cannot be given or taken away or shared and that any organized effort to interfere with this power through a process such as collective bargaining is irreconcilable with the idea of sovereignty and is hence unlawful. [Hanslowe, 1967, 14–15]

Another formulation of the view is provided by Neil W. Chamberlain:

In Hobbesian terms, government is identified as the sole possessor of final power, since it is responsive to the interests of all its constituents. To concede to any *special* interest group a right to bargain for terms which sovereignty believes contravenes the *public* interest is to deny the government's single responsibility. The government must remain in possession of the sole power to determine, on behalf of all, what shall be public policy. [Chamberlain, 1972, 13]

* Reprinted from Mary Gibson, *Worker's Rights* (Totowa, N.J.: Rowman & Allanheld, 1983), 108–21, Copyright © 1983 by Mary Gibson.

Applying the doctrine specifically to the right to strike, Herbert Hoover said in 1928 that "no government employee can strike against the government and thus against the whole people" (Aboud and Aboud, 1974, 3). And in 1947, Thomas Dewey stated that "a strike against government would be successful only if it could produce paralysis of government. This no people can permit and survive" (Aboud and Aboud, 1974, 3).

On the other side, Sterling Spero wrote in 1948:

When the state denies its own employees the right to strike merely because they are its employees, it defines ordinary labor disputes as attacks upon public authority and makes the use of drastic remedies, and even armed forces the only method for handling what otherwise might be simple employment relations. [Spero, 1948, 16]

Even if one accepts the doctrine of sovereign authority, it has been argued, it does not follow that collective bargaining or striking by public employees must be prohibited. Legislatures have often waived sovereign immunity in other areas of law. In most jurisdictions, individuals are now able to sue public bodies for negligence, for example. And since sovereignty refers to the people's will as expressed in legislative action, the concept does not preclude—indeed, it seems to require—that the people may, through their representatives, enact legislation authorizing government to engage in collective bargaining and permitting public employees to strike.

A related objection to the claim that sovereignty precludes strikes by public employees distinguishes between what might be called legal and political sovereignty. Legal sovereignty, according to this view, exists in order to meet the need for a peaceful, final, and enforceable means of settling disputes within society. Political sovereignty, on the other hand, refers to the process by which decisions are made in a political system. The American political process, it is pointed out, provides for no ultimate sovereign authority.

It might be added that the role attributed to government by the idea of legal sovereignty—that of a neutral or impartial third party for settling disputes—is clearly inappropriate where government itself is one of the parties to the dispute, e.g., as the employer in a labor-management dispute. This is so whatever one may think, in general, of the depiction of government as a neutral in disputes between private parties.

It has also been pointed out that the sovereignty argument as advanced by governmental units sounds suspiciously like the management prerogatives arguments private employers advanced against the rights of workers in the private sector to organize, bargain, and strike. If those arguments are properly rejected for the private sector, it is not clear why they should be accepted for the public sector. It is worth asking, moreover, what our reaction would be to the sovereignty argument if it were advanced by the government of another country as justification for prohibiting strikes by its citizen-employees. As the Executive Board of the Association of Federal, State, County, and Municipal Employees (AFSCME) has said, "Where one party at the bargaining table possesses all the power and authority, the bargaining process becomes no more than formalized petitioning" (Eisner and Sipser, 1970, 267).

A somewhat different version of the sovereignty argument relies on the claim that the public has rights, and these rights outweigh the right of public employees to strike. Hugh C. Hansen, for example, says:

In a democracy, the people should decide what services the government will supply. The right to strike is a powerful weapon, subject to abuse, which would indirectly give workers the power to make those decisions. A public employee strike is only successful if it hurts the public. . . . The public has rights; it should not be reluctant to assert them. [Hansen, 1980]

This sort of appeal to the rights of the public, however, is subject to what seems to me a decisive objection. As Ronald Dworkin has argued, it eliminates the protection which recognition of individual rights is supposed to provide:

It is true that we speak of the 'right' of society to do what it wants, but this cannot be a 'competing right' of the sort that may justify the invasion of a right against the Government. The existence of rights against the Government would be jeopardized if the Government were able to defeat such a right by appealing to the right of a democratic majority to work its will. A right against the Government must be a right to do something even when the majority thinks it would be wrong to do it, and even when the majority would be worse off for having it done. If we now say that society has a right to do whatever is in the general benefit, or the right to preserve whatever sort of environment the majority wishes to live in, and we mean that these are the sort of rights that provide justification for overruling any rights against the Government that may conflict, then we have annihilated the latter rights. [R. Dworkin, 1978, 194]

Thus, if we take seriously the claim that workers in general have a right to strike, we cannot justify abrogating that right by appeal to a conflicting right of the public to decide what services government will supply. (Note that Dworkin is not here objecting to the idea of group rights in contrast to that of individual rights; it is only the idea of the rights of society as a whole, or of a democratic majority, as potentially competing with the rights of individuals, corporations, or other corporate-like entities within the society, that threatens to annihilate the latter rights.)

If we reject the argument from sovereignty, then, there are two further arguments against the right of public employees to strike that pick up different threads from the arguments discussed so far. One appeals to preservation of the normal American political process, and the other to the essentiality of government services. The former may be dealt with more quickly, so let us consider it first.

What sovereignty should mean in this field is not the location of ultimate authority—or that the critics are dead right—but the right of government, through its laws, to ensure the survival of the " 'normal' American political process." As hard as it may be for some to accept, strikes by public employees may, as a long run proposition, threaten that process. [Wellington and Winter, 1969, 1125-26]

But what is this normal political process? "Is something abnormal because it does not operate in conjunction with the standard political process and procedures of a particular era? Does the normal political process automatically exclude any methods or goals which will disrupt existing power relations?" (Aboud and Aboud, 1974, 4). And if a group "distorts" the political process by having more power than the average interest group, are public sector unions the only, or even the most salient examples? (Note that, by Dworkin's argument above, the "right of government. . .to ensure the survival" of the normal political process cannot be understood simply as a right to prevent individuals or groups from affecting and influencing the political process through the exercise of their rights.)

Is it true that recognizing the right of public employees to strike would give them such irresistable power that the political process would be seriously enough distorted to justify denying them that right? To argue that it would, it seems to me, one would have to base one's case on one or more independent reasons for thinking such disproportionate power would ensue. One of these—essentiality of government services—we shall examine next. Two others—absence of a competitive market in the public sector, and the idea that public employees have influence over their wages and working conditions through lobbying and voting—we shall consider briefly below.

The claim that government services are essential may be thought to provide support for prohibition of strikes by public employees in one or more of at least three ways. First, it may be argued that, since these services are essential, it is intolerable that they be interrupted, even temporarily, as they would be by a strike. A second argument is that if essential services are interrupted, the public will put enormous pressure on government to restore them, and government will have little choice but to cave in to union demands, no matter what they are. Thus, if such strikes were permitted, public employee unions would be in an extraordinarily powerful position. Indeed, one opponent of the right to strike in the public sector likens public employee strikes to sieges or mass abductions because, in such a strike, an "indispensible element of the public welfare, be it general safety, health, economic survival, or a vital segment of cultural life such as public education, is made hostage by a numerically superior force and held, in effect, for ransom" (Saso, 1970, 37). A third argument is that, since government services are essential, the individual recipients of those services have a right to receive them. A strike that interrupted such services would, therefore, violate the rights of the would-be recipients, and, since the services are essential, the right to receive them must be an important right. These rights of individual recipients, then, may be said to compete with and outweigh any right of public employees to strike. (This appeal to the rights of individual members of the public does not run afoul of Dworkin's objection, above, which rejects only appeals to the rights of society, or the majority, as a whole.)

Clearly, however, not all government services are essential in the ways required for these arguments to be sound. In addition, somewhat different kinds and degrees of essentiality may be required by each of the three different arguments.

First, from the fact that a given service, such as public education, for example, is essential to society and its members over the long term, it by no means follows that any temporary interruption of such a service is intolerable. Public education is routinely interrupted for summer vacation, spring and fall breaks, holidays, and snow days. Time lost due to (legal or illegal) strikes by school employees can be, and is, made up by scheduling extra days and/or hours of classes. Are transportation services provided by municipal bus lines essential in ways that those provided by privately owned bus companies are not? If hospital workers in voluntary hospitals have the right to strike, why are public hospital employees different? Are their services any more essential? Upon reflection, it appears that few, if any, public services are essential in the way required to make the first argument sound, i.e., that even temporary interruption of them would be intolerable. Many who reject the first argument as applied to most government services do, nonetheless, accept it for two specific categories of service, those provided by police and firefighters. We shall return to these possibly special cases below.

In response to the second argument, that enormous public pressure to end a strike and restore services would force government to yield even to unreasonable union demands, there are at least three things to be said. First, in the absence of the economic pressure that a strike in the private sector exerts on the employer, public pressure to restore services is the only real leverage public employees can bring to bear on management to come to terms. Striking workers, of course, forfeit wages and place their jobs on the line in the public sector just as in the private sector. So the pressure on workers to arrive at an agreement and end a strike is very strong indeed. In contrast, the public sector employer is likely to have tax revenues continue to accrue during a

strike, while saving on the wage bill. Without public pressure for the restoration
of services, management could comfortably wait out almost any strike, thus
rendering the strike weapon totally ineffectual.

Second, the impact on tax rates of wage and benefit packages provides a
strong incentive for public sector employers to bargain hard. "For the public
employer, increases in the tax rate might mean political life or death; hence,
unions are not likely to find him easy prey" (Aboud and Aboud, 1974, 6).
And, as AFSCME's Victor Gotbaum points out:

An automobile can increase in price 300 percent. Your food can go up 200 percent.
If your taxes go up even less of a percentage, somehow the public is being raped
by public employees. That is not so. In fact, our own studies show that the wage
bill has not been going up that high since the arrival of unionism, taxes have not
increased at a greater pace than costs in other areas, and yet we get this funny
comparison that somehow when workers in the public sector strike, they get a
helpless hopeless citizen. [Gotbaum, 1978, 161]

A third response to the second argument is that it is essential to identify
the source of the public pressure. As Ronald Dworkin's argument above
establishes, public disapproval or displeasure at being inconvenienced or made
somewhat worse off does not justify the abrogation of a right. Certainly,
then, the anticipation of public pressure arising from such displeasure cannot
justify the abrogation of the right to strike. Thus it seems that prohibition
of public sector strikes could be justified only by showing that they constitute
a very direct and serious threat to the public safety or well-being, or that
exercise by public employees of the right to strike would somehow violate
more important rights of other members of society, as the third argument
from essentiality of government services maintains. The claim that *any* strike
would seriously and directly threaten the public safety or well-being does not
seem at all plausible applied across the board to public employees. Again,
it appears most plausible in the case of police and firefighters, although even
here a blanket prohibition may be far more restrictive than is justifiable. We
shall return to this question below.

Now let us consider the third argument, that the individual recipients of
government services have rights to those services which would be violated if
they were interrupted by a strike. First, from the fact that an individual has
a right to a government service it does not follow that the right is violated
if the service is temporarily interrupted. Even a very important right to a
given service need not be violated by a temporary interruption, as it would
be, let us suppose, by permanent cessation of the service. Moreover, from
the fact that individuals have very important rights to certain services it does
not follow that the onus is entirely upon government workers to provide

those services without interruption under whatever conditions management chooses to impose. The right is against government or society as a whole, whose obligation it is to create and maintain conditions in which qualified workers are willing to work and provide those services.

It is worth noting, too, that in many instances the issues over which government employees are likely to strike are issues on which the interests of the recipients of government services coincide with those of the providers. Welfare workers demanding lighter case loads, teachers insisting on smaller classes, air traffic controllers complaining about obsolete equipment, under-staffing, and compulsory overtime are all instances of government workers attempting to secure adequate conditions in which to do their jobs. The rights of the recipients of these services are not protected by prohibiting the providers from using what may be the only effective means of securing such conditions—quite the contrary. Even where this is not the case, there appear to be no grounds for a general claim that strikes by public employees would violate the rights of the recipients of govenmental services. If such a case is to be made, it must be made in much more particular terms with respect to specific categories of service. Once again, the chief candidates presumably will be policing and firefighting, to be discussed below.

Let us now briefly consider two additional reasons which have been offered in support of the claim that recognizing the right of public employees to strike would give them such power as to seriously distort the political process: absence of a competitive market in the public sector, and the claim that public employees have the opportunity to influence their wages and working conditions through lobbying and voting. The absence of competitive market forces in the public sector has been said to lend disproportionate power to striking public employees in two ways. First, it is argued that in the private sector market forces such as elasticity of demand for the employer's product and the extent of nonunion competition limit the ability of an employer to absorb increased labor costs. Since employees recognize these limits, and have no interest in putting the employer out of business, they have reason to limit their demands accordingly. In the absence of such forces, it is held, public employee unions have little reason to restrict their demands to reasonable levels. This argument seems to ignore the fact that all striking workers have a very direct incentive to reach a settlement—they lose wages each day that they are out. Even with a strike fund, strikers' incomes are drastically reduced, and in a prolonged strike, any existing strike fund is in danger of being exhausted. Moreover, unions in the public sector are not entirely insulated from competitive labor. The threat of permanent job loss through layoffs or even complete elimination of public agencies is very real. Santa Monica, California, for example, ended a strike of city employees by threatening to contract out its sanitation work. In Warren, Michigan, a similar threat was carried out (Burton and Krider, 1972, 277).

The second way in which the absence of market forces is said to result in greatly increased power for potential of actual strikers in the public sector is that public employers, not needing to minimize costs to remain competitive and profitable, will not bargain hard. As we saw above, however, the pressure to keep tax rates down can also provide an effective incentive for hard bargaining. Indeed, in many cases, the absence of a competitive market can work to strengthen the hand of the employer rather than that of the union, since the economic pressure a private sector strike brings to bear on the employer is absent, or greatly reduced, in the public sector.

Our final candidate for an argument showing that granting public employees the right to strike would seriously distort the political process is the claim that, unlike private sector workers, public employees and their unions have the opportunity to affect their wages and working conditions through the political process, so that if they had the right to strike as well, they would wield undue power. Thus it has been argued that, through collective bargaining, public employee unions can acquire the maximum concessions management will offer at the bargaining table, and then they can apply political pressure, through lobbying efforts and voting strength, to obtain additional concessions. If the right to strike were added, according to this argument, public sector bargaining would be heavily weighted in favor of employees.

But the capacity of public employee unions to influence legislative decisionmaking is a necessary (and often inadequate) counterweight to the tendency of legislators, responding to public pressure to keep taxes down, to solve difficult and ubiquitous fiscal problems at the expense of public employees. Representatives of each of the different categories of government workers must attempt to bring their concerns to the attention of legislators in an effort to avoid being lost in the budgetary shuffle. Further, although they constitute a growing percentage of the workforce, public employees as a group are unlikely to constitute anything approaching a voting majority in any given jurisdiction. And, although public employees as a group may constitute a potentially significant voting block, those workers directly affected by negotiations over any particular contract will almost certainly be a tiny minority. Thus, whatever truth there may be to this argument, it seems grossly inadequate to the task of showing that if on top of their right as citizens to participate in the political process they had, as workers, the right to strike, the political process would be so seriously distorted as to justify prohibiting the exercise of one of these important rights.

We have been unable to find any justification for a general prohibition of strikes by public employees. I conclude that public employees generally, like workers in the private sector, have the moral right to strike, and the right ought to be recognized and protected by law, as it is for all other workers.

We must turn now to consider whether police and firefighters constitute a special case where prohibition of strikes may be justified, even though it is not justified for other public employees. We shall not be able to give this complex and admittedly difficult question adequate discussion here, but we can try at least to identify some of the relevant considerations.

Of the various arguments discussed above, only those appealing to essentiality of services may apply differently to police and firefighters than to other public employees, so those are the only arguments relevant here. As you may recall, there were three arguments from essentiality of services. First, it may be argued that police and firefighting services are essential in a way that makes it intolerable for them to be interrupted, even temporarily. The second argument claims that, if such services were interrupted by a strike, public pressure to have them restored would be so strong that even outrageous demands would be agreed to. Thus police and firefighters are in a position to "hold hostage" the public safety. And, third, individual members of the public may be said to have very important rights to protection of their lives, safety, and property that police and firefighters provide, rights that would be violated if those protections were suspended by a strike.

Concerning the second argument, the burden of proof must be on those who would deny an important right to show that there is more than a theoretical possibility that the right would be abused in seriously harmful ways. More than that, many of our important rights and freedoms are occasionally abused in ways that result in serious harm to others. In most cases, we reluctantly accept the risks in order to preserve the freedoms. Proponents of prohibition of strikes by police and firefighters must, then, provide convincing evidence that legal recognition of their right to strike would create a serious *practical* threat that is out of proportion to the other risks we endure out of respect for rights. I have so far seen no reason to believe that such evidence can be produced. Note, too, that the fact that the restriction in question applies to a minority of the members of society, in contrast to many other possible restrictions of rights that might be adopted, is a reason to be suspicious of it.

Let us grant, though, that one or more of these arguments may have some force in the case of police and firefighters. Is that force sufficient to justify flatly denying to these individuals an important right? The answer to this question seems to depend on what the available alternatives are. It may be that, with some constraints, the right to strike could be retained by these workers without serious threat to the rights or safety of the public. If so, outright prohibition of such strikes still would not be justified.

For example, provision might be made for partial work stoppages with emergency services continued for life-threatening situations. Police functions include many that could be interrupted with some inconvenience but little serious danger to the public; for example, traffic control, parking violations, paper work not immediately essential to protecting the rights either of victims of crime or of the accused. Firefighters might respond to alarms but limit their firefighting to those measures needed in order to carry out all possible rescue efforts.

Another possibility is to provide for a mandatory "cooling off" period of, say, thirty or sixty days. This could be either automatic or available to be invoked by the appropriate public official if he or she deemed it necessary. During this period, mediation could take place in an effort to help the parties reach voluntary agreement. (A mediator is a third party who attempts to help the disputants find a resolution they can agree upon. A mediator has no power to impose a settlement.) Also, during such a period, public officials would have the opportunity to make contingency plans for protecting the public in the event of a strike. It may be objected with some justification that such a "cooling off" period is, or should be, unnecessary. Mediation efforts could be undertaken before, rather than after, a contract runs out, and contingency plans could be made when officials see that negotiations are not going well and the contract is within a month or two of running out. Nevertheless, supposing that public officials sometimes lack wisdom and foresight, and that the public safety may be at stake as a result, there may be some grounds for such a provision.

I see no reason why some such constraints would not suffice to eliminate any serious special threat to the rights and safety of the public that the prospect of a strike by police or firefighters poses. But since some will no doubt remain unpersuaded, and since the precise nature and degree of constraints justifiable on these grounds will be controversial among those who are persuaded, it may be worthwhile to look briefly at what the alternative is if the right to strike is entirely denied. Some procedure must be provided for arriving at a settlement when contract negotions are at an impasse.

The principal alternative is compulsory binding arbitration. Arbitration differs from mediation in that an arbitrator investigates a dispute and issues a decision which is binding on both parties. There are two sorts of labor disputes in which arbitration may be used. It is most commonly used as a final step for resolving individual grievances that arise under an existing contract. Frequently, the contract itself provides that grievances that are not resolved by the other measures provided in the grievance procedure will go to arbitration. The second kind of dispute is that in question here, where the parties are unable to reach agreement on a contract. We shall be discussing only arbitration of the latter sort.

In the most usual form of arbitration for settling the terms of a contract, the parties present and argue for their positions on the issues that are in dispute, and then the arbitrator draws up terms that he or she considers most fair. Thus the arbitrator may impose terms that were not proposed by either party. It has been objected against this sort of arbitration that, since arbitrators most often "split the difference" between the two sides, there is little incentive for the parties to bargain in good faith, since the more extreme the position they present to the arbitrator the more they are likely to get in the compromise. To avoid this problem, another form of arbitration has been proposed. It is called final-offer arbitration because the arbitrator is restricted to a choice between the final offers of the two parties on all unresolved issues. The arbitrator may not pick and choose among the offers of the parties on different issues—the choice is between one total package or the other. The purpose of this restriction is to provide a strong incentive for each party to make the most reasonable possible proposals—with the hope that, in so doing, they may even arrive at an agreement without going to arbitration. A serious problem with this procedure is that one or both of the final offers may contain some provisions which are eminently reasonable and others which are not. An employer's final offer, for example, might be very reasonable in terms of wages and benefits, but contain a change in the grievance procedure that would be disastrous for the union. In addition, an arbitrator, who is not familiar with the day-to-day operations and problems, may not be in a position accurately to assess which proposals—especially non-economic proposals—are reasonable.

This latter problem constitutes an objection against compulsory arbitration in any form. The parties themselves know best what the issues mean in terms of what it would be like to live and work under a given provision for the next year, two years, or three years, depending on the duration of the prospective contract. They know which issues are so important to them that they are worth risking a strike over, and which provisions they can live with. No third party can know these things as well as the disputants themselves. Thus, both practical considerations and appeal to the right of self-determination argue in favor of allowing the parties to settle their disputes themselves, even if that means strides will sometimes occur.

Another potential problem with final-offer arbitration is that a different form of "splitting the difference" would tend to arise. Since both parties generally have the right to veto the appointment of an individual arbitrator—and surely they must have this right, since this individual will determine the terms and conditions that will govern their working lives for, typically, one to three years—there will be a strong tendency for arbitrators to decide half of their cases in favor of management and half in favor of unions. An arbitrator with a record of decisions going too often either way would soon be out of work. Now it may be thought that this pressure should be welcomed, since it amounts to a strong incentive for arbitrators to be even-handed, and hence fair. But it must be noted that there is little reason to expect that, over any given period of time, for any particular arbitrator, management will have made the most reasonable offer in just 50 percent of the cases he or she hears, and the union in the other 50 percent. Yet the pressure is to build a record that appears to reflect just this situation.

Finally, whichever form of arbitration is used, some opponents of compulsory arbitration argue—with a good deal of plausibility, in my view—that arbitrators tend to have backgrounds, educations, life-styles, and social contacts that lead them, consciously or unconsciously, to identify more with supervisors, managers, and public officials than with workers. This identification cannot help but influence their sympathies, their assessment of the arguments put forth by the parties, and hence, ultimately, their decisions. Thus, a system of compulsory arbitration is, probably inevitably, biased in favor of management and against workers. Note that this objection is compatible with the previous one, although it may at first appear not to be. If unions are aware of the pro-management bias of arbitrators then they will risk going to arbitration only when their case is particularly strong. They will settle voluntarily in many cases where they ought to win in arbitration but probably would not. In such a situation, unions would have a better case than management in significantly more than 50 percent of the cases that actually got to arbitration, so a fifty-fifty split of the decisions would reflect a promanagement bias.

For all of these reasons, then, compulsory binding arbitration is unsatisfactory as a substitute for the right to strike. As a matter of political reality, however, it may be that, given the kinds and degrees of constraint likely to be placed on their right to strike by legislators in a given jurisdiction, police and firefighters do better to accept a system of arbitration than to retain a right to strike that would be rendered utterly ineffectual.

To conclude this discussion of the right of public employees to strike, it must be emphasized that prohibition of strikes does not prevent strikes. Indeed, it can be argued that it is likely to have the opposite effect. New Jersey's Commissioner of Labor and Industry said in 1965 that "it may be more critical to have the strike weapon available to workers to alert management, government, the customers of the government, and the public that they must do something; they cannot go on ignoring the problem" (Male, 1965, 109). (As we noted above, New Jersey still has not recognized the right of public employees to strike.) Allan Weisenfeld develops the argument as follows:

Strikes in the public sector will be no more frequent, probably less, than in the private sector and cause no greater inconvenience and dislocation. . . . It is the denial of the right to strike in the public sector . . . which invites strike threats. Anti-strike laws create a tendency on the part of public managers to rely on them to bail them out, and hence, they tend to contribute little to help solve the problems before the bargainers. [Weisenfeld, 1969, 139]

Prohibition of strikes may thus exacerbate the very problems it is intended to solve.

A Kantian Utilitarian Approach*

R.M. Hare _____

How should a legislature decide which rights should be protected in the workplace? According to a typical utilitarian approach, the legislators have to consider what legal provisions about rights will, if adopted, maximize the satisfactions of the preferences of the affected parties. Who are the affected parties? Obviously the employees concerned, and other employees; the employers, including their shareholders if any; and, most of all, the general public, which consumes the products and services that they provide. This same public has an interest not only in continuity of production and service, and in avoiding price rises, but also in the preservation of public order and a smoothly working economy.

In Britain and other countries, starting in the nineteenth century, permissive legislation has been increasingly enacted conferring various immunities and powers on trade unions. I am convinced that this has had, on the whole, great utility; it has tended to further preference satisfactions all round. It has been, along with the factory acts regulating employment practices, the main factor in bringing about improvements in conditions of work and greater equality of wealth, power, and status. Since these improvements and this greater equality can be justified on utilitarian grounds, utilitarians should, and did, support the legalization of trade unions and the conferring on them of certain privileges (especially freedom from liability to be sued for acts which would render anybody else liable for damages). Present disputes about labor laws are largely concerned with the question of whether the process has gone too far—whether the immunities (which are a kind of legal rights) given to trade unions are now greater than utility can justify.

From the beginning, the question has frequently been discussed in terms of rights, legal or moral; I see no harm in that, provided that we keep a good grip on the argument. The permisive legislation I have been speaking

---

of conferred certain *legal* rights on trade unions. The conferring of them could be justified in two ways, but it is important to see that they come, in effect, to the same. The first way is directly utilitarian. We say that the introduction of a certain legal right (for example, to combine against an employer) will, all in all, maximize the preference satisfactions of all those affected, considered impartially. As I said, I think the earlier legislation can be justified in this way.

It is quite usual to teach beginner philosophy students that there are two approaches to moral questions, the utilitarian and the Kantian, which are poles apart and between which they have to choose. The present question illustrates the falsity of this dogma. A "Kantian" (a name often claimed by antiutilitarians) is likely to base his arguments on the existence of certain *moral* (not *legal*) rights, or on *justice,* used as a term of moral approval. It may be said (speaking morally) that the workers have a right to seek to improve their conditions and wages by such and such means. Or it may be said that it would be unjust to prevent them. People who say this are usually appealing to their own intuitions and to those of people who they hope will share them. That is why appeals to justice and to rights are such a powerful rhetorical weapon if the intuitions, or even the prejudices, are there to be appealed to. Again, I see no harm in this, provided that we keep a grip on the argument.

A utilitarian can give an honourable place to intuitions and even prejudices. But the crucial question is, "*What* intuitions and prejudices in particular ought to be allowed this honourable place?" There have been, after all, those who insisted with equal vehemence on the right of employers to manage their own businesses on their own property and employ anybody they wish to on whatever terms they can negotiate. How are we to argue about what moral rights people have, and what legal rights they morally ought to be given?

It is here that the Kantian and the utilitarian approaches begin to converge. Kant's 'Categorical Imperative' was formulated by him in various ways, but they are all ways of giving reasons for moral "maxims," or answering the question of what moral maxims we should adopt and act on. All these ways are directed to securing impartiality in our treatment of other people; we are to adopt maxims we are prepared to will universally, whatever role we were to occupy in the situation, and in so doing are to treat other human beings as ends, just as we treat ourselves. That means treating their ends as if they were our ends, or, in other words, treating the satisfaction of their preferences as if they were the satisfaction of our own.

Among the maxims we shall be led to adopt by this Kantian utilitarian method are maxims requiring the respecting of certain rights. Both the moral rights and the legal rights we morally ought to accord to people will depend on whether according them will do the best to maximize the satisfaction of the preferences of people, treated impartially as ends (as if *we* were in their position). By using this criterion, we are being *fair* to all those whose interests are affected by the according or the withholding of the rights. It is reasonable to ask anybody who rejects this way of arguing about rights, what other way he is going to suggest. I cannot see any promise in the way which is commonly followed, and which I have already described: the appeal to intuitions unsupported by any argument about what are the best intuitions, as we have seen, is mere rhetoric and leads to no firm conclusion, because intuitions, when not criticized and amended in the light of argument, will conflict.[45]

[This short extract comes from a longer paper on the rights of employees, in which I discuss the judgment of the European Court of Human Rights in the case of Young James and Webster (Strasbourg, 13 August 1981). These applicants had been dismissed by the nationalized British railroad in pursuance of a union shop agreement, they having refused on conscientious grounds to join a union. The court, by a majority, found that their rights had been infringed, on the ground that a right to join a union, protected by the European Convention on Human Rights, implied a right not to join a union if unwilling. Three dissenting judges, all Scandinavian, held that in logic there was no such implication. Although they agreed with the majority that the applicants had been wronged, they held that they had no remedy under the convention, but that the matter rested with the British legislature (which, in fact, had already by that time brought in amending legislation to cover such cases). In agreeing with the dissentient judges, I argue that in general, where there are conventions or bills of rights couched in very vague terms, courts are easily tempted to stretch the law in conformity to their own moral opinions or even prejudices, usurping powers which belong properly to a democratically elected legislature.]

Notes

1.   Albert Soboul, *La Revolution Francaise,* Editions Sociales (Paris, 1982), 196.

2.   Francis Place quoted in G.D.H. Cole and Raymond Postgate, *The British Common People, 1746–1946* (London: University Paperbacks, 1961), 177–78.

3.   Michael Harrington, *Socialism* (New York: Saturday Review Press, 1972), chaps. 6 and 11.

4.   Herbert Gutman, *Work, Culture and Society* (New York: Vintage Books, 1976), 26.

5.   Quoted in Thomas Brooks, *Toil and Trouble,* rev. ed. (New York: Delacorte Press, 1971), 145.

6.   John Kenneth Galbraith, *The Great Crash* (Boston: Houghton Mifflin, 1961), 181–82.

7.   Ibid., 180.

8.   Robert Reich, "Collusion Course," *The New Republic,* 27 February 1984.

9.   Morgan O. Reynolds, *Power and Privilege* (New York: Universe Books, 1984); Richard O. Freeman and James L. Medoff, *What Do Unions Do?* (New York: Basic Books, 1984); Lester Thurow, *On Generating Inequality* (New York: Basic Books, 1977).

10.   "The De-unionisation of America", *The Economist,* 29 October 1983.

11.   Harry Braverman, *Labor and Monopoly Capital* (New York: Monthly Review Press, 1974).

12.   Andre Gorz, *Farewell to the Working Class* (Boston: South End Press, 1982; (French original, 1980.)

13.   Charles Sabel, *Work and Politics* (New York: Cambridge University Press, 1982).

14.   *New York Times,* 11 December 1983, 7.

15.   Milton Friedman, *Capitalism and Freedom* (Chicago: University of Chicago Press, 1971), 120.

16.   Ibid.

17.   Frank Knight, "Wages and Labor Union Action in the Light of Economic Analysis," *The Public Stake in Union Power,* ed. Philip D. Bradley (Charlottesville: University Press of Virginia, 1959), 44.

18.   F.A. Hayek, "Unions, Inflation and Profits," in *The Public Stake in Union Power,* 47, ed. Philip Bradley (University of Virginia Press, 1959).

19.   Mancur Olson, *The Logic of Collective Action* (Cambridge, Mass: Harvard University Press, 1975), 68–69.

20. Ibid, 71.

21. Friedman, *Capitalism and Freedom,* 124.

22. Milton and Rose Friedman, *Free to Choose* (New York: Avon Books, 1981), 221.

23. Albert Rees, *The Economics of Trade Unions* (Chicago: University of Chicago Press, 1977), 74.

24. Friedman, *Capitalism and Freedom,* 124.

25. Rees, *The Economics of Trade Unions,* 89.

26. Ibid., 90-91.

27. Milton and Rose Friedman, *Free to Choose,* 224.

28. Olson, *The Logic of Collective Action,* 83.

29. Ibid., 88.

30. Ibid., 89.

31. Lawrence E. Blades, "Employment at Will vs. Individual Freedom: On Limiting the Abusive Exercise of Employer Power," *Columbia Law Review* 67 (1972): 1404, 1405-6. For authorities referred to, see Ibid., 1406-10; Clyde W. Summers, "Individual Protection Against Unjust Dismissal: Time for a Statute," *Virginia Law Review* 62 (1976): 481; "Protecting Employees at Will Against Wrongful Discharge: The Public Policy Exception," *Harvard Law Review* 96 (1981): 1931.

32. Josph Rosenfarb, "Protection of Basic Rights," *The Wagner Act: After Ten Years,* ed. L. G. Silverberg (1945), 91, 93.

33. NLRB v. Jones & Laughlin Steel Corp., 301 U.S. 1, 45–46 (1937).

34. Quoted in Jack Stieber, "Protection Against Unjust Discharge: The Need for a Federal Statute," *University of Michigan Journal of Law Reform* 16 (1983): 319, 320.

35. Quoted in Janet R. Bellace, "A Right of Fair Dismissal: Enforcing a Statutory Guarantee," *University of Michigan Journal of Law Reform* 16 (1983): 207, 214.

36.   U.S. Commission on Industrial Relations, *Final Report of the Commission on Industrial Relations* (1915), 80–81 and Del. Coates, *The Founding Convention of the Industrial Workers of the World: Proceedings* (1905, repr. 1969), 246.

37.   Vegelahn v. Guntner, 167 Mass. 92, 104 (1896); Plant v. Woods, 176 Mass. 492, 504 (1900) (diss. opinions of C. J. Holmes)

38.   Sec. 1 of the National Labor Relations Act, 29 U.S.C. 151.

39.   United Steelworkers v. Warrior & Gulf Nav. Co., 363 U.S. 574, 578–82 (1960) and see Gateway Coal Co. v. United Mine Workers, 414 U.S. 368 (1974).

40.   Frank Elkouri and Edna Asper Elkouri, *How Arbitration Works,* 3d ed., BNA, Washington, D.C., (1973), 611–12, 632–34.

41.   Paul R. Hays, *Labor Arbitration: A Dissentive View* (New Haven, Conn.: Yale University Press, 1966), 37–75.

42.   Summers, "Individual Protection," 483.

43.   Benjamin F. Fairless, *It Could Only Happen in the United States,* n.p. (1959), 44.

44.   Sidney & Beatrice Webb, *Industrial Democracy* (London: Longmans, Green & Co. Ltd., 1897, repr. 1920), 217.

45.   For Kant's views, see his *Groundwork of the Metaphysic of Morals* (available in many translations). For a full explanation of the Kantian utilitarian approach, see my *Moral Thinking* (New York: Oxford University Press, 1981). For more about labour legislation, see my "Liberty and Equality: How Politics Masquerades as Philosophy," *Social Philosophy and Policy* 2 (1984).

PART 5 _____

TECHNOLOGY, UNEMPLOYMENT, AND THE FLIGHT OF FACTORIES

Alternatives to Industrial Flight*

Staughton Lynd _____

A shutdown is a devastating experience for the victims. . . . As one
Youngstown steelworker put it to me, "You felt as if the mill would always
be there." Because steelworkers felt this way they put up with boredom, and
danger, and humiliating harassment from supervisors every day, trading off
these indignities for the fringe benefits which would come to them from long
service at a particular plant. Now that bargain has been broken, and workers
in Youngstown and elsewhere are beginning to ask: Why is the company
allowed to make a shutdown decision unilaterally? Since the decision affects
my life so much, why can't I have a voice in the decision?

The communities in which shutdowns occur are starting to ask the same
questions. A plant closing affects more than the workers at the plant. City
income from industrial property taxes goes down, schools start to deteriorate
and public services of all kinds are affected. Layoffs occur in businesses which
supplied raw materials for the shut down plant and in businesses which
processed the product, retail sales fall off. All the signs of family strain—
alcoholism, divorce, child and spouse abuse, suicide—increase. Why may a
corporation unilaterally decide to destroy the livelihood of an entire community?
Why should it be allowed to come into a community, dirty its air, foul its
water, make use of the energies of its young people for generations, and
then throw the place away like an orange peel and walk off? . . .

The steel industry says that plant closings are unpleasant but necessary,
just like surgery.

The basic idea put forward by the industry is that capital must be free
to go wherever the rate of profit is highest. The industry argues that only
if businesses are free to shut down, and free to move elsewhere, will American

* Reprinted from Staughton Lynd, *The Fight Against Shutdowns: Youngstown's Steel Mill
Closings* (San Pedro, Calif.: Singlejack Books, 1983), 3–217 excerpts, Copyright © 1982
Staughton Lynd.

industry be modernized so as to compete effectively with European and Japanese imports.

As the steel industry sees things, maximizing profit means closing down old facilities and building from the ground up in new ("greenfield") locations.

As the steel industry sees things, maximizing profit may even mean investing outside the steel industry entirely, so as to earn the money which then can be invested in steel. (We should ask industry spokesmen: If it is more profitable today to invest in real estate, or chemicals, or oil, rather than in steel, won't the same thing be true five years from now?)

Many people in public life agree with the steel industry. Mayor Caliguiri of Pittsburgh admits that Pittsburgh has no specific plans for retraining unemployed blue-collar workers. He suggests, in fact, that it might be a good idea if the city's unemployed moved somewhere else. "I'd rather have less people with high incomes than more people with relatively low earning and spending power," he has said. . . .

Three Arguments Against Industrial Flight

Youngstown workers have struggled to find words to express a different point of view. Ed Mann said in meeting after meeting: "We're not gypsies." John Barbero recalled how British labor leader Aneurin Bevan told about the uprooting of his family from the coal mining country of Wales. "When do we stop running?," Barbero asked. It was common in Youngstown to meet steelworkers who had lost one or more other jobs in shutdowns before the mill closed. . . .

Out of the meetings, the kitchen-table arguments, the leaflet writing, and the law suits, workers in Youngstown spelled out an argument for modernizing industry in existing communities ("brownfield" modernization). The argument makes the following points:

1. Even from the standpoint of the single firm, greenfield modernization is more expensive than brownfield modernization.
2. When costs to the community as well as costs to the firm are considered, the case for brownfield modernization becomes overhwelming.
3. In the last analysis, the question of brownfield versus greenfield modernization is a question of what kind of society we want. There is no economic necessity for the reindustrialization of America in new towns rather than in old ones. The strongest motivation for industrial flight from the cities in which plants presently exist appears to be anti-unionism. Management grows tired of labor troubles, and imag-

ines that new hires in a community which lacks a history of struggle will solve its problems. A second motive for industrial flight appears to be simply the American habit of scrapping last year's car, last year's community, and last year's spouse, and moving on. The concern for family and community so much talked about nowadays should express itself in a program for modernizing industry in existing sites because it is better for human beings. . . .

Two comprehensive Federal studies of the steel industry have reached the conclusion that it is cheaper for a steel company to modernize in existing, brownfield sites than in new, greenfield locations. . . . (But) one must also consider human costs. Even if greenfield modernization were cheaper than brownfield for the company, it might be more expensive for society as a whole.

Late in 1978 an analysis was conducted of the socio-economic effects of the Campbell Works shutdown. It found that in addition to the employees at the Works who were terminated, at least another 3,600 jobs would be lost through the secondary multiplier effect on suppliers, retail businesses, and others. Loss of wages to the former Campbell Works employees during the first three years after the shutdown was estimated at $50–70 million, and loss of wages to those in other businesses during the same period at $63.5 million. The study projected costs to the public sector during the same three years of $60–70 million. About half of these public costs were expected to take the form of local, county, state, and Federal tax losses. . . .

City after city in the Mahoning Valley has experienced a budgetary crisis followed by wage cuts and layoffs for public employees, and cutbacks in social services. Frank Fasline, treasurer of the Campbell school board, told Carol Greenwald and Dorie Krauss:

This thing is wrecking the school system here in Campbell. It is really a drastic situation. We're down to the state minimum in every area. We've had layoffs; we've curtailed purchasing supplies; we're down to the bare necessities. We've reduced all the extra-curricular activities. We have to make kids pay for some of their own football equipment. We're borrowing every year to pay the deficit from the previous year.

In May 1980, nearly all of Youngstown's municipal employees, including firefighters and police officers, went on strike for pay increases the city said it could not provide because of revenue lost in the shutdown of the Valley's steel mills.

By January 1981, unemployment in the Youngstown-Warren Metropolitan Statistical Area had reached 15.4 percent, the highest level since the Depression. . . .

Statistics cannot convey the full human costs of the Youngstown shutdowns. This was a community in which the generations of a family cared for one another, in which grandparents did babysitting, and were themselves cared for by families rather than institutions. Now, as a result of the shutdowns, young people feel compelled to leave town. . . .

And what balance sheet can adequately reflect these lines by a son about his unemployed father?

He's losing his mind with nothing to do,
because he got laid off from the Sheet & Tube . . .
Dad sits around the house, all worried and sick,
with nothing to do the dog he does kick.
It's all Lykes fault and dad knows it by now,
he just wants to go and blow his brains out.
Yet he sits in his chair, impatient and worried,
I guess he'll be there until the day he is buried.

Felix Rohatyn, the financier who engineered New York City's "survival," echoes the analysis developed by Youngstown steelworkers in the following ways:

In a world where capital will be in shorter supply than energy, is it really a valid use of resources to have to build anew in the Sun Belt the existing schoolhouses, fire houses, transit systems, etc., of the North for the benefit of the new immigrants in the South, instead of maintaining and improving what we already have in place here? Is it rational to think that northern cities teeming with the unemployed and unemployable will not be permanent wards of the federal government at vast financial and social cost? . . . Doesn't the notion of "taking the people to the jobs" completely ignore that many of those people, in large parts of this country, are unwilling and unable to move?

Sweden Provides One Alternative

Twenty-five years from now, no doubt too late for many, many Youngs-towns, this is how every civilized nation will modernize its industry. Several of us in Youngstown had a glimpse of that future when we met at the Local 1462 union hall with Per Ahlstrom, editor of the weekly magazine of the Swedish Metal Workers Federation. Ahlstrom began by emphasizing that Sweden, like the United States, is a capitalist economy. Then he went on to describe the Swedish steel crisis and how it was resolved. Several years ago, he said, Sweden faced the same problems of overcapacity and low profitability which now exist in the United States. There were three Swedish steel companies, two privately owned, and one owned by the government. Each was trying to carry on the whole steelmaking process from blast furnace to rolling mill, and all were losing money. Accordingly, the Swedish government insisted that the three enterprises coordinate their activities. At the same time, however, it was decided as a matter of principle that rather than concentrate all steelmaking in a single location it would be socially preferable to preserve each of the three, traditional steel towns if a way could be found to do so. The resolution was that each company remained where it was, but each henceforth was responsible for a single phase of steelmaking. The mill closest to sources of iron ore in northern Sweden did the initial processing. The mill located on the sea-coast did most of the finishing. Meantime, since all modernization and rationalization tends to eliminate jobs, imaginative programs were designed to help people leave the steel industry, not in shock and defeat, but with a sense of moving forward in their lives. All Swedish employers were required to list all job openings, and a computerized printout of currently available jobs was posted each day in the mill itself. Persons who wanted to visit other communities where there were job openings were paid to do so, as were their spouses. Every steel worker was guaranteed two years' pay during the period of transition. The social objective, our visitor stated, was that no one ever be compelled unwillingly to leave a job.

Sweden does what it does for essentially "political" reasons. Helen Ginsburg says this well in an article in *The Nation*. She quotes an unnamed Swedish official: "Swedes are not particularly religious but one thing we do hold almost sacred is everybody's right to work." The result, she continues, is that the unemployment rate in Sweden was 1.7 percent from 1960 to 1970, and 2.1 percent from 1971 to 1979. This is not because the Swedish economy in general or its steel industry in particular are immune to the shocks affecting other capitalist economies. On the contrary, Sweden is more dependent than the United States on exports, and has no coal of its own.

The answer is that the Swedish commitment to full employment is politically unassailable. Even though it has traditionally been regarded as an important means of raising the output of goods and services, and hence living standards, it is not viewed solely in economic terms. It is also linked to other vital social goals. . . . [The] concept of "normalization" is fundamental to the Swedish social welfare system; that is, the goal is to enable everyone to live as normal a life as possible and "to reduce the risk of isolation, loneliness and alienation." And work is considered the key to a normal life. In short, a job is considered a basic right.

Listening to Per Ahlstrom in Youngstown, Ohio, was like hearing a fairy tale. For instance, early retirement, which is the objective of the United

Steelworkers of America in its collective bargaining about shutdowns, is, according to Ahlstrom, considered a defeat in Sweden because it deprives a person of years of contribution to society as a worker. . . .

It remains to be seen whether tax breaks and other subsidies, granted on condition that the money provided be reinvested in steel, would induce U.S. Steel and other steel companies to rebuild aging mills in places like Pittsburgh, Gary, Indiana, and Lackawanna, New York. If not, the people of the United States will have to consider doing the job themselves. In the 1930s, the government created the Tennessee Valley Authority to provide electric power to areas that private utilities could not profitably serve. Frank O'Brien, former president of Local 1843, USWA, representing production and maintenance employees at J & L's plant in Pittsburgh, has suggested formation of a "Monongahela Valley Authority" that could acquire and operate steel mills that the industry did not wish to modernize. . . .

O'Brien has described his idea this way:

When you work in a mill, and you see all these guys with the know-how, all together right there, then you see that you have the ability to operate the mill no matter what top management does.

The company says, "Hey, it's not profitable for us any more to produce steel here." But we still need jobs. Companies like J & L are making money. They are moving because they don't make enough money to suit them. They've let their plants run down like an old automobile: you run it into the ground, and then you take the license plate off and walk away from it.

So we should think about forming an Industrial Development Authority and running the mills ourselves. . . . The companies have used this . . . for their own purposes. In the 1950s J & L used it to evict people from their homes in Scotch Bottom in Hazelwood. They said they needed the land to expand, but when they had evicted the people and gotten the land they didn't expand. They just let the land sit there and stored raw materials on it.

So I'm thinking the law can be used in reverse.

I think back to the time when the Port Authority was born. Pittsburgh Railways was the big operator transporting people in the City of Pittsburgh. They ran into a financial bind. So the Port Authority was formed, taking in all the bus companies in Allegheny County as well. It bought up the railway and the bus companies because people still had to be transported.

Recently they decided to close down the J & L hot strip mill. A thousand people lost their jobs.

A couple of Sundays later the Mayor was out to our father-and-son communion breakfast at St. Stephens in Hazelwood. He made a little speech and then he opened it up for questions.

So I got up. I said the Mayor had better start worrying now about the U.S. Steel mills, that when they build that plant in Conneaut they're going to shut down every plant up and down the river.

He said, "Well, what would you do?" I told him: "You, and the County Commissioners, sit down and form an authority, like the Port Authority. We can run the plants ourselves."

On Alternatives to Industrial Flight: The Moral Issues

*Judith Lichtenberg**

Staughton Lynd writes: "Workers in Youngstown and elsewhere are beginning to ask: Why is the company allowed to make a shutdown decision unilaterally? Since the decision affects my life so much, why can't I have a voice in the decision? The communities in which shutdowns occur are starting to ask the same questions."[1]

The thrust of Lynd's questions is moral, not practical. He is asking why companies *ought* to be allowed to exclude workers and communities from shutdown decisions, and he is suggesting that the latter have a *right*—a moral right, which ought perhaps to be made a legal right—to participate in these decisions.

From some perspectives, these questions seem to answer themselves. The free market defender may say: "It is the company that owns the factory, makes the investments and takes the risks; in accepting jobs, workers freely consent to certain ground rules." Thus, the firm has the right to move whenever it chooses. The committed democrat, on the other hand, may insist that in matters that crucially affect a person's life, that person ought to have some say: "What touches all must be decided by all."[2] A shutdown decision touches deeply the lives of workers, their families, and their communities; they ought to have a say in what happens to the factory on which their livelihoods depend.

These are polar views, framed in the strongest terms—in terms of rights, moral "musts." But there are positions short of the poles that, though expressing some of the same underlying concerns, do not state the issues as inescapable moral imperatives. Defenders of laissez-faire may think not that firms have a natural or God-given *right* to make shutdown decisions uni- laterally, only that our kind of economic system is preferable (for which they may have a variety of reasons), and for it to work, firms must completely

* A portion of this article appeared in Center for Philosophy and Public Policy's newsletter, *QQ* v. 4, No. 3 (Fall 1984). Permission for publication in its entirety granted by author.

control investment decisions. Similarly, advocates of workers' participation in company decisions may think not that they have a *right* to participate, but simply that the possibly disastrous consequences of plant closings make a moral claim on our concern.

How can we adjudicate between these conflicting points of view? Suppose we go back to Lynd's questions and the view implicit in his essay—one that challenges the status quo, in which workers have no voice in shutdown decisions. What reasons are there for thinking that the status quo is not as it should be, that workers and communities ought to have some say in decisions about whether a plant stays or goes?

At least two basic kinds of arguments support worker participation. One focuses on the idea that, although in our legal system factories belong to stockholders, workers may acquire a kind of moral property right, a moral claim to some control over their workplaces. The other emphasizes that, through their relationships over time with workers, firms have incurred obligations to them that preclude unilateral shutdown decisions.

The first view rests on the labor theory of property, originally developed by John Locke.[3] The germ of the theory is that property rights are acquired by "mixing one's labor" with, and thereby adding value to, external objects. To make this view workable requires many qualifications, but its essential core is persuasive: Having worked on an object and transformed it into a socially valuable commodity gives one *some* claim to the fruits of one's labor. How much of a claim, and how it compares to that of the entrepreneur who has mixed a different kind of labor and has taken risks the worker has not, are questions a complete theory of property must address.

The second argument for workers' rights to a say in shutdown decisions expresses the idea that when a company has dug deep over generations into people's lives, perhaps affecting a whole community, it incurs obligations to those people and that community. Although the company may have entered freely, it is no longer at liberty simply to withdraw from relationships that have developed over years or even generations.

These are mere sketches of arguments, and I shall not flesh them out here. For some, no elaborate argument is necessary; for others, none will be convincing. Here I shall assume that, as matters of abstract moral right, these views seem persuasive; it seems plausible at least in the abstract that workers have some moral claim to the factories in which they labor and that companies have incurred obligations to these workers and communities that they are not free simply to renounce.

The sticking point is in the phrase *in the abstract*. I said earlier that the thrust of Lynd's questions is moral, not practical. But this is too simple; moral questions are not altogether separable from practical ones. Indeed, much of the controversy about employee versus management claims in plant shutdowns rests precisely on disagreement about what would in fact happen if owners were not free to make such decisions unilaterally. To decide, then, whether the abstract moral arguments for worker participation are plausible when concrete, we need to know more about the consequences of such legal and institutional changes.

What obstacles, then, do abstract moral right and obligation encounter? What arguments can be made against the rights of workers or the duties of owners?

One important argument is that plants like those in the Youngstown area are no longer sufficiently profitable; therefore, it is both natural and right (or at least not wrong) to abandon them for more profitable ventures.

Not sufficiently profitable; that looks like an easy cover for greed. What profits are sufficient? What the traffic will bear?

But this cynical response may be misguided—or at least premature. The idea that a company can be profitable, yet not sufficiently profitable, can be explained in terms other than sheer avarice; it can be explained by the economics of investment. Unless a plant's rate of return equals the standard rate—that is, unless it is competitive with other ventures in which investment might be made—it will not endure beyond the short run.

This is not to deny that corporations may seek profits above the standard rate of return. It may be their natural tendency to seek the highest profits possible; to suppose so is not to ascribe to them base motives, only the desire for gain often found among human beings. But many economists argue that the tendency to seek higher profits, though it may be motivated only by self-interest, benefits others too. They say that the profit motive leads to the creation of more wealth, and in the long run, not only firms and corporations, but also workers and the general population benefit. The wealth spreads or trickles down. If companies are prevented from closing and seeking higher profits elsewhere, it is argued, in the long run the total pie will shrink, and everyone, workers included, will suffer.

Two claims are implicit here. First, permitting companies to move when they deem fit is *efficient,* that is, will produce more wealth overall.[4] Second, this greater overall wealth will be *distributed* in a way that benefits workers. Each of these claims needs to be considered more carefully.

Does Management's Freedom to Move Increase Efficiency?

The idea that if owners, rather than workers, are legally entitled to make shutdown decisions, the economy will be more efficient, is refuted by a well-known theorem of economics. According to this theorem, if the two parties (in this case, owners and workers) are free to bargain with each other, and each is guided only by economic motives, the most efficient outcome will be reached no matter who possesses the legal entitlement.[5] For whichever side stands to benefit most will simply buy out the other side's entitlement if it doesn't possess the entitlement itself.

Take a simple example. Suppose a company will realize savings in labor costs of $4 million a year if it moves a plant from Ohio to South Carolina. Suppose also that the Ohio workers will lose $3 million, the difference between their present wages and their income, from other jobs or from unemployment compensation if the plant moves. In this case, it is efficient for the factory to move, for efficiency is a matter of realizing the greatest net benefit overall. Now whoever is legally entitled to make the shutdown decision, the plant will move. Suppose the owners have the entitlement. It won't be in the workers' interests to pay more than $3 million to get the plant to stay, and it won't be in the owners' interests to accept less than $4 million. No agreement will be reached, and the plant will move. Now suppose the workers possess the entitlement. Then it will be in the owners' interests to pay up to $4 million to the workers to be allowed to move, and it will be in the workers' interests to accept something above $3 million to allow the plant to move. Owners and workers will reach an agreement under which the plant moves—the efficient outcome.

Now imagine instead that the owners will realize savings of $4 million if the plant relocates, but the workers will lose $5 million. Then it is efficient for the plant to stay. Suppose the workers possess the entitlement. It won't be in the owners' interests to pay more than $4 million to be permitted to move, and it won't be in the workers' interest to accept less than $5 million. No agreement will be reached, and the plant will stay. What if the owners possess the entitlement? Then it will be in the workers' interests to pay up to $5 million to prevent the plant from going, and it will be in the owners' interests to accept something above $4 million. Owners and workers will come to an agreement under which the plant stays—again, the efficient outcome.

There is, then, no merit to the claim that allowing workers to have some control over shutdown decisions is bad for the economy because it is inefficient. The difference between the system in which owners are entitled to make these decisions and the system in which workers are is not a difference in the *total* amount of wealth produced, but in *who* gets the better economic deal. So, for example, in the first case, where owners will save $4 million if the plant moves, but workers will lose $3 million, if the owners have the entitlement, they will move straightaway, saving $4 million while the workers lose $3 million; whereas if the workers have the entitlement, they will be able to bargain for a better deal. The question is not how much wealth, but in whose hands?

Does Management's Freedom to Move Benefit Workers?

Now if it is a question of improving the lot of already well-off owners as against much less well-off workers, many people will see no dilemma. And yet it will be argued that the issue is not so simple. For it is often said that if the company realizes higher profits, it will invest them in ways that are good for the economy, and so in the long run for all Americans. But if it pays out what would have been those profits in the form of higher wages, the income will not be saved and invested. Since workers do not have enough income to save, they will spend it on consumer goods, groceries and the like, which do the economy no good.

This argument depends on the assumption that income spent on consumer goods is not invested. True, it is not invested by the consumer. But money spent on groceries increases the profits of the supermarket, which in turn may invest those profits. Some would argue that this sort of investment does not benefit the economy in the way investment by steel companies (and similar producers) does. But this is a disputed question among economists, and it ought not to be assumed without argument, therefore, that money spent on consumer goods has no effect on savings and investment.

There is a more important argument for the view that corporate autonomy benefits workers. When factories close down in the old industrial centers of the North and Northeast, they move to places that have traditionally been poorer: to the South, now fashionably called "the Sunbelt," or to Third World countries whose standard of living is much below that of the average American. The new factories create jobs for workers in these places and may greatly improve their standard of living. This fact seems to confront us with a discomforting dilemma. We are now forced to weigh not the welfare of workers against that of owners, but rather the welfare of Youngstown workers against that of workers in South Carolina or Korea. And framed in these terms, it may seem there are good grounds for preferring South Carolinians or Koreans. For these people, especially those in the Third World, are generally much poorer than workers in Ohio, even laid-off workers. Shouldn't we give more weight to the welfare of the worse off than the better off?

So the concern with Youngstown workers might appear to rest on a partial view; when we extend our vision beyond one town or one region, a different picture seems to emerge.

Or does it? Will workers worldwide be better off on balance if plants are permitted to move when they choose, or not? We are interested in what will happen *in the long run,* and predicting what will happen far in the future is extremely difficult. The controversy is at this point in danger of degenerating to mere assertion and counterassertion, for we do not have the tools to settle this dispute empirically.

The argument must proceed at a different level. We can begin by asking why it is that Ohio workers are better off now than their counterparts in the American south or in the Third World. There seem to be several reasons. When the Northeast became industrialized in the nineteenth century, practical necessity dictated the location of factories; they were built close to the source of raw materials, or convenient to waterways or railroads. Labor was relatively scarce, so workers were in an advantageous bargaining position compared to most modern factory workers. But the position of these earlier American workers was improved immeasurably by the facts of their coexistence under the same management, their similar interests, and the forces making it necessary for factories to be where they were. It became clear that collectively they could exert a power they didn't possess as individuals. They formed unions and were able to extract concessions from the companies. Owners and managers were no longer able to say, "take what we offer or leave it." They were forced to operate partly on workers' terms.

So the situation remained as long as there was no viable alternative to the factories staying where they were; companies could not set the terms of work unilaterally. But as technology developed the situation changed; the reasons keeping factories in the Northeast (such as convenience to waterways) were less weighty, and the attractions of moving (primarily, cheap, unorganized labor elsewhere) became increasingly compelling. There was at this point only one way the company could avoid having to come to a mutually satisfactory agreement with its employees, and that was to move, or threaten to, if workers did not accept management's terms.

Now it is obvious what the effects of shutdowns or relocations are on workers in threatened factories. But we are at the moment considering their effects on workers elsewhere; we are considering the claim that such workers, in greater need, may benefit by such actions. But the two issues are not separate. When Ohio workers have achieved a certain degree of power, companies undermine that power in the only way now available to them: by threatening not to "play the game" anymore. But this has consequences far beyond Ohio. It means undermining the hard-won strides labor has made over the years, and that affects not only the communities in which shutdowns occur, but workers elsewhere as well. For there will always be unorganized workers to act as a magnet for companies when their own employees get into a position to make unwelcomed demands.

Thus, even though in the short-run workers in South Carolina or Korea might benefit from Ohio plant closings—and might benefit from them more, economically, than Ohio workers are harmed—over time, corporate autonomy in shutdown decisions is a setback for labor, not an advance. This is even more obvious if we think not only in the narrowest economic terms, not simply in terms of dollars, but also in terms of self-respect and the ability to determine important aspects of one's own life. What workers benefiting from plant closings would gain in the short-run are jobs and money—nothing to sneeze at, to be sure. But what they would not gain and what Ohio workers and ultimately all workers would lose is the power to affect in any way a crucial aspect of their lives, their work and livelihood. For they would be forever at the mercy of employers who can say: "take it or leave it."[6]

Freedom to Move and Fair Play

"Take it or leave it" is not only *harmful* to workers, but also *unfair* to them.

Consider an analogy. A child with a Monopoly game offers to play with other children. They play contentedly for a while, but eventually some of the other children are putting hotels on Pennsylvania Avenue and Boardwalk, and the game's owner is broke. He's a bad sport, declares the game at an end ("It's my game"), takes his game and goes home.

Obviously, the child is acting unfairly. He was free to play or not play. But having agreed to play, he is not free to quit simply because the terms no longer suit him. (It would be different if he began to feel sick or had to finish his homework.) Similarly, we may conclude that the company is acting unfairly if it says, "You play our way or not at all." But the analogy may appear to have its limits. For although in quitting, the child is clearly being unfair, most people would probably say that it would be wrong to force him to continue to play. Would it be similarly wrong to force the company to stay? If so, our conclusion may seem innocuous: the company is acting unfairly, but nothing can be done about it. (After all, "life is unfair.")

The question is this: What is the difference between those situations in which we think, "He's being unfair, but it would be wrong to force him not to," and those in which we conclude, "He's being unfair and should be made to act otherwise"? There are, I think, two conditions relevant to answering this question. One has to do with the costs, of various sorts— economic, moral, political—of forcing people to be fair. It may be literally too expensive to force them, or it may involve trampling on other values, like privacy or personal freedom. The other condition concerns how much is at stake for the participating players.

Obviously, it would be ludicrous to consider bringing the coercive power of the state down upon our poor, unsporting child. It would be ludicrous because not enough is at stake for anyone and because the implications of such a policy in terms of state interference in people's private lives would be monstrous.

What about prohibiting companies from making unilateral decisions to abandon factories? We have argued above that there are no clear economic costs of doing so in terms of efficiency and the like. Nor would it seem to be especially expensive or unwieldy to set into motion the necessary enforcement apparatus. Already existing government agencies, as well as the negotiation structures of management and labor unions, can perform the relevant tasks. Without a compelling argument for owners' exclusive property rights to factories, there do not seem to be any other obvious costs of enforcement. As for the other condition, it seems clear that the stakes for participating players are very high. Obviously some people (company stockholders, perhaps) may be made worse off by the decision, but workers in the affected plants will be spared grave economic and personal hardships. And, in the long run, we have argued, so will workers in general.

There is a further similarity between the Monopoly case and plant closings. Although it would be absurd to force children legally to fulfill agreements to play Monopoly, it is at least plausible that parents would be justified in forcing them. The difference between the Monopoly case and the plant closings case, then, seems to be not that it is wrong to force in one case and not the other, but rather that the morally appropriate agents of force are different.

These considerations bring us back to our earlier discussion. We began by mentioning two (not unrelated) kinds of arguments for the conclusion that workers ought to have a say in decisions about plant shutdowns and relocations. The first, rooted in the labor theory of property, supports the view that not only owners but workers may come to have property rights in their workplaces. The other argues that in view of relationships developed over years and even generations, companies come to have certain obligations to workers that are incompatible with abrupt withdrawal. We abandoned these matters of "abstract moral right and obligation," in the belief that the controversy about factory closings hangs mostly in more pragmatic considerations. Having, we hope, dispelled some of these concerns, we have returned, in these last arguments about fairness, to the more purely moral substance of the earlier arguments. For the idea that it is unfair for companies to "play the game" only as long as it suits them and that it is legitimate to force them to do otherwise, really amounts to the view that, having agreed to play the game at all, companies have incurred obligations they are not at liberty to abandon, and workers have as a result of their investments of labor acquired rights. The Monopoly example and our inquiry into the conditions under which it is legitimate to "coerce fairness" are steps toward fleshing out further the arguments for owners' obligations and workers' rights.

The connection between fairness and the earlier arguments can now be made more explicit. In the Monopoly case as in the plant closings case, the response of "It's mine" (my game, my factory) is no longer an argument-stopper. We can interpret this in either of two ways: (1) It may be yours, but that doesn't mean you can do with it whatever you please; or (2) it may have been all yours once, but other people have now acquired rights to it, so it is no longer just yours to do with as you please. The first interpretation grants the original owner an exclusive property right, but asserts that it has been limited or qualified by his own actions;[7] the second interpretation denies the original owner an exclusive property right. The difference between these may be more semantic than substantive, but which interpretation we choose may determine whether we frame the argument in terms of workers' rights or just companies' obligations.

The practical conclusion is the same in either case: Companies should not be permitted to make decisions about plant closings and relocations unilaterally. This conclusion is supported by a variety of moral considerations having to do with fairness, self-respect, autonomy, and the interests of workers in general over the long run. It is, in addition, a conclusion that seems to survive the harsh scrutiny of economics.

Robotry, Unemployment, and Work-Sharing

Dan Lyons _____

Rumors sweep through the press periodically that robots and computers are replacing human workers in industry. Some say we are going through a superrapid "Second Industrial Revolution." In the first Industrial Revolution, machines largely replaced human muscles, in the second, machines might replace the human mind, in many useful functions.

Of 20 million U.S. factory workers, it's said that one-third to one-half of all hands-on factory jobs in the United States could be done now, in theory, by robots.[8] By 1990 the leasing price for some robots might be down to $1 per hour.[9] Twenty million workers here might need retraining in the next decade because their skills will be obsolete.[10] One observer predicts that 20 million out of 70 million workers here and in Europe will be replaced in the next twenty-five years.[11] All 8 million U.S. manufacturing operators, plus other workers, could be replaced by the year 2025. Not only will fewer people be hired, people will be fired.[12]

Unhelpful Pollyanna Statements

"Robots will do the nasty, boring jobs, freeing humans for creative work." But a nasty, boring job is better than no job at all; besides, there won't be many creative jobs available. For example, only 350,000 new American jobs are expected among computer programmers and systems analysts—whereas 1.3 million new jobs are predicted in three unskilled service roles: janitor, hospital orderly, and nurse's aide.[13] Nor is there any social force now visible in America to stop robots from taking over interesting jobs such as drafting.

Let's look at another statement: "Any increase in technical productivity makes more jobs than it destroys by lowering the price of goods so aggregate demand goes up. The same number of workers, or more, will end up making far more goods cheaper for mankind." This much is surely true: If America doesn't use robots in its industries, then its goods will likely be undersold by the robotic industries abroad; thus, even more of our jobs could be lost by not robotizing.

Dramatic increases in output per worker must tend at first to decrease the jobs available to humans—unless there is a tremendous worldwide increase in total goods consumed, and that would presuppose a great increase in people's ability to buy goods. People in developing countries need more goods, but often can't pay for them. Nor is there any visible tendency to increase the buying power of the average world citizen.[14]

It's said that the workers will have to inspect the work of the robots, but robots can already inspect finished parts better than the average human.[15] Computers can now diagnose some problems in their own internal workings just as they can successfully diagnose some human ailments. Robots can be programmed to notice when their working tools wear out and call for replacements from other parts of the automated system; the robot can remove the bad part and screw in the replacement. There are already factories using robots to make robots; the ideal will be to build into robots as many cheap, discardable modules as possible in order to minimize the cost of repairs.

One observer predicts that by the year 2010, up to 20 million of the 70 million blue-collar workers in America and Western Europe will be displaced by machines;[16] another predicts that robots might remove three jobs for every one they create.[17] So we can't just assume automatically that these dramatic new changes will undo any damage they do to the human social fabric. Optimists must explain exactly how the robotic revolution will create more jobs than it will destroy in the long run.

The final statement is: "The main function of robots is not to replace workers! What's at stake is a totally automated factory, with higher-quality production, more flexibility for modifying products, and lower costs for maintaining parts-inventories."[18] As noted before, companies now using or planning to use robots cite cutting labor costs as the main reason for automating.[19] In fact, the other admitted advantages of automated production mean this: Even if a human could do the robot's work as well and as cheaply, the robot would still be preferred, as part of a generally automated system that offers other savings. Where robots and humans compete as equals, the robots will prevail.

The Job-Sharing Remedy

One remedy comes to mind: We could minimize joblessness simply by sharing more evenly the hours of work available. If 100 million U.S. workers somehow worked thirty-five hours instead of forty hours each week, up to ten million new jobs would become available. While this remedy may appear fair, theoretically, serious drawbacks turn up in every specific workshare proposal.

Suppose we mandate a thirty-five- instead of a 40-hour standard workweek by law. Then employers would face a new incentive to hire more workers, instead of working their present workers extra: they'd want to avoid the extra surcharge on overtime pay.[20]

However, only 60 percent of U.S. workers are covered by overtime laws at all![21] Second, now that fringe benefits make up almost 40 percent of the payroll, the company might have to pay full benefits for each part-time worker;[22] this gives the firm reason to fill in with regulars working overtime. Third, many firms are even now breaking the law, offering desperate (or greedy) workers extra hours at regular rates, on the QT. A shorter standard workweek might simply encourage such cheating.

We should probably cut down on employers' fixed costs per worker for fringe benefits to lessen the firm's tendency to substitute overtime for new hiring; perhaps the government should provide health insurance in such a situation. Tax breaks could be given to firms in proportion to the total number of workers on their payroll.

Partial Unemployment Pay

A serious proposal to promote job-sharing has already been tested in many places. The "partial unemployment-pay" scheme works as follows: If a firm has to cut its labor costs by 10 percent, it cuts each worker's hours a little in order to prevent having to fire one worker in ten. The government partially compensates each worker for income lost by the shorter hours. (After all, if a worker gives up some work hours, why shouldn't he get a partial subsidy? The government saves an equivalent amount on the subsidy for the person who would otherwise be fired.) Two people get partial subsidies and have the self-respect of being employed, instead of one worker being totally subsidized and humiliated.

Schemes like this have proved feasible in various European countries, and also in California, though the jobs thus created have not been enough to solve unemployment problems.[23]

Seniority Rights

It might be thought unfair to ask long-time workers to share the burden of underemployment in order to avoid laying off new workers. But it's not clear why workers should automatically have additional rights to job security just because they have additional years of employment with one company. (If a worker's contract specifies such entitlement, then of course he has a legal right to such security, but it's not at all obvious that he has a prior moral right to have such a clause included.)

Perhaps some job preference should be shown to *older* workers; it is more difficult to overcome hardships later in life than when one is young. However, that's a different issue. Seniority might just as easily favor a younger, single worker over an older worker who must provide for a family.

But the issue here is not whether long-time workers should be fired; the issue is whether they should accept a cut in yearly hours, partially compensated by insurance payments, to save new workers from being laid off. It's understandable that senior workers would hesitate to tell their families that they have volunteered for a (slight) cut in income to help other workers. But if the company announces a policy such as this, it's hard to see how the long-time workers have any valid complaint. A slight financial hardship for them (balanced by extra leisure hours!) means job security for newer workers.

A basic difficulty with all job-sharing schemes is "skill-compatibility": We can't just decide that a brain surgeon should share his job with a carpenter. But some observers feel that there will shortly be a surplus of trained or trainable workers in many types of jobs that will survive the robotic revolution;[24] job-sharing should pose no problems especially with unskilled service jobs. (And of course the partial unemployment pay schemes involve substitution of fully qualified peers.)

On the other hand, a basic advantage of job-sharing overtime is in terms of productivity: Common-sense tells us that workers will work harder if they put in fewer hours per week.

One can find technical difficulties with every specific proposal designed to encourage work-sharing. But we should not abandon the general idea. It is obviously a good partial remedy for universal job shortages; we must simply work to minimize its disadvantages.

Is Work-Sharing Fair To Workers?

Donald Levy _____

Massive unemployment is expected to result from the widespread introduction of robots into the workplace. Indeed, some observers project a consequent loss of four million jobs in manufacturing alone by the end of the eighties.[25]

Three types of remedies have been proposed for such unemployment: (1) worker reeducation programs, such as the training of production workers in computer and allied technology; (2) creation of publicly funded, public interest jobs to repair our neglected bridges, roads, waste disposal services, harbours, and so forth; and (3) work-sharing as an alternative to dismissal. I shall confine myself here to identifying a serious, and in my opinion decisive, moral defect of the work-share solution.

Proposals for work-sharing include taxing overtime pay, legislating a reduced workweek, having the state pay unemployment compensation to workers on partial shifts (instituted in California, Oregon, and Arizona). Such schemes have the common intended effect of keeping the number of workers up by reducing the individual worker's wages. Unlike the first two remedies (worker reeducation and creation of new public interest jobs), schemes for work-sharing appear to impose the whole burden of the new technology upon the workers, that is, upon those least responsible for its introduction, least likely to reap its financial rewards, and least able to bear it.

The moral inappropriateness of work-sharing as a remedy for unemployment resulting from robotics can be seen from the following analogy: Suppose a new technology had a foreseeable side effect of polluting the air to a measurable and seriously harmful degree. Would it be fair to require the cost of cleaning the air to be paid by the government alone, or to leave the air uncleaned, allowing the population at large to suffer its ill effects? Of course we would regard the polluters, those *responsible* for introducing the new technology, as having a prima facie obligation to bear all or more of the cost. In the past, ignorance of the effects of pollution and lack of any means to control it may have excused much harm done by its producers. However, by contrast, the harmful effect of robotics—massive unemployment—is, to some extent, fore-seeable, and plausible alternative proposals for handling it are known. Even if unemployment does not result from robotics, as some economists predict,[26] declining income for large numbers of workers forced to move from man-ufacturing to service jobs is expected.[27] The unfairness in that case would obviously be very similar.

The work-sharing remedy means that employers who are responsible for causing robotry-induced unemployment would be exempt from paying its cost. The entire burden would be borne by their workers. I conclude that the work-share remedy is, for this reason, extremely unfair.

Notes

1.   Staughton Lynd, *The Fight Against Shutdowns: Youngstown's Steel Mill Closings* (San Pedro, Calif.: Singlejack Books, 1983), 3.

2.   See Michael Walzer, *Radical Principles: Reflections of an Unreconstructed Democrat* (New York: Basic Books, 1980), 275.

3.   *Second Treatise of Government,* chap. 5.

4.   It is important to realize that the economist's notion of efficiency concerns the total amount of wealth irrespective of how it is distributed. The situation where A has $100 and B has $1 is more efficient in this sense than the situation where A and B each have $50.

5.   This is Coase's theorem. R.H. Coase, "The Problem of Social Cost," *Journal of Law and Economics* 3 (1960). The theorem assumes also that transaction costs—in this case the costs of bargaining—are zero. Since the structures for collective bargaining are already in place, transaction costs will in fact be close enough to zero in this case to make the theorem practically applicable.

6.   George Steinbrenner, owner of the New York Yankees and chairman of the board of American Ship Building, told shipbuilding union leaders in Lorain, Ohio, that if they did not agree to wage and other concessions, he would close down the shipyard and throw union members out of work. "I don't know about you boys, but *I'll* be eating three meals a day," Steinbrenner said. (*Washington Post,* 5 February 1984, Fl.) What is disturbing is that the same outcome can be achieved without the assumption of maliciousness; it results naturally from structural features of the situation.

7. Property rights are, of course, always limited and qualified: To say "It's mine" never means "I can do with it anything I please." I am not at liberty to burn down my house.

8. Sara Levitan and Clifford M. Johnson, "The Future of Work: Does it Belong to Us or the Robots?" *Monthly Labor Review,* U.S. Labor Department, Bureau of Labor Statistics (September 1982), 11.

9. William R. Tanner, *Industrial Robots,* Dearborn, Michigan, Robotics International of the Society of Manufacturing Engineers, 1981.

10. P. DuPont, "Retooling the Workforce," *Vital Speeches* 49 (15 February 1983):269.

11. L.D. Harmon, quoted in *USA Today,* 25 November 1983. *Business Week* was quoted as predicting that 25 million manufacturing jobs will be 'robotized' by 2010 ('Hearings', 58).

12. Robert U. Ayres and Steven M. Miller, "Robotics and the Conservation of Human Resources," *Technology in Society* 4 (1982):187.

13. Tanner, *Industrial Robots,* 43.

14. Henry Levin and Russell Rumberger, "The Low-Skill Future of High Tech," *Technology Review* (August–September 1983).

15. *The New York Times,* 28 March 1983, 21.

16. L.D. Harmon, quoted in *USA Today,* 25 November 1983.

17. Henry Levin and Russell Rumberger, "The Low-Skill Future of High Tech," 21.

18. Ayres and Miller, "Industrial Robots on the Line," 40. (Also, 'Hearings', 29.)

19. Robert U. Ayres and Steven M. Miller, "Industrial Robots on the Line," 41–42.

20. If one-fifth of all present overtime jobs were converted into new jobs, the job total would rise by 1.7 percent; R. Ehrenberg and P. Schumann, *Longer Hours or More Jobs,* (Ithaca, N.Y.: The New York State School of Industrial Relations, 1982), 1.

21. Ibid., 63.

22.   Ibid., 6.

23.   However, Fred Best estimates that a mature "Partial-Unemployment Payment" program, implemented nationally, might reduce unemployment by perhaps 16 percent during a recession, (in *Work-Sharing: Issues, Policy Options and Prospects,* Kalamazoo, Michigan, The Upjohn Institute for Employment Research 1981, 192). For a later report on the California experiment, see J.D. Vasche, "Unemployment Benefits for Work-Sharing," *Business.*

24.   Fred Best, *Work-Sharing,* 27.

25.   G. G. Schwartz and W. Neikirk, *The Work Revolution* (New York: Rawson Associates, 1983), 125.

26.   No rise in unemployment is foreseen in W. W. Leontief and F. Duchin, *The Future Impact of Automation on Workers* (New York: Oxford University Press, 1986).

27.   This effect is discussed in R. M. Cyert, "The Plight of Manufacturing: What Can Be Done?" *Issues in Science and Technology,* vol. 1, no. 4 (Summer 1985), 87–100.

PART 6

THE RIGHTS OF HEALTH CARE WORKERS

Notes From A Hospital Strike*

Patricia Sexton _____

> Remember the dignity of your womanhood.
> Do not appeal, do not beg, do not grovel.
> Take courage, join hands, stand beside us,
> fight with us.
>
> Emmeline Pankhurst, feminist, 1888

When a strike was called at Penn hospital over the terms of the first contract, only RNs, clericals, doctors and administrators continued to work. Few of the strikers had ever engaged in any kind of direct action before, so it was a new and daring experiment for them. Most had the backing, not only of the union but of their husbands, fathers and sons who, in this Pennsylvania mining-steel community, gave solid support to the strike.

Despite such backing, most women admitted to being frightened by this unprecedented public challenge to authority, but some mastered their fear, came forward, and led the strike. Most of the women strikers had serious grievances of their own, but some walked the picket line out of concern for coworkers. . . .

Comments by Rosemary Trump, Local President

At Penn hospital the union won two units by majority votes. The hospital continued to fight us with their anti-union consultant firm. They made up wild accusations and tried to undo the election results. But we mobilized the community, our own members and labor reps in the area, to put pressure on the hospital.

---

* Reprinted from Patricia C. Sexton, *The New Nightingales* (New York: Enquiry Press, 1982), by permission of the publisher. Copyright © 1982 by Enquiry Press.

Finally we staged a demonstration to force bargaining. The local police and hospital officials over-reacted and the police chief threatened to get dogs and fire hoses to chase us off. We had a very heated exchange, and I said, "Will you guarantee me this in writing? I always wanted to be on national news. I'll make sure that NBC and ABC are here to see this. You with your big badge and big billy club, batting down our women and their babies."

I called the state police because I could see this guy was paid off by the hospital to give us a bad time. Fortunately we got a community relations person from the state police to intervene. So we were able to force them into bargaining. They created the union for us, the employer did.

Very good leadership came forward. The employer finally made an offer but our members considered it inadequate. So we had our first strike and we got our first contract. We made big gains in that contract and we've worked hard with the stewards to iron out the problems you have in the first year of marriage.

We struck for 12 days and we picketed around the clock. The hospital admitted no additional patients during the strike, only emergency cases, and they released patients as they got better. They had the top floor completely closed and part of the third floor. So a big building was sitting there without money coming in. It puts pressure on the administration to get back to the table and negotiate.

Comments By Strikers

During the strike the hospital told us they were admitting all new patients, just to make us feel guilty about not being there to take care of them. It was an out-and-out lie. They also said the picketers were responsible for deaths in the hospital during the strike. They even got families to blame the picketers for their relatives passing away. Of course, the patients were all being taken care of by the RNs, the doctors, and the others. For once, the nurses weren't just parked at their desks. . . .

All of the aides were for the union. We had nothing. Supervisors could fire you for anything. No questions asked, no recourse. The LPNs were really being degraded. "You're just an LPN, so you can't do this and that." The hospital had hired a lot of new graduate LPNs, and that helped get the union in. They had never been treated like that, anywhere, and they were very upset. They were doing a good job and being told they were dummies. When somebody new came on the floor, the head nurses would show their authority and tell them off in front of everybody. It's no fun to be degraded in public.

I was working in the kitchen when I joined the union. Then I went to housekeeping, but I couldn't forget about my friends in the kitchen who had it so bad. I tried to sign up people in housekeeping. Half of them wouldn't talk to me because they were so set against the union. That's funny; they were against it until the contract was signed. Then they loved what they got out of the strike. A few are still bitter. Most of them were just scared to death. At first they would run and hide when they saw us coming. A lot of them still say, "Oh, I don't want to talk to you. I'll get fired." When we started to picket, more and more of the housekeeping ladies came out. One thing was nice. None of our people crossed the picket line. We had only one that stayed in the hospital. For 12 days she didn't come out. . . .

A few were told by their husbands and sons, "The union's in, and you're better off with it." The women would come out to the line and say, "My husband told me to come out, so I'm going to help you." It was really nice. I was tickled that they stood up and came with us. And they were tickled when they saw that the union got them their bonus, better pay and a pension.

They're older women in housekeeping, and they're scared about their jobs. A lot of them lost their husbands, or their husbands divorced them, so they feel insecure. It's the only job they ever had, and they are so thankful the hospital gave it to them. That's why they didn't want to fight for a union. . . .

The hospital pushed us into a union. It was a matter of fairness. We were discriminated against, harassed and pressured. We wanted to be able to talk. It was like being in jail. We weren't allowed to discuss certain matters with certain people. The wage scale was locked in a drawer. We had to get permission to see it. They had no seniority list. They just went by who they liked. If they liked you better than me, you got the job. They had no open bidding on jobs. Strictly a buddy system. We wanted the security of knowing they couldn't fire us because they didn't like us. Before the contract, only three Blacks worked in the hospital. They were always given the nasty jobs. They used to complain, "Niggers down South don't work this hard." You can't run a floor on bigotry. Everything has to be divided equally, which is what we wanted. . . .

My father got me involved with the union. He used to work in the mines, but he got sick and spent a lot of time at the hospital as a patient. He said, "What you need is a union. You people are worked to death." So when local 585 came in, I decided to work along with them. I helped organize. I talked to people. I went to union meetings. I stuck my neck out. I sat in on negotiations. You can't believe how bad your employer is until you sit in there and listen to what people say.

During the strike, the "volunteers" would almost run us down trying to cross our line. They were the worst. Some crawled up over the hill and snuck in. It was ridiculous. One truck went in and out of the hospital just to agitate us. If we said anything to them, they called the police. People in the community volunteered for strike breaking. The ministers even went in to do the cooking. A few doctors were behind us and would tell us to keep up the good work. They even said they'd transfer some patients to other hospitals.

I don't think there should be strikes. But if that's what it takes, I'm all for them. . . .

Myself, I wasn't scared for my job during the strike. If you don't help yourself, who's going to help you? You have to take a step forward somehow. People respect you much more when you stand up for yourself. They'll stand back and say, "Oh, well, maybe we can't do this to her. She'll fight back, She won't lay down."

Job security was a huge problem before we got our contract. People were afraid of losing their jobs. When we started to organize, supervisors would say, "Don't talk to that union organizer or you'll lose your job." That's why we lost the first two union votes.

The union guaranteed us that if we showed the others not to be afraid to vote union, we'd never get fired. So I picketed, got my picture taken like everybody else, and never got fired or punished. I didn't have a family to support, so I didnt' need to worry. . . .

My husband's been a union man since he started at the steel mill. He says, "A union's as strong as its members. If the members aren't strong, you might as well throw the union out the door." He wouldn't go to work without a union. I was out on the picket line, and got my picture taken. I was worried about that picture. My husband said, "Don't worry. I've had my picture taken on picket lines and I'm still working after 32 years." . . .

The union organizer was a terrific talker. He could tell us what we wanted and needed, but he didn't stand on a pedestal and say, "You've got to do this or that." A lot of people get turned off if union officials come on too strong.

You have to talk to people, not above them or down to them. Then you can grow. You have to have women organizers too. Definitely. It isn't a man's world, it's a people's world. We had two organizers, a man and a woman, so we got both points of view. . . .

You get a lot out of it. You beat them. It's a terrific feeling to win and know there's nothing else they can do.

I loved being on the strike committee and negotiating the contract. Everyone should sit in on negotiations. You understand the contract much better when you help write it. I kept thinking, "Oh, I'm stupid and I don't know how to answer what the hospital says." But you learn more than you think you can. When you give them a good answer, you say, "Did that come out of me?" You surprise yourself. You do it and you wonder how.

The twelve of us on the negotiating team all came from different departments, so you learn a lot about other departments in negotiations. We sat across from management. I got so mad at them sometimes I could have wrung their necks. It wasn't like we were asking a lot. Instead of saying, "We'll try to work it out," they'd say, "No way. No way."

You meet people during a strike that you've never seen in the hospital, and you get to be friends. I enjoyed it even though it took me away from home an awful lot. We held meetings sometimes twice a week. Sessions might last until two in the morning. And then we had to drag outselves to work the next day.

I became a steward after the strike, and I've learned how to handle grievances. Now I can talk to people that have problems and answer their questions. I couldn't have done that before. If you're a steward, the minute you sit down in the cafeteria everybody converges on you. It's a chance to air their complaints. Stewards should have an office and certain hours to talk to people. I like being a steward because I want people to get a fair shake, but it does take a lot of time. Stewards should really be paid. I could be doing my chores or taking care of my child in my time off.

At least the hospital listens to us a little now. Before the union, we wanted a suggestion box. No names, no nothing, just suggestions. I never knew they had one until last week. They had put it in a year ago. It was hidden behind the cashier's office. They didn't tell anybody it was there. They do things like that.

Before the union came in, whenever you got reprimanded or written up, it went into your personnel record. You couldn't check that record to see what it said. Now you can, and you have grievance procedures to protect you.

The strike got us a lot of what we wanted. Nobody could have gotten more than we did in a first contract—a dental plan, paid pension, a bonus, a wage increase. We got every third weekend off. We asked for every *other* weekend, but we knew we wouldn't get it. We got protection against being fired or disciplined without cause. I'm not satisfied with everything, but it's a good stepping stone. Each time we negotiate, the contract will get better. Some day there'll be a big management turnover, and the people with a big mental block about unions will go. Then we'll work together. The union's everywhere. They have to accept it.

The Right of Health Care Workers to Strike*

James Muyskens _____

The 1974 Amendments to the National Labor Relations Act (NLRA) opened a new era in health care workers' legal rights. The Amendments extended rights to health care workers that had long been held by others in the private sector, including the right to organize in trade unions and a qualified right to strike. The exclusion of health care workers from coverage by the NLRA prior to 1974 reflected the view that the methods of collective bargaining were incompatible with the moral demands of the health care worker-patient relationship. The no-strike stance taken by both the American Medical Association and the American Nursing Association in this earlier period testifies to the acceptance of the view within as well as without the professions. However, as early as 1958 when New York City interns organized over wage issues and during the 1960s when many new associations were formed, the view that bargaining strategies borrowed from industrial workers should not be used by health care workers was under challenge.

With the weakening of the legal and professional constraints against health professionals' strikes, concerns about the moral force of the duty to obey the law or the duty to honor a no-strike pledge are no longer central to the debate. Thus, in this essay, we turn to other moral considerations that, on the one hand, may place restrictions on the right of health professionals to strike and, on the other, may provide the basis in certain situations for a duty to strike. We begin, however, with a practical constraint.

As a pressure tactic, a strike is less likely to be effective if it challenges public opinion than if it can tap into it. Public sympathy for one's goals

* Revised from James Muyskens, "Nurse's Collective Responsibility and the Strike Weapon," *Journal of Medicine and Philosophy*, vol. 7, no. 1 (1982), 102–112, by permission of the publisher. Copyright © 1982 by D. Reidel Publishing Company, Dordrecht, Holland, and Boston U.S.A.

must be carefully nurtured. Having it is often the key to victory, lacking it, the ground for defeat. Public opinion sets the broad parameters for strike activity.

Whatever their legality, health care workers' strikes called *exclusively* for economic gain find little public support. There is wide-spread agreement that economic demands of striking health professionals must be coupled with demands for better patient care or at least with persuasive arguments that better pay and working conditions will lead to better care. Since highly paid professionals will find it difficult to make a convincing case that increased pay for them is necessary for better patient care, their ability to win salary concessions by means of a strike is very limited. Strikes over non-economic issues (e.g., increased availability of laboratory services, additional para-medical workers) may be more successful. Poorly paid professionals can more successfully make the case that increased pay for them is necessary for better patient care. Thus they are in a far better position to use the strike as a means for exacting economic concessions. Whereas the housestaff strikes in the late fifties and the sixties were primarily devoted to economic interests, typically health care workers' strikes in the 70s and 80s have been called over issues of quality care for patients and improved working conditions as well as higher wages.

Of course, we can question the sincerity of the demands for better patient care. They may simply be strategies for winning public symparhy. For example, a nurse is quoted in an article in the *New York Times* (March 25, 1980) as saying that when nurses strike "they talk about better patient care, but the bottom line is 'How much are you going to give me?' " Nevertheless, the sincerity of health professionals' pleas for quality care for patients cannot be dismissed so summarily. Some strikes by health care workers have not involved economic issues at all. The seven-day strike by housestaff of seven municipal and two voluntary hospitals in New York City in 1981 was over hospital conditions that, the union claimed, were "so bad that poor patients were dying unnecessarily because of inadequate staffing and equipment" (Gapen, 1981, p. 18). When the strike occurred, a wage settlement had already been negotiated. Strikes such as this cannot be plausibly described as cleverly disguised strategies for economic gain.

Of course, in most strikes, especially by the lower paid health care workers, the demand for better wages will be of great importance. Since bill collectors are as persistent with nurses, x-ray technicians, para-medics, and interns as with professors, plumbers, and police officers, it would hardly be surprising if, for most individual health care workers on strike, wage demands were of greater and more compelling concern than demands for improved patient care. Yet it would be a mistake to conclude from this that the expressions of concern about quality patient care are no more than smoke screens.

Health care professionals have been trained to do a job that includes such activities as diagnosing disease, caring for the terminally ill, treating those with curable disease, comforting the discouraged, and rehabilitating the injured. As is true for anyone with a skill, they get satisfaction from doing it well. One cannot perform well if services are drastically understaffed, if laboratories are not accessible when needed, if support services are lacking, and so on. Thus, even a professional with only self-regarding concerns would have reason to support quality care for patients. But surely many, if not most, health care professionals are committed to doing the best they can for their patients and recognize that they have the collective responsibility of maintaining and improving the quality of health care. They want to meet these obligations. With these considerations in mind the question we are addressing in this essay can be made more precise: When is the strike a morally acceptable weapon for health care workers to use in attempting to maintain and improve the conditions necessary for the proper delivery of health care?

Too often discussions of the moral duties of health professionals give the impression that the list of duties is exhausted when one has gone through those that pertain to the health professional as individual practitioner—e.g., the duty to respect a patient's autonomy, the duty to maintain confidentiality, the duty to safeguard privacy. But health professionals do not work in a vacuum. Because of society's interest in their activity, their practice is regulated by the state. The various health professions are given the legal status of protected monopolies (for example, no one may practice nursing unless licensed by the profession) and the authority to control their own practice. In exchange, society asks the profession to deliver high quality services. To take, one example, by accepting the role of nurse, one—along with one's colleagues— assumes responsibility (1) for maintaining and improving standards of nursing, (2) for maintaining conditions of employment conducive to high quality nursing care, (3) for contributing to the development and implementation of community and national health needs, (4) for making the most efficient and effective use of nursing resources. Analogous duties extend to all health professions.

To exercise these collective duties, it is necessary for health professionals to act in concert—for example, to work through professional associations or unions or to form independent groups within one's employment setting. If these collective efforts meet resistance or prove ineffectual, it may be difficult or impossible to fulfill these duties without taking further action—such as engaging in a strike or work slowdown. However, such action may come into conflict with a variety of other duties of health professionals including their collective duty to provide health care to all in need of it and their duties as practitioners to specific patients currently under their care. This potential for conflicts of duty is what makes the question of the health care worker's right to strike a morally difficult and complex one.

The issue is compelling because many find themselves in situations in which it is next to impossible to fulfill their collective responsibilities. In this respect, the nurse's situation is a paradigm for nearly all health care workers and warrants special attention. Frequently nurses lack power relative to administrators and other health professionals (such as doctors). Often their proper place is seen as being "at the physician's side"—a position of low esteem. Many times nurse supervisors have neither the ability nor the desire to defend members of their staff in disputes with other health professionals or administrators. Far too often nurses are assigned too many patients or ordered to do tasks which lie outside the range of their training or expertise. To say the least, these and many other factors such as the pervasive sexism of our culture, the class background of nurses, and their relatively low pay militate against high quality nursing care.

In contrast to nurses and many other health care workers, interns and residents do not find themselves in a struggle against sexism and classism. Yet frequently they too are caught in the middle and are unable to exercise their responsibilities as health care providers. On the one hand, as hospital employees with little institutional power they must carry out the duties assigned to them and are accountable to the institution. On the other hand, as new physicians committed to the traditional values of the profession they feel primary loyalty to their patients.

If a larger number of patients have been admitted to their service than can be properly cared for, the conflict between the duties to the institution and to one's patients becomes as acute for housestaff as it does for nurses. Circumstances of employment make it impossible to carry out insitutional requirements, duties to individual patients, duties to contribute to quality care more generally, and to maintain integrity as a person and as a professional. No matter how hard the housestaff try, the situation dictates substandard care for most, if not all, their patients. And without intervention the substandard care will continue with future patients. (Housestaff cannot do what private practice physicians can do to insure quality care for their patients, namely, turn away new patients when the patient-load threatens to get too heavy.)

We must ask whether, in situations such as this, the strike is an appropriate weapon to use in the fight for better patient care. There are those who argue that recourse to a strike cannot be defended for, in seeking to fulfill one duty, more compelling duties are violated. We must consider their argument. Yet we shall argue to the contrary. Before doing this, however, we shall examine strikes by health care workers that are more heavily weighted toward economic issues than toward those of patient care *per se*. The strike, after all, is a technique most closely associated with labor organizations exacting *economic concessions* from management.

In strikes by nurses, given their relatively low pay, it is very unusual for a strike not to be premised in large part on demands for better pay and benefits. If such "self-serving" goals are incompatible with exercising professional responsibility, a strike by nurses cannot be condoned. However, far from being incompatible with professional responsibility, the demand for better wages in the lower paid health professions such as nursing (I shall argue) is a requirement of professional responsibility.

An increase in compensation must go hand in hand with upgrading the nursing profession. Just as low pay is correlated with low esteem and low status, low status is linked to the lack of quality nursing care. Low status is a nearly insurmountable impediment to quality care. The economic issue is *not* detachable from the quality of care issue. The quest for higher wages as well as better working conditions is part and parcel of the struggle to fulfill the collective responsibilities of the profession.

However, it may be objected that this line of reasoning blurs an important, traditional distinction between the professional and the laborer or worker. The worker does his or her job for pay, in part because the required tasks lack intrinsic worth. A professional's motives, it has often been argued, should be different. A professional is committed to his or her profession for its own sake and for the sake of those who are its recipients and beneficiaries. Therefore, the argument continues, a professional must refrain from using the strike weapon.

Is this argument persuasive? Its persuasiveness depends on our being able to detach the economic isssues from the quality of care issues. I have suggested, to the contrary, that they are not detachable. Let's consider this issue further. It would appear to be an empirical fact that we are unlikely to get many quality people to enter a profession which has poor working conditions, low esteem, and low pay. Even if we were to succeed in attracting highly qualified and highly motivated people it is unlikely that their enthusiasm and morale could be sustained over the years. High drop-out rates, cynicism, and discouragement—all of which presently obtained in nursing—would have to be expected. If all professionals were motivated solely by love of their art and service to humanity, as proponents of the view under challenge wistfully imagine, indeed, a strike would be incompatible with professional standing. However, since professionals are humans of complex motivation, the image of the professional on which the argument rests is unrealistic.

Especially since other professional groups (e.g., school teachers, college professors, even well-to-do surgeons) now engage in strike action and appear not to have lost their professional standing, attempts to show that striking is incompatible with professionalism are not likely to be effective. If we are to find that striking is incompatible with the professional duties of a nurse or any other primary care giver, the conflict will arise from specific duties rather than general professional obligations.

Before we turn to these specific duties of primary care givers, it will be helpful to look more closely at what one is doing when striking. To strike is to take collective action, including the refusal to work, with the aim of extracting concessions from one's employer. The refusal to work imposes inconvenience and possibly hardship on those in need of one's services. In the case of strikes by employees such as nurses, the detrimental effect of the strike on the public (those in need of nursing care) is often more immediate and more grave than on the employer. The public's inconvenience is the means of which pressure is put on the employer to come to a settlement agreeable to the striking employees. Were the public in no way inconvenienced the strike would likely be ineffectual.

Consider the conflict that appears to arise for the striking nurse or intern, given that the means for achieving admittedly worthy goals is the inconvenience and perhaps even the hardship of patients. As professionals, they are committed to put the interests of their patients first. The nurse in the large, modern medical center has the special task of caring for the patient as a person, of humanizing an otherwise impersonal and sometimes demeaning health care system. Of all health professionals, the nurse may be uniquely situated so as to be the most effective guardian of the patient's interests and rights. Perhaps, then, it is this special role of the nurse that makes it especially wrong for nurses to strike. The intern or resident in today's large medical center may be the focus of the patient's hopes, having no family doctor or perhaps even family to whom to turn for advice and support. For those who have such a fundamental obligation to the patient to be willing to sacrifice that patient's interests in order to achieve higher salaries for oneself and one's colleagues or better care for future patients at least appears to be contradictory and wrong.

If—contrary to usual circumstances (as we have discussed)—strikes by nurses or housestaff were *solely* for higher wages (i.e., no quality of care issues were on the table and the situation happened to be such that the salary issue was unlikely to affect quality of care (say, for example, that the pay scale already was relatively high), we can see that a strike would be incompatible with the health professional-patient relationship. Patients are being used as means for advancing health professionals' interests. Patients' interests (which the health professional has pledged to advance) are being held hostage. What makes matters most difficult is that the especially stringent duty not to treat patients in this way is not counter-balanced by any other compelling moral duty. The moral duty of the care provider to her or his patients stands in conflict with self-interest—which, of course, does not provide one with a moral basis for failing to do one's moral duty.

On the other hand, if the strike is undertaken with an aim of advancing patient care, the case is quite different. We have the makings of a classic conflict of duty situation. The on-going, collective duty to maintain and improve the quality of health care appears to be in conflict with specific duties to one's current patients and the collective duty to provide health care to the public. When all of these duties cannot be fulfilled, one has to decide which duty ought to take priority over the others.

For those who find themselves in work contexts in which wages, standards, and practice are deficient, our earlier discussion has made clear that concerted action to correct these conditions is obligatory. As is well-known, the recent experience of many groups of health care workers within specific health care facilities is that the only effective way they can find to affect the needed changes is strike action. If, as a matter of fact, a strike is the most effective way, or indeed, the only effective way in a particular situation to make the changes necessary for quality care, the collective responsibilities of care providers require them to strike—*unless* there are other more stringent duties (to be considered below) which are binding on them and which would be violated were they to engage in a strike.

An initially appealing yet (as we shall see) unacceptable argument for giving priority to the duty to maintain and improve the quality of care (and, hence, to strike) is the following: The sacrifice of patients' interests resultant from a strike is for the future improvement of health care of patients. That is, the sacrifice required of patients is for the good of patients. It would be short-sighted not to see that this is a reasonable price for patients to pay in order to have better care available in the future. Therefore, as in many other areas of our lives, it is reasonable to sacrifice the short-term interests for the long-term ones. Hence, patients cannot reasonably object to a strike under these conditions.

This argument would have some force if the *same* patients whose present interests and needs are sacrificed were the ones to benefit from the future gains. It is one thing to make X sacrifice now for X's (his/her own) later benefit. It is quite another to make X sacrifice now for Y's (another's) later benefit. But with most strikes, the sacrifice required now is for the benefit of others later. It is the yet unknown patient of the future rather than the present patient whose welfare a strike can advance. The weakness of the argument is that it fails to consider the crucial question of justice (fair treatment of individuals to whom one already had obligations) and simply considers that of over-all consequences.

Taking up the question of justice, David Bleich argues that no argument in favor of striking can be successful. The health professional always has some other more stringent conflicting duty. He asks:

May a person on the way to a class on first-aid instruction ignore the plight of a dying man, on the plea that he must perfect skills which may enable him to rescue a greater number of persons at some future time? . . . No person may plead that an activity designed to advance future societal benefits is justification for ignoring an immediate responsibility. . . . The "here and now" test is a general rule of thumb which may be applied to most situations requiring an ordering of priorities (Veatch and Bleich, 1975, p. 9).

No doubt we can all agree that the person failing to give aid on his way to first-aid instruction stands defenseless. Bleich suggests that his action violates a general principle to the effect that commitment to a course of action designed to increase future good is not a weighty enough reason to exempt one from immediate duties. Were we to apply this principle to the issue at hand in the manner Bleich proposes, we would conclude that a health care provider going on strike even for the highest of motives, namely, to benefit future patients, is in the wrong for she or he is violating immediate responsibilities to patients in need of care by inappropriately appealing to future benefits.

However, such a conclusion need not be drawn even if we accept Bleich's argument. The sort of strike that would be analogous to his case of the man on his way to a first-aid class would be a strike to improve emergency care and refusing to respond to an emergency. In order to improve conditions so that more lives can be saved later, a life is lost here and now. Such a strike could not be morally justified—a fact that is generally recognized and honored by strikers by seeing to it that care in emergency rooms and intensive care units is not withdrawn. Bleich's example is useful in making it clear why withdrawal of services necessary for the maintenance of life cannot be justified.

The central moral question concerning health care workers' strikes, however, is whether the withdrawal of non-emergency and non-lifesaving health care services can be shown to be an acceptable means to the end of better care for future patients. Bleich's general principle cited above (that one may not plead that one's attempt to advance future good exempts one from any immediate responsibility) rules out withdrawal of these services as well *if* doing so entails ignoring any immediate duties to patients.

Is Bleich's principle one we should accept? Whether or not we accept it will depend on how important we take considerations of consequences to be. We can imagine any number of cases in which greater over-all good would be served if we are free to fail to meet an immediate conflicting responsibility.

For example, suppose one is ready to proceed with a research project which, if successful, will probably provide us with the means to save numerous lives in the future. It is determined that the only way the project can go forward is by selecting subjects from whom truly informed consent is not possible (for whatever reason). Most people would agree that at least in general one's immediate duty to his or her research subjects is to obtain genuine informed consent. Most would also agree that this is a very stringent requirement. Yet if the risk to the research subjects were truly minimal and the potential for gain for those benefiting from the research were immense, we may feel that it is appropriate at least to consider whether an appeal to future societal benefits is sufficient to outweigh this immediate and serious responsibility. If we feel such a consideration is appropriate, our position entails a rejection of Bleich's principle. On the other hand, we may feel consideration of consequences is illegitimate here. A Kantian, for example, takes the principle of autonomy as basic and absolute. No consideration of consequences could justify treating any person or persons as means only. Using persons as research subjects without obtaining genuine informed consent would be to treat them merely as means. Bleich's principle is a vigorous affirmation of the Kantian view which extends the veto of consideration of consequences to every conflict of duty situation. The implications of holding a view such as Bleich's are far-reaching. It denies the moral efficacy of numerous policy trade-offs made daily, for example, deciding to put money into medical research and training rather than into the treatment of those already ill.

In deciding for or against Bleich's principle, the crux of the matter is how weighty we consider the duty to work for future societal benefits to be. As we have seen, this depends in part on our basic moral intuitions or beliefs but also on our social or professional roles and concomitant commitments. I have argued that health professionals have a clear and compelling duty to see to it that future care will be better than the sub-standard care available in certain facilities and locales. Contrary to Bleich, I contend that this is too stringent a duty for us to be able to determine *a priori* that all other immediate duties must take priority in conflict of duty situations. What must be determined is whether the duty to work toward better care in the future should, in the particular situation at issue, take precedence over any other duty with which it conflicts.

In place of Bleich's principle, I propose the following procedural rule: All the various duties of health care providers put forth in the ethical codes of their professions and accepted by practice and tradition are initially binding on them. The only time one is excused from fulfilling any of these duties is when doing so conflicts with fulfilling a more stringent duty. For example, if one can continue to care for his or her current patients and simultaneously work toward better care for future patients, both duties are binding. Only when circumstances prevent doing both (doing one conflicts with doing the other) is an individual justified in failing to perform one of these. As we have seen in the research example, how we determine which of several conflicting duties is the most stringent is a complicated issue that must be decided by an independent procedure (more on this later).

An implication of this procedural rule is that a strike can only be defended in conflict of duty situations. Even if conditions permit no more than being available and minimally carrying out duties to patients, a strike will still put current patients at somewhat greater risk and deny care due to them. Where better care is available, patients stand to lose much more, if their health care providers go on strike. Failure to fulfill the duty to provide care to current patients is defensible only if it is countermanded by a more compelling one.

A second implication of the rule is that even when one cannot perform a particular duty because it conflicts with a stronger one, an individual is not excused from all responsibility concerning that duty or the persons to whom the duty is owed. Ways must be found to minimize the adverse effects of our being unable to perform conflicting duties—for example, by directing non-emergency patients during a strike to other accessible facilities that provide service and where workers are not on strike and by continuing to provide intensive care and emergency services.

A strike satisfying these conditions (i.e., those striking find themselves in a conflict of duty situation and they take responsibility for providing for emergency and alternative care) would not be morally objectionable. That is, it would be morally permissible. If other conditions obtain, however, it will be far more difficult to justify a strike. For example, if one were in a facility far from any other facilities and a strike would leave many without the possibility of care, the duty to the public "here and now" may be the stronger duty.

Since strikes involve conflicts of duties and we cannot say *a priori* that one duty, the duty to care for one's current patients, is in every situation the most stringent, in some situations strikes may even be morally mandatory. If they are the only means or clearly the most effective way to change prevailing conditions that are incompatible with high quality care, then they are morally mandatory.

The moderate position developed in this essay—condoning strikes in certain carefully circumscribed situations, claiming they are morally mandatory in others, yet not justified in others—is a position that would be taken were health care providers and the public drrawing up an original contract. Consider the following hypothetical situation, following John Rawls, in which members of the public cannot know when or what health care they may need (they are under a veil of ignorance) (Rawls, 1971, pp. 136–42) and providers also do not know in what situation they will find themselves. Health care professionals as professionals would want to be able to provide the best care under the best conditions. They would seek sufficient power to be able to overcome any impediments to quality care. The public would be concerned to have available to them the best care possible within the limits of allocated resources. Under no conditions would they be willing to barter away a constant availability of emergency or lifesaving care. (They never know when such care may make the difference between life or death for them.) If it were determined that in some situations—due to factors outside the control of either health care professionals or the public—the only way quality care could be obtained would be by use of the strike weapon, health care professionals would insist on the right to use it and the public would concur as long as emergency and lifesaving care could not be withdrawn. The public would agree to suffer the necessary inconveniences and hardship of a strike in the event that it were the only way to achieve high quality health care.

The way to determine in a particular situation whether health care workers' obligations to their patients and the public are weightier than their collective and future-oriented duty to take strike action is to appeal to the original contract. Would the public as party to the agreement be willing to make this required sacrifice in order to benefit from this goal being sought? If so, the duties to one's patients or to the public that conflict with strike activity can justly be set aside in favor of the strike action. If not, they cannot.

Even if a strike can be morally justified, everyone would agree that it is an awkward and tortuous means of settling disputes. A better way would result from a three party initial compact—a compact which also included the health care workers' employers. Such an agreement would commit both workers and employees to binding arbitration. That is, if a dispute between workers and their employer could not be resolved by collective bargaining, it would be agreed that it would be turned over to a mutually acceptable arbitrator. (The mechanics of this could be worked out in a variety of ways.) Strikes could be avoided while achieving the end of improved care. Clearly such an agreement would be advantageous to the public. They would not have to pay the price for the failure of other parties to reach an agreement. Health care workers would also find this to be in their best interest. They could avoid being forced into the extremely awkward position of causing hardship or at least inconvenience to those whose interests they have sworn to protect. Employers in the original position would also see that they stand to gain. They could not count on health care workers' inability or disinclination to vigorously press their demands. Faced with the prospect of having to concede just as much or more to striking workers as in binding arbitration, they would prefer binding arbitration. That would avoid the loss of income and goodwill which inevitably result from a strike.

Of course, in the present real life situation the employer's lot is quite different. He or she has little to gain by accepting binding arbitration. Perhaps through moral suasion employers will come to see that they ought to accept it. More likely, however, binding arbitration will be accepted only when it is in a particular employer's interests to do so. This will be the case if health care workers are able to exact as many concessions from their employer by striking as would be possible through binding arbitration. Only strong, united action on the part of health care workers will achieve such a breakthrough.

Health care workers should do all in their power to avoid strikes. But, paradoxically, the best way to accomplish this is to be ready and able, in appropriate situations. to execute an effective strike.

Nursing Ethics and Hospital Work

Tziporah Kasachkoff ⎯⎯⎯⎯⎯⎯⎯⎯⎯⎯⎯⎯⎯⎯⎯⎯⎯⎯⎯⎯

Until World War II, almost all hospital nurses were employed as private duty nurses whose salaries were paid by the hospitalized patient whom they served. In this context, nursing care was usually "primary care nursing"— the care of a patient was primarily the responsibility of one particular nurse; as a result, although different nurses served on different shifts, a hospitalized patient could count on seeing the same daytime nurse and the same nighttime nurse—both in the patient's and not in the hospital's employ—day after day, night after night.

Today, however, almost all nurses not only work in but are employed *by* some health care facility, such as hospitals (which employ 75 percent of all practicing nurses), clinics, or nursing homes. And in most such facilities, nursing services are organized around specific tasks rather than around specific patients, with the result that each patient is attended to by a variety of nurses, each of whom is assigned a specific nursing task, but none of whom is responsible for the total general nursing care of any one patient. Nursing care in the form of medication, alleviation of discomfort by physical manipulation (back rubs, bathing, massage, and so on), health care education, medical monitoring, dietary counseling, help in personal hygiene, and psychological support is carried out not by one nurse but by many nurses, each of whom the patient sees for only a short time, and all of whom have many other patients besides. Today's hospital or clinic has very few primary-care nurses.[1]

The way in which nursing care is presently delivered makes the moral situation of today's nurse much more complicated than before. For when the nurse was both employed and paid for by the patient, her* primary and overriding interests were clearly the patient's. Now, however, the nurse's

---

* Instead of referring to nurses awkwardly as "him/her" I shall throughout use the feminine pronoun. At present, about 3 percent of the profession are males.

contract is not with the patient, but with the hospital that pays her; as a result, notwithstanding the nurse's professional commitment to serve as "advocate" for the patient,[2] the circumstances of the nurse's employment make it sometimes seem as if the nurse's primary relationship is with her hospital-employer, the patient being relegated to "third-party" status.

Moreover, the nurse's moral position today reflects not merely the tensions implicit in her dual role as hospital employee on the one hand and patient care provider on the other; the nurse's services and loyalties are due also to the physicians under whose medical directives she works, as well as to coworker nurses and other health care personnel with whom she works. It is not surprising that in this setting the nurse often faces ethical dilemmas that arise out of conflicting moral obligations. In fact, so numerous are the moral conflicts that the nurse experiences in her work because of the special complexity of her institutional and professional role, one writer has dubbed these conflicts "problems of the nurse in the middle."[3]

Here we shall look at some of the ways in which a nurse may be caught "in the middle," and we shall deal only with problems that arise for the nurse because of her relationship to both patient and hospital. But we should keep in mind that the moral issues surrounding nurse/hospital, nurse/patient, nurse/physician, and nurse/nurse (or other coworker) relationships are only artificially separated: nurse/hospital/patient conflicts arise (in many cases) only because the nurse has moral obligations that arise out of other relationships as well. However, for the purposes of our analysis, we shall try to disengage some of the issues from the others.

Let us turn to the problem of the nurse who may be caught in the middle between the needs (and perhaps the rights) of the patient for whom she cares and the demands (and perhaps the rights) of her hospital employer.

First, let us note that not every way in which a nurse may be caught in the middle because of her simultaneous relationship with her employer and her patient is a way that involves her in a moral conflict unique to the nursing situation, or even to situations that arise most typically within health care facilities. For example, it may be that the nurse and hospital are in conflict over the best way to treat a given patient because they have made different assessments of the factual consequences of treating the patient one way rather than another. Or they may agree about what constitutes the best treatment for a particular patient and yet disagree over whether the nurse should follow a hospital policy that interferes with that treatment. A conflict between a nurse and a hospital over whether to follow the hospital's policy of waking up patients at 6 A.M. to take their temperature might be such a case. The problem represented by a case of this sort is more intractable than is the problem concerning a disagreement based on different views about *how* a given treatment will affect a certain patient. For the question of how a patient will be affected by a given treatment is a straightforwardly empirical matter, even if in a particular case it may be difficult to answer this question in advance of the decision that must be made. But a conflict over whether a particular patient's welfare should have priority over a hospital's policy (even when that policy is directed towards the efficient management of an institution whose job it is to serve *many* patients) is a conflict over which *values* should have priority in the treatment of patients in a hospital setting. Furthermore, the issue here is complicated by the fact that not only is it values and not mere facts that are in dispute, but, in addition, the different values held by the parties to the dispute are held by them as matters of professional interest. The nurse is professionally committed to the welfare of the patients who are entrusted to her care. Hospital administrators, on the other hand, have as their professional concern and charge the setting of hospital policies that will promote the efficient running of the hospital as a whole. Conflict over hospital policy may arise because in hospitals, as in all bureaucratic establishments, the efficient management of the *system* may be at odds with the best treatment of individuals. It is important to see that the nurse is professionally obligated both to follow the policies set by her employer and also—by the stated objectives of her profession—to protect her patients from harmful practices; however, the sort of conflict under discussion does not *necessarily* place the nurse in the middle of a morally problematic situation, or even in a situation that is uniquely troublesome to her because of her role as a professional nurse working in a hospital setting.

To see why this is so, let us suppose that the hospital administrators in our example take the position that although waking patients up at 6:00 A.M. is indeed poor nursing practice, unless all patients have had their temperatures taken by 6:30 A.M. other nursing tasks that must be done before the 8:00 A.M. shift begins will be rushed or sacrificed with the result that the general efficiency of the entire operation will be lowered. If we grant this point, as the nurse might, then we can see that a nurse might well agree that even though a given hospital policy may require blatant interference with good nursing care, that policy need not necessarily be a source of conflict for the conscientious nurse. For although a given hospital policy may result in the lowering of the quality of nursing care for some (and maybe even for all), the nurse may view the system that the policy serves as having a moral value that overrides the sacrifices the policy requires.* We all do sometimes sacrifice a particular good in order to preserve a system whose failure would undermine some important value. (Decisions to allow publication of tasteless and objectionable material in order to preserve a free press is an example.)

---

* Of course, it is an open and empirical question whether the hospital organization does *in fact* require all the sacrifices of individual care that are made in its name.

Granted then that *some* of the problems the nurse faces as a result of her employment situation are problems that, in some ways at least, are endemic to *all* settings in which the having or doing of something of value is threatened by a policy or feature of an institution whose existence and preservation is also of value, let us look at some specific problems that may arise for the nurse as a result of her hospital work.

Suppose that a nurse works in a (typical) hospital in which (1) nurses are expected, as a matter of routine, to wake patients up at 6:00 A.M. in order to take their temperatures; (2) nurses are expected to help resuscitate terminally ill patients regardless of the expressed wishes of the patient; and (3) nurses are required to work in units that are so chronically understaffed that the situation is judged to be potentially injurious to patients. Let us ask with respect to each of these situations whether, *given that patient interest is undermined by them,* it is a nurse's moral right, or even her moral duty, to refuse to cooperate with the hospital's policy or even to try to change the policy. (The question we are asking here is *not* whether the nurse is under a moral obligation to do what is wrong. Rather, what we are asking is how the nurse is to *decide* which of several alternative courses of action *is* the right thing to do.)

Let us begin by noting two things: (1) the three situations noted above pose problems for the nurse because there is a felt tension between the moral duties owed the patient on the one hand and those owed the hospital on the other; and (2) whatever duties the nurse has in these situations, they are not necessarily her duties *merely* because she is a nurse. Some of the nurse's duties are her duties in virtue not only of her professional role but of her more general and personal role as a responsible moral agent. The duty not to harm a patient, for example, is subsumable not only under a nurse's professional responsibility to care for her patient, for it is a moral duty not to cause harm to another whether one is a nurse or not and whether the other is a patient or not. Thus, the nurse's moral obligation not to harm a patient is not merely a consequence of her professional role; we are *all* under the obligation not to cause harm to others. But this duty has *special* stringency for the nurse because of her special professional commitments.

The question of what a nurse's moral rights and duties are with respect to hospital policies that require her to do what is detrimental to patient interest, might be answered as follows: Since the only moral justification for the existence of health care institutions (notwithstanding the fact that they may be profit-making bureaucracies) is their objective in promoting patient health, and since it is only because the nurse helps the hospital to meet this objective that she is hired, it follows that in accepting such employment the nurse puts herself not only under the obligation to provide good nursing care, but also under the obligation to try to make sure that conditions exist that make that care possible; any features of an employing institution that interfere with the fulfillment of one's employment obligations ought to be ignored, contravened, or changed.

Suppose we agree with the premise of this argument that, as one philosopher has put it, "It is (the) moral right of the patient that is ultimately the principal justification of any professional duties the nurse has . . .,"[4] does it follow that the nurse's professional duties to the hospital must *always* be overridden when fulfilling these duties runs contrary to the best interests of a particular patient? After all, we saw that it may be the case that sometimes ignoring a particular patient's interest or even a particular interest of patients in general *may* be the best way to preserve a system whose efficiency works to the ultimate benefit of all, patients included. A hospital's policy, say, of waking patients up at 6:00 A.M. is, in itself, clearly not in patients' interests, but it *may* be necessary to preserve something of *greater* value to patients *generally* than the sleep it costs them. On the other hand, in cases where the good achieved by following the policy is bought at the price of ignoring some fundamental right of the patient (for example, following "Do Not Resuscitate" orders which go contrary to the wishes of the patient) or of risking his life (for example, continuing to work in a unit of a hospital that is chronically understaffed), the loss or potential loss to the patient in following the policy may be of sufficient gravity that whatever is gained in institutional efficiency by following the policy may not offset it.

A nurse's duties then concerning given hospital policy depend on the relative value of the good sacrificed by following the hospital policy compared with the good that the policy serves. Thus, conflicts between a nurse and hospital regarding following policies that counter patients' interests must be decided on case by case. Sometimes commitment to patient welfare will require contravening hospital policy detrimental to particular patients' interests and sometimes it will not. However, what is important to notice here is that in every case it is *patients' interests*—patients viewed at least as a general class and interests viewed at least as long term—that are the final arbiters for the nurse of whether hospital policy is justifiably contravened.

Suppose, however, that someone counters as follows: The position outlined above, based, as it is, solely on the good of the patient, completely ignores the fact that as an employee of the hospital, the nurse has at least the presumptive moral duty to follow hospital orders. As a result, it wrongly treats as morally irrelevant the fact that the policies at issue are set by an employer who is paying the nurse to follow them. But the nurse who works in a hospital has professional commitments to her patients only *because* of her employment by the hospital; that is, her professional commitments are contingent *on her being a hospital employee*. It would be paradoxical indeed if the obligations imposed by her employment contract morally bound the nurse to change the employing institution's policies so that she could fulfill her contract. One physician has put this point as follows: "Although a professional, dedicated nurse is committed to the best care of the patient, that person's job is essentially to carry out the job as *defined* by the hospital and physician who is directing care. The nurse's contract lasts for the duration of the time clock."[5]

How shall we assess this argument? Let us look at how the above argument would apply to three other cases:

(1) Carpenters under contract to build desks for a furniture manufacturer do not have the right (much less the obligation) as a result of their contract to demand of the manufacturer that they be given building materials of sufficiently high quality so that the desks can be built to a standard that the carpenters see fit.

(2) Automobile workers are employed by a car manufacturer to construct gas tanks that have a defect in their design that makes them potentially dangerously explosive. The workers are under no professional obligation to do more than their contract requires and are thus not required to demand that a well-designed gas tank be provided.

(3) Preparatory high-school science teachers who are asked, for the purpose of cutting costs, to use old, outdated texts that contain erroneous information have no moral duty to try to change their conditions of employment so that they can teach in the way that they, rather than their employer, thinks adequate.

Clearly there seems, at least in some of these cases, to be something wrong. Let us look at two issues that will help indicate what it is: The issue of professionalism and the issue of public trust.

Issues of Professionalism

There is a difference between being a worker and being a working professional. Working as a professional commits one not only to one's employment contract, but also to certain ethical ideals and standards associated (either explicitly or implicitly) with the profession. These ideals and standards not only set the limits of acceptable behavior within the profession, they are an announcement both to the profession itself and to the public at large of the guiding principles of the profession and of its moral purpose. To be a professional, then, is to be bound by certain professional and ethical principles—

promises, if you will—that transcend the requirements of specific employment contracts.

The reason professional principles supercede the demands of specific employment contracts is that professions are characteristically concerned with work that is of considerable public and social value. Their principles, therefore, reflect the recognition that the conduct of professionals is a matter of public concern and affirm that those whom the profession presumes to help will not be compromised by considerations either of interest or of mere convenience to others, be the others oneself or one's employer.[6]

What is wrong with the claim that teachers are under no obligation to ignore or try to change the terms of their employment contract so that they can do their jobs as they rather than as their employers see fit is that their jobs are only *partially* defined by their employment contract. More fundamental are the terms of their practice *as defined by the principles of their profession.* These principles, as principles of no occupation whose areas are of great social concern, commit the professional to the welfare of her client over and above any employment contract to the contrary.*

However, with respect to the cases of the carpenter and the automobile worker, it is clear that in the sense that we have been using the term, neither the carpenter nor the automobile worker can be said to be working "professionals," nor can either appeal to professional norms in order to justify the demand that he be permitted to do his job responsibly. This does not mean, however, that the carpenter and automobile worker may not be entitled, and perhaps (under certain circumstances) even obligated, to override employment contracts or policies that interfere with the job as they responsibly view it. Nor does it mean that they cannot be said to be "acting professionally." After all, given what being a professional means, it is not an accident that acting "professionally," even when one is not a member of a profession, involves doing one's work with an attitude of responsibility and a concern for quality.

Issues of Public Trust

It is clear that the public's trust is invested in the service professions. But sometimes matters of public trust are involved in work that lies outside the service professions as well. In fact, there is an issue of public trust whenever the public is offered a good or service whose assessment involves technical or esoteric expertise and whose faulty assessment poses significant risks to the

---

* Indeed, it follows from this that certain kinds of professionals have the moral responsibility, if they cannot change the conditions of their employment, to avoid or withdraw from employment contracts that would force them to violate their professional norms.

public's welfare. With respect to public trust, the automobile worker, the teacher, and the nurse, seem all in the same position. For the consuming public cannot reasonably be expected to judge the quality of what is offered with respect to their work. The average consumer cannot, by looking, identify a defective gas tank, nor can students or patients reasonably be expected to be judicious consumers of the services they need. High-school students cannot be expected to judge the adequacy of teaching materials concerning a subject about which they are ignorant; hospital patients, already made anxious and vulnerable by the unfamiliarity of the hospital setting, are not typically in a position to judge objectively the adequacy of their hospital care. Furthermore, in all these cases the consequences of bad service may be grave. Faulty gas tanks, like understaffed hospitals, put the consumer at risk to life and health. (The consequences in the teaching case are, admittedly, less severe, for here it is educational objectives that are thwarted and, perhaps, educational futures compromised.)

The carpentry case, however, is unlike the others. For here we are *not* dealing with esoteric items about which the public is ignorant. Furthermore, there is no issue of public trust involved in desk manufacturing because the welfare of the public is in no way at risk.

Now keeping in mind what we have said concerning both professionalism and public trust, let us turn again to the question of whether a nurse has the right, or even the obligation, to contravene hospital policy that undermines her patient's welfare. From our discussion we might say the following: In so far as following hospital policy insures the efficient organization of hospital procedures for the purpose of providing better overall patient care, the nurse is *not* clearly in the right (nor does she have the obligation) to ignore or try to change the policy unless the policy betrays the general public's (or the patient's) trust. Waking patients up early for the purpose of taking their temperature does not do this. But following a hospital's policy of, say, ignoring a patient's wishes to not resuscitate, or working in a chronically understaffed critical-care unit, does risk patient welfare and does subvert his or her ultimate interests. The nurse, therefore—both by professional commitment and by public trust—is entitled, and perhaps to some extent even duty-bound, to try to change the policy.*

---

* One very large and important issue (which will not be touched on here) is just *how far* morality requires the nurse to go in such situations as these. Sometimes doing the right thing will be tantamount to doing what is heroic. If doing the right thing involves risking one's job or one's professional future, does this attenuate the stringency of the nurse's duty. This is a large question, and in the context of nursing practice today, not one of theoretical importance only.

Before concluding, one feature should be mentioned that is endemic to the nursing situation and, though not unique to it, has uniquely poignant significance in it.

We saw that where there is an issue of public trust it derives (in part) from the fact that the consumer is not in a position, knowledgeably and confidently, to judge the quality of the service he procures. While this is true in different ways not only of patients but also of students and of consumers of certain other services (and products) too, it is true of the hospitalized patient, who is especially susceptible to exploitation in such a way that the nurse's professional involvement seems at times to commit her to what may be called "extra-professional" moral concern.

Hospitalized patients are not only in a position of ignorance; typically they are in very real distress, or in pain, filled with anxiety and feelings of vulnerability and fear, and always aware both that control of their environment is in the hands of others and that they are not even in an adequate position to evaluate the care they receive.

Clearly the suffering and emotional fragility that the nurse is faced with imposes obligations on her that, though they have traditionally been termed the "virtues" of her profession (compassion, benevolence, and patience), go beyond simple professional duties. In this respect, nursing, like teaching, but to a much greater degree, is a profession whose requirements are not easily separable from the requirements of generally responsible moral agency.

In conclusion, we might note how ironic and unfortunate it is that, given the pervasiveness and importance of ethical issues in nursing practice, until quite recently questions of the nurse's moral responsibility and accountability were not viewed as appropriate issues for nurses to address. Nurses were viewed as simply lacking the ethical autonomy necessary for moral agency. As traditionally defined and perceived (by physicians, hospitals, and the public at large), nurses were subordinate to and dependent upon physicians' directives—a role that seemed to place the nurse in a dependent moral position as well. The 1970 American Medical Associations' Committee on Nursing statement that nurses should remain under the supervision of physicians for the purpose of "extending the hand of the physician" made explicit the view that issues of both nursing practice and patient care were essentially issues of what it is that *physicians* decide. The implication was clear: The ethics of the nursing profession were essentially the ethics of obedience to physicians' demands. Of course such a view could do nothing actually to absolve nurses from the necessity of making ethical choices and from being morally responsible for the implications of their behavior. For even *if* the nursing profession *were* to be defined by its dependence on physicians' directives, the moral responsibility of the nurse could not thereby be relinquished in the interests of professional subordination. Absolution from moral wrongdoing cannot be affected merely because one commits a wrong based on the order of another.

Notes

1. The specialization of nursing services that fragments the care of the patient into discrete and isolated units is not due solely or even especially to the specialized knowledge or expertise required by all the different tasks performed. Though technical expertise no doubt plays some part in the way that nursing (and other hospital) services are compartmentalized, more telling is the way that nursing and other services have been institutionalized as a result of the hospital bureaucracy—because of the way in which hospitals function as hierarchies of authority and the way in which payment for hospital services is determined.

2. Point 3 of the American Nurses' Association Code for Nurses: "The nurse acts to safeguard the client and the public when health care and safety are affected by incompetent, unethical or illegal practice of any person."

The accompanying interpretive statement (3.1) is entitled "Role of Advocate" and refers to the nurse's role as that of "client advocate."

3. Andrew Jameton, "The Nurse: When Role and Rules Conflict," *Hastings Center Report,* vol. 7, no. 4 (August 1977).

4. Dan Brock, "The Nurse and Patient Relation: Some Rights and Duties," *Nursing Images and Ideals: Opening Dialogue with the Humanities* (New York: Springer Publishing Company, 1980), 119.

5. Robert H. Bartlett, "When Nurse and Doctor Disagree" *Troubling Problems in Medical Ethics,* ed. Marc D. Basson, Rachel Lipson, and Doreen L. Ganos (New York: Alan R. Liss, Inc., 1981), 195.

6. For discussion of the meaning of professionalism and of some of the ethical implications for nurses, see Andrew Jameton, *Nursing Practice: The Ethical Issues* (Englewood Cliffs, New Jersey: Prentice-Hall, 1983), chap. 2. See also Edmund D. Pelligrino, "To Be a Physician," *Medical Ethics: A Clincal Textbook and Reference for Health Care Professions,* ed. Natalie Abrahams and Michael D. Buchner (Cambridge, Mass.: MIT Press, 1983), 94, 95.

PART 7 _____

DISCRIMINATION AND AFFIRMATIVE ACTION

Comparable Worth*

Helen Remick and Ronnie J. Steinberg _____

Cultural beliefs underlying the differentiation of men's and women's work are so strong (though obviously changeable) that widespread debate on a comparable worth policy would have been unthinkable twenty—perhaps even ten—years ago. The concept of comparable worth was introduced as "equal pay for work of equal value" at the close of the Second World War. The Equal Pay Act, passed only twenty years ago, in 1963, without a comparable worth standard, was as radical a reform as the political system could then tolerate. . . .

Criticisms of Comparable Worth

As the goal of comparable worth has evolved from a political demand into a policy with serious economic consequences for employers, opponents have developed a number of arguments against it. . . .

Apples and Oranges

Fortune magazine article described comparable worth as "a fallacious notion that apples are equal to oranges and that prices for both should be the same" (Smith, 1978:58). The apples-and-oranges comparison refers to the supposed impossibility of finding a method to describe, evaluate, and establish equivalencies among dissimilar jobs. However, both suggestions—that no method for comparing dissimilar jobs can be found and that apples could not be equal to oranges—are themselves fallacious.

* Reprinted from Helen Remick and Ronnie J. Steinberg, eds., *Comparable Worth and Wage Discrimination* (Philadelphia: Temple University Press, 1984), by permission of the publisher. Copyright © 1984 by Temple University Press.

Of course, any particular apple may not be equal to any particular orange, nor are all apples identical. Yet there are general characteristics of fruit, such as the number of calories, the vitamin and mineral content, and so on, that make it possible to compare specific apples with specific oranges. Along some of these dimensions of comparison, the apples and oranges compared may, in fact, be equivalent, and therefore be of equal value.

Likewise, certain dissimilar jobs may comprise functional tasks and characteristics that, from the employer's point of view, are equivalent in value. Job evaluation systems describe and analyze jobs in terms of an array of underlying features such as prerequisites, tasks, and responsibilities. While far from perfect, these systems have been and continue to be used to classify dissimilar jobs, especially in large firms and at the management level. It is surprising, then, that the same employer groups that have supported job evaluation systems when they have been used to create and justify an existing organizational hierarchy and wage structure, contend that such systems cannot be used to compare male-dominated and female-dominated jobs within that wage structure. . . .

The Cost

Critics of comparable worth policy also argue that the financial costs of adjusting female wages up to male standards would be prohibitive: employer advocacy groups have presented estimates that range from $2 billion to $150 billion (Newman and Vonhof, 1981:309). But the assumption underlying these estimates is that all wage discrimination in all work organizations is going to be rectified all at once and tomorrow. This assumption has no basis in history; nor does it reflect the approach thus far taken within work organizations to correct for systematic undervaluation or for other forms of discrimination.

Most legal reforms that impact upon the labor market have been implemented in stages; either the scope of coverage is initially restricted and gradually expanded to cover a larger proportion of employees overtime, or the legal standard is introduced in steps. . . .

Should comparable worth policy become incorporated into Title VII, it would no doubt be implemented as are policies designed to correct for other forms of employment discrimination. Currently, work organizations found to be in violation of the law must present a plan for eliminating discrimination that includes reasonable goals and timetables based on the probable availability of employees and the probable rate of turnover. Similarly, to comply with a comparable worth policy, firms would first have to determine the scope and form of wage discrimination in their organization. They would then have to develop a plan for removing it . . . there is no reason to believe that a firm would be required to correct all inequities immediately if doing so would have serious financial consequences. Rather, the cost of implementing comparable worth policy will probably be spread out at the very least over the next two decades. While no doubt costly, the length of this implementation process should reduce the impact of its cost for any year or even any decade. The goal of the proponents of comparable worth is to balance fairness with fiscal responsibility. . . .

Integration of Jobs

Opponents of comparable worth frequently tout the integration of the work force as a better solution to the salary differentials between men and women. When most people speak of integration, they mean bringing women into male-dominated jobs by eliminating the few remaining barriers to their entry. It would then be totally up to the women to pursue these new careers if they wished to improve their earning power. While this process is, of course, important, full integration requires that men enter female-dominated fields as well. While some women are motivated by economic reasons to seek nontraditional work, these same reasons discourage men; because of the low wages and low status of female-dominated occupations, men have no incentives to seek this work.

Moreover, the segregation of our work force is so extensive that fully two-thirds of all men and women would have to change fields of employment to bring about an equal distribution of the sexes across all occupations. The sheer numbers involved point out the impossibility of integration alone as a reasonable solution. For example, almost 20 percent of the U.S. workforce are clerical workers, virtually all of whom are female. Obviously only a small portion of the 5 million typists can become one of the 800,000 carpenters. The emphasis on women seeking men's jobs also raises questions about the men doing this work: are they to be asked to give up their jobs so that women may have them; if so, do we retrain them to be typists, and at whose expense? . . .

One implicit message in the push for an integration strategy to equal employment is, once again, that women are the cause of their own exploitation; if they had just chosen the correct field of work, they would be making a reasonable wage. After all, if women's jobs are not systematically underpaid, then their assigned wages are a fair measure of the true worth of the jobs and of the workers in them. Many factors go into the choice of an occupation, and these factors affect both the hirer and the applicant. Whatever the reasons, these factors are obviously difficult to modify. In any case, men's jobs should not be the only ones that can be done with dignity and fair pay. Our society needs nurses, day care workers, waitresses, and typists. It is unreasonable to underpay these workers simply because they had the misfortune not to be born male and not to choose traditionally male jobs.

Groups and Justice*

George Sher _____

In this essay, I want to discuss one argument in favor of preferential treatment for the members of groups whose past members have suffered discrimination. On the argument in question, such preference is said to be justified by the fact that it compensates for injustices *done to the relevant groups themselves.* By focusing on wronged groups, and not their individual members, the argument may seem to avoid the problem of justifying preference for group members who were not themselves the victims of discrimination. However, despite this apparent advantage, I believe the argument should be rejected. In particular, I shall argue that it fails because (1) racial and sexual groups are not enough like persons to fall under the principle of distributive justice, and (2) even if such groups did fall under it, that principle could not possibly justify preferential treatment for their current, undeprived members.

I

There is some initial appeal to the claim that discriminated-against groups have received "less than their fair shares" of good jobs, educational opportunities, and other benefits in the past, and so deserve more of these benefits than they ordinarily would as compensation now. We have a fairly firm grasp of what constitutes fair sharing among individuals, and it is not unnatural to think that this notion might extend to groups as well. But there are also pitfalls here. What constitutes an individual's fair share is determined by a principle of distributive justice which seems to dictate that goods should be distributed equally except when persons differ in need or merit. Hence, a person's fair share is inextricably bound up with, and cannot be determined

* Revision of George Sher, "Groups and Justice," *ETHICS, an International Journal of Social, Political and Legal Philosophy,* vol. 87, no. 2 (January 1977) by permission of the publisher. © 1977 by the University of Chicago. All rights reserved.

without a knowledge of, his merits and needs. If our notion of fair sharing is to be extended to groups, then this connection will have to carry over. What constitutes a group's fair share will have to be bound up with that group's needs and merits in a manner at least strongly analogous to that in which an individual's fair share is bound up with his needs and merits. It seems to me, however, and I shall argue in this section, that racial and sexual groups simply do not *have* needs or merits of the appropriate sorts. If they do not, then the seemingly natural claim that discriminated-against groups were denied their fair share of goods will make no sense.

Consider, first, the sense of "need" that is relevant to the principle of distributive justice. To say in this sense that an entity needs a good is just to say that the good is necessary for the entity's well-being. Hence, only those entities which in principle can attain states of well-being can possibly have needs of the appropriate sorts. For human beings, this restriction poses no difficulty. Human beings are equipped, physiologically and psychologically, to benefit in indefinitely many ways. Hence, the only problem about determining *their* needs is to decide which levels of well-being should be considered minimally acceptable for them. But for racial and sexual groups, the situation is dramatically different. Such groups, unlike their members, do not satisfy the preconditions for attaining any of the states of well-being with which we are familiar. They do not have single organized bodies, and so can neither sustain good bodily health nor suffer illness. They do not have nervous systems, and so cannot experience the various states of comfort and discomfort which these systems make possible. They do not have consciousness, and so cannot experience either amusement, happiness, interest, or self-esteem, or the less pleasant states which stand opposed to these. They do not even have the degree of legal or conventional organization that is shared by corporations, clubs, and other legal persons. Hence, they cannot increase or decrease their wealth or holdings as these other composite entities can. Because racial and sexual groups lack the sorts of organization which alone confer capacities to attain states of well-being, they can hardly have the sorts of needs which presuppose these capacities. Any statements which appear to attribute such needs to them must therefore be elliptical. Such statements must either attribute needs to some of the groups' members (in which case no additional properties will be attributed to the groups as wholes), or else must be ways of speaking about *average* degrees of need within the groups (in which case additional properties will in a sense be attributed to the groups as wholes, but those properties will not be relevant to the distribution of goods: average needs are no more genuine needs than average citizens are citizens).

It is also difficult to see how racial or sexual groups could satisfy any of the criteria for *merit* relevant to distributive justice. Those criteria are notoriously diverse. We sometimes tie merit to pure ability (however measured), but at other times we consider also, or instead, efforts expended, degrees of skill acquired, and goods produced. Despite this diversity, however, and whatever the logical and historical relations among them actually are, our criteria for merit are at least unified by one common presupposition. To satisfy any of them, an entity must in some sense be capable of *acting*. Skills and abilities are exercised only through actions. Hence, it would be senseless to speak of either the abilities or the skills of a non-agent. For similar reasons, non-agents can neither exert effort nor produce goods. Once again, this requirement hardly restricts our application of the criteria of merit among human beings. Persons are the source of our concept of action, and so of course it applies to them. The requirement does, however, seem to rule out our application of the criteria of merit to racial and sexual groups. These groups do not have the organization required to act at all. Hence, they cannot possibly perform the sorts of actions through which alone efforts are made, skills exercised, abilities demonstrated, and goods produced. Once again, therefore, it seems that any statements which appear to be about racial or sexual groups' merits must really be about something else. Such statements must be about either the merits of individual group members or else the average degrees of merit within groups.

These considerations show that racial and sexual groups cannot have the sorts of needs and merits which justify deviations from strictly equal distribution of goods. But even if no racial or sexual group can deserve *more* of any good than any other, it might still seem that each group can deserve the *same* amount of goods as every other. If this were so, then questions of fair sharing among racial and sexual groups could still arise. To suppose this, though, would be to overlook the common roots of the different elements of our concept of distributive justice. As Gregory Vlastos has made clear,[1] equal distribution under ordinary circumstances and unequal distribution when needs differ are both ways of achieving the single goal of *equalizing benefits*. The first is appropriate when each recipient would benefit equally from the good in question, the second when some would benefit more than others. If equal treatment and special treatment under special circumstances do both aim at equalizing benefits, then desert of each must alike presuppose the capacity to benefit. Hence, the proper conclusion is not merely that racial and sexual groups do not qualify for exemptions from equal treatment, but rather, and more radically, that such groups do not fall under the principle of distributive justice at all.[2] There may indeed be circumstances in which justice dictates preference for each group member; but if there are, this must be because each group member has suffered deprivation in the past. In any such case, it will be the affected individuals, and not the group itself, to whom the principle of distributive justice applies.

II

Thus far, the argument has been that racial and sexual groups lack the sorts of organization they would need to deserve goods, and so that all talk of unjust distributions of goods among them is out of place. In this section I want to make a further point: even if it *were* possible to distribute goods unjustly among these groups, a policy of preferential treatment extending to their undeprived members could not possibly compensate for such injustices.

It seems obvious enough that the principle of distributive justice cannot apply only to racial and sexual groups. If it is to apply to groups of these sorts, it will have to apply also to cultural, religious, and geographic ones. But, having widened our horizons this far, why should we stop even here? There are really as many groups as there are combinations of people; and if we are going to ascribe claims to equal treatment to racial, sexual, and other groups with high visibility, it will be mere favoritism not to ascribe similar claims to all these other groups as well. Moreover, if all groups do have the same claim to equal treatment, then all groups must also have the same claim to compensation for unequal treatment. Any compensation that is deserved by a deprived racial or sexual group must also and equally be deserved by any other similarly deprived group. Once these natural assumptions are granted, however, it is easily shown that any case for the preferential treatment of undeprived members of deprived racial or sexual groups would be precisely matched, and so destroyed, by similar cases for the preferential treatment of all other undeprived individuals.

For suppose that G is a group composed of all the individuals with a given racial or sexual characteristic. Moreover, suppose that most, but not all, of these individuals have suffered the privations of discrimination in the past. Let Adams, Brown, and Carpenter be the *non*-deprived members of G, and let Edwards, Frederics, and Gordon be a similar number of non-deprived members of non-G. If deprived groups do deserve compensation, and if preferential treatment of their undeprived members is a proper way of effecting such compensation, the past deprivation of G will justify preferential treatment for Adams, Brown, and Carpenter. However, since all deprived groups must deserve compensation if any do, and since the "mixed" group consisting of the deprived members of G plus Edwards, Frederics, and Gordon (call this group M) was precisely as deprived as G itself, the case for preference for Adams, Brown, and Carpenter will be precisely matched by a similar case for preference for Edwards, Frederics, and Gordon. Moreover, since the same reasoning must justify preference for the undeprived members of all other mixed groups—and since everyone belongs to one or another of these—the ultimate conclusion must be that all undeprived individuals (as well, of course, as all deprived ones) deserve preferential treatment now. But this is plainly absurd. If everyone deserved preference, there would be no one to whom anyone deserved to be preferred, and so no one would deserve preference.

It might seem possible to avoid these difficulties by showing that Adams, Brown, and Carpenter deserve preference over Edwards, Frederics, and Gordon in a slightly different way. It seems no less reasonable that groups which were overprivileged in the past deserve less than their ordinary fair shares, than it does that groups which were underprivileged deserve more. Hence, since non-G has been precisely as overprivileged as G has been underprivileged, it might seem that non-G's members, Edwards, Frederics, and Gordon, deserve less than equal treatment now, and so, indirectly, that Adams, Brown, and Carpenter deserve preference over them. But this argument is just as vulnerable to refutation by generalization as its twin. If discrimination is called for against the current members of any overprivileged groups, then it must be called for against the current members of all of them. And since the mixed group M was precisely as underprivileged as G in the past, its complement, non-M, must have been precisely as overprivileged as G's complement, non-G. Hence, any case for discrimination against Edwards, Frederics, and Gordon because of their membership in non-G will again be precisely matched by a parallel case for discrimination against Adams, Brown, and Carpenter because of their membership in non-M.

If these remarks are correct, then even granting that deprived racial and sexual groups were denied distributive justice will not establish that the current, undeprived group members should be afforded preference now. However, there may appear to be a problem with my argument's pivotal claim that artificially constructed groups like M are as deserving of compensation as deprived racial or sexual groups like G. Even though M has undoubtedly suffered the same amount of deprivation as G, the fact remains that it was prejudice focused upon the relevant racial or sexual characteristic, but not prejudice focused upon the arbitrary characteristic of M-ness, that was responsible for the deprivation of the two groups. For this reason, G may still seem to be the group that is the more deserving of compensation. But if so, then there will indeed be a reason to afford Adams, Brown, and Carpenter preference over Edwards, Frederics, and Gordon.

However, I do not think this objection can be sustained. To see the difficulties it involves, consider first the claim that certain intentions on the part of discriminatory agents can increase their victims' degrees of desert. The most plausible version of this claim is that desert of compensation increases when discriminatory acts are performed with the intention of harming their victims. However, there are at least two reasons why the claim, thus interpreted, is not likely to establish that G deserves compensation more than M. First, many of those who discriminated in the past held stereotyped views of their victims. Blacks were perceived as possessing criminal tendencies and lacking industry, women as being unable to do a full day's work, etc. In light of these stereotypes, it seems reasonable to suppose that much discrimination was practiced not with the intention of harming blacks or women, but rather only with the intention of denying goods to anyone with those legitimately desert-cancelling characteristics which blacks and women were mistakenly thought to possess. To the extent that this is so, it is hard to see how the intention behind the discrimination could increase the desert of these groups now. Moreover, second, even when discrimination has been guided by the intent to do harm, the intention is hardly likely to have been to harm any racial or sexual *group*. Only a very sophisticated bigot could intend to harm a group as opposed to its members; and yet in the absence of any intention to harm G itself, the principle that discriminators' intentions to harm their victims increase those victims' degrees of desert will not distinguish G's desert from M's.

There is also a deeper difficulty with the claim that the intentions behind past discrimination make G more deserving of compensation than M. This difficulty emerges when we recall the point of compensating for breaches of distributive justice. To compensate someone for receiving less than his proper share of a given good is simply to restore to him, as far as is possible, the good of which he has been unjustly deprived, or which he has been unjustly prevented from attaining. Since this is so, his desert of compensation must depend on precisely the same considerations as those which determined his initial claim to that good. But, except perhaps in some freakish and irrelevant cases, initial claims to goods are never a function of the (future) intentions of disruptive agents. Hence, subsequent desert of compensation for unjust distribution can hardly be affected by those intentions either.[3] Because desert of compensation for unjust distribution is independent of the intentions of those who acted unjustly, the fact that the common members of G and M were deprived because they belonged to G but not because they belonged to M cannot possibly bear on the degrees to which the two groups deserve compensation. Thus, it remains true that no breach of distributive justice involving a group could call for a preferential policy extending to that group's current undeprived members.[4] If past violations of distributive justice are to license preference for all current group members, this can only be because each of these individuals has himself or herself been treated unjustly.[5]

Individual Candidate Remedies: Why They Won't Work

Gertrude Ezorsky _____

Discrimination against blacks in America has exemplified a caste system, marked by fear of contamination from "inferior" caste members, their segregation into the lowest paid, most miserable occupations and their consequent impoverishment.

Today the laws banning white contact with blacks in personal facilities are gone, but race prejudice has far from disappeared. The disinclination of most whites to form friendships and intimate relationships with blacks, and the widespread resistance to neighborhood and school integration, causing violence in some cities, are indicators of a pervasive racial bias. Although a few blacks have moved up, occupational segregation into the lowest jobs, and even into unemployment, is still fundamentally intact. Today a white high-school dropout is less likely to be unemployed than a black with some college education.[6] Where employed, blacks are overrepresented at the bottom of the occupational ladder.

Nathan Glazer warns us that unrepresentative racial distribution in occupations may only reflect ways in which racial groups have "expressed themselves."

Distinctive histories have channeled ethnic and racial groups into one kind of work or another, and this is the origin of many of the "unrepresentative" work distributions we see. These distributions have been maintained by an occupational tradition linked to an ethnic community which makes it easier for the Irish to become policeman, the Italians fruit dealers, Jews businessmen, and so on.[7]

But Glazer fails to note the kind of work that blacks have traditionally performed: hot, heavy, and dirty jobs in the foundries and paint pits of the automobile plants, the boiler rooms of utilities, the dusty basements of the tobacco factories, and in the murderous heat of the coke ovens of the steel mills. Today every other person involved by occupation with dirt or garbage is black.

I suggest that black people have not "expressed themselves" by such labor. Moreover, while Glazer reminds us that the Irish have by historic tradition been policemen, he fails to mention the "distinctive" history that has "channelled" blacks into their "kind of work"; that history is slavery.

Two ways of reducing occupational segregation may be distinguished: the group method—known as affirmative action—and the individual candidate method. Affirmative action is exemplified when an employer sets a numerical goal for hiring, promoting, or retaining black employees during layoffs. Taking affirmative action does *not* require that the blacks who benefit from its use be victims of past discrimination by this same employer. The point of affirmative action in employment is to reduce occupational segregation of blacks as a group; as U.S. civil rights enforcement officials learned—before the drastic decline of affirmative action enforcement began in the seventies— the notable absence of blacks from a work force is remedied not by vague employer promises to look for blacks, but by setting a reasonable, *specific* numerical goal for hiring them.

The individual candidate method is exemplified when a black applicant makes a legal complaint proving that he was denied a position because of an employer's bias. The black applicant is then restored to the position he would have held with that employer, but for discrimination. Thus, unlike affirmative action, the individual candidate method [hereafter, the individual method] requires that the blacks *prove* that they were discriminated against by the employer.

Some persons who agree that occupational segregation is unfair, also think that it can be undone without affirmative action. They believe that use of the individual method to rectify specific acts of discrimination will eliminate occupational segregation. I shall confine myself here to criticizing that belief in the effectiveness of the individual method. As I shall show, that method has inherent weaknesses. Moreover, it is often irrelevant to situations where the consequences of social practices, past and present, sustain occupational segregation.

Inherent Weakness of the Individual Method

First, the black complainant must prove that the employer denied him a position because of race prejudice. But the existence of pervasive race prejudice is compatible with great difficulty in proving prejudice in an individual case, a difficulty due in part to effective counter-strategies by employers. How does a black applicant know whether the the job has really "just been filled"? How can a qualified black driver prove that a delivery company's new policy—hiring only college graduates—was devised to exclude black candidates? How can an experienced black worker demonstrate that announcement of a managerial opening was canceled because the employer learned that she—a *black* employee—was clearly the most qualified candidate. The difficulty of proving biased intent, when employers have power to cover up such bias, reduces the effectiveness of the individual method.

A second weakness of that method is that employees who assert their rights are often labeled "troublemakers" by their supervisors. (Many of the rights we now take for granted were won by such troublemakers.) However, that label can damage a person—especially a black person—for her entire working life. A realistic assessment of that damage to themselves and to the families they support often stops black people from initiating perfectly justified discrimination complaints.

Two Societies

Contemporary social practices contribute to occupational segregation. White and black people still live, for the most part, in two different societies. They have personal and intimate relationships with persons of their own color. Such social separation from whites creates disadvantages for blacks in the world of work that cannot be dispelled by the individual method. Here is why:

As vocational counselors know, "connections"—friends, family and neighbors—lead people to jobs. "It isn't what you know, but who you know" expresses a profound social truth. Today the better jobs are still held predominantly by whites. They tell their white associates about vacancies in their line of work; such hiring through social connections, although a disadvantage for blacks, is for employers a cheap form of personnel recruitment.

Blacks also lack access to the white gatherings where political candidacies and well-paying patronage jobs are dispensed over lunch, dinner, and drinks. As a prominent U.S. official said recently, "To get a job" in Washington, "you have to know someone."

Thus, the existence of two societies, a white and a black, reinforces occupational segregation. However, the individual method cannot remove the damage to blacks caused by their exclusion from white society. First, because choice of one's personal associates is rightfully exempt from the laws that prohibit racially biased acts. Even prejudiced persons have a moral right to choose their own friends and spouses. Second, because the individual method presupposes the *candidate* model of discrimination: A black candidate competing for a position is rejected because of race. His discrimination complaint granted, he is awarded the position that he should have been given in that competition. But where positions are dispensed behind the scenes in white society, no competition exists. Hence, blacks have no opportunity to become candidates for such jobs. When a white employer gives his nephew a comfortable position with the firm, usually no one knows which individual would have been hired in a fair competition. Therefore, no black individual can complain that he or she should have been given that position. Since the individual method is usually irrelevant to hiring through white social connections, that method cannot reduce the adverse impact of such behind-the-scenes hiring on black people, an impact that serves to reinforce occupational segregation.

Another social practice that contributes to such segregation is racial separation by neighborhoods. That separation is a palpable barrier to establishing white connections that lead to better jobs. Moreover, excluded from residence in distant white suburbs, ghetto blacks have no access to many jobs in newly created suburban enterprises. In some cases, where openings exist, no public transportation is available, or the carfare is prohibitively expensive for a black youth. But the individual method is an ineffective tool for opening up all white neighborhoods to black residents. Landlords and realtors, like employers, use effective strategies to defeat individual complaints of housing bias. Does a black apartment seeker have *proof,* or the time to assemble proof, that a landlord's excuses ("The apartment isn't available because it needs repair") are conjured up to exclude blacks, or that a real estate agent is steering black clients away from white neighborhoods? Moreover, the individual method cannot eliminate ostensibly race-neutral practices that tend to exclude blacks from white areas, such as zoning laws that ban multiple unit dwellings— more affordable by blacks—or the prohibition by public referendum of government subsidized housing where, as it happens, more black people live. Complaints of biased acts against specific individuals are irrelevant to such practices. Yet the segregated housing they sustain cuts off employment possibilities for blacks.[8]

Nor can individual complaints create effective vocational training for black youths in ghetto schools, which as segregated are visible targets for inadequate state funding.

Consequences of Past Discrimination

Black people, as the saying goes, have been the "last hired and first fired." Hence, they have usually been overrepresented among job losers during economic recessions. However, that higher job-loss rate has persisted into the present, a persistence that is due in part to the consequences of past discrimination. But as I shall show, the individual method is of no use in remedying this situation.

After the 1965 Civil Rights Act, many public and private employers, because of affirmative action regulations, hired more than their usual token (or zero) number of blacks. However, due to the employer's *past* hiring discrimination, blacks still remained noticeably absent among the more senior workers. Thus, during the economic recessions beginning in the seventies, the jobs of the more recently hired black workers tended to be eliminated by seniority-based layoffs. (In the mid-seventies the black male job-loss rate was twice their work force ratio.) Thus, where blacks have been hired as municipal police, teachers, fire fighters, and in private enterprises because of recent affirmative action measures, layoffs by seniority tend to make the work force— as before the Civil Rights Act—all white.[9] However, although a seniority system in fact tends to sight blacks first for layoff, it is race blind. Hence, individual complaints of biased acts cannot reduce its devastating impact in employment on black people.

When blacks lose their jobs during an economic recession, they usually move down the occupational ladder into unskilled, temporary jobs or no jobs at all. Once again the individual method is irrelevant to the reinforcement of occupational segregation.

Civil Rights and Group Preference*

Morris B. Abram _____

There were to key principles that united the civil-rights movement in the 1940's, 50's and early 60's, and that gave it the moral force needed to win the people's "hearts and minds." The first was a steadfast commitment to equality of opportunity: All Americans should have an equal chance to excel at work, at school and across the spectrum of American institutions. Neither government nor the private sector should be allowed to erect barriers on the basis of ethnic or racial groups. Martin Luther King articulated this principle in his unforgettable statement of his dream that "my four little children will one day live in a nation where they will not be judged by the color of their skin, but by the content of their character."

But with the new battle cry of equality of results, ethnic groups began demanding not equal access, but rather a fixed percentage of admissions, jobs and other goods. The definition of discrimination changed. Where once it meant barriers designed to thwart equal access, the new definition held that unless an employer had a particular proportion of minorites in his employ, he had the burden of proving he was not guilty of discrimination. Whenever different racial groups showed different outcomes—for example, on a test— the new movement claimed that racial discrimination was going on in violation of the 14th Amendment. The accepted goal of equality of opportunity was replaced by a creed of equality of results. Equality as a ground rule for how the contest would proceed gave way to the idea of equality as an agreement, ahead of time, that the contest would come out a certain way.

Though these new arguments were advanced in the name of integration, they were in fact of a piece with the old spirit of segregation. Equality of results depends fundamentally on a "group"conception of rights, precisely the

* Reprinted from Morris Abraham, "What Constitutes a Civil Right," *New York Times,* 10 June 1984. Copyright © 1984 by The New York Times Company. Reprinted by permission.

conception the old movement stood against. Everyone knows that people are different, and that you cannot expect identical results from any two individuals. So the new movement, in order to demand equality of results, had to claim instead that once you mass people together in groups, they are no longer different and should produce the same results. Moreover, the "remedy" urged when the new "discrimination" was uncovered was not taking steps to insure that all could compete equally, but rather to impose a strict racial balance— in sum, to treat individuals on the basis of their race.

This threatened to pit ethnic group against group, with each race clawing at another for education, jobs and professional opportunity. This new policy of group preferences, at first justified as compensation for slavery and its aftermath, became increasingly irrational and divisive as political muscle pushed government to include in preferred classes groups that had never experienced slavery, including Hispanics, Asians, Aleuts, women and eventually the handicapped and homosexuals

Affirmative Action*

Herman Schwartz _____

The American civil rights struggle has moved beyond simply banning discrimination against blacks, women and others. It is now clear that centuries of discrimination cannot be undone by merely stopping bad practices. Some kind of affirmative action is necessary to provide members of the disadvantaged groups with equal opportunities to share in the good things society has to offer.

The question of what kind of affirmative action is appropriate has generated intense controversy in the United States. One view is that it is necessary to provide actual preferences to members of disadvantaged groups in hiring, educational opportunities, government benefits and programmes, and the like, often in arrangements calling for specific minimum goals and timetables or quotas to achieve certain proportions of jobs, or other benefits.

In the famous *Bakke* case, Justice Harry Blackmun wrote:

I suspect that it would be impossible to arrange an affirmative action program in a racially neutral way and have it successful. To ask that this be so is to demand the impossible. In order to get beyond racism, we must first take account of race. There is no other way. And in order to treat some persons equally, we must treat them differently. We cannot—we dare not—let the Equal Protection Clause perpetuate racial supremacy.[10]

And Justice Thurgood Marshall emphasized that "It is because of a legacy of unequal treatment that we now must permit the institutions of this society to give consideration to race in making decisions about who will hold the positions of influence, affluence and prestige in America."[11]

* Reprinted from *Israeli Yearbook on Human Rights,* v. 14, (1984) by permission of the publisher. Copyright © 1984 Faculty of Law, Tel Aviv University Israel. (Original title "Affirmative Action: The American Experience.")

Others, including certain American Jewish organizations, find this kind of race or gender preference immoral and illegal, preferring instead to rely on finding and training disadvantaged group members for the desired opportunities. Thus, United States Civil Rights Commission Vice Chairman Morris Abram declared:

I do not need any further study of a principle that comes from the basic bedrock of the Constitution, in which the words say that every person in the land shall be entitled to the equal protection of the law. Equal means equal. Equal does not mean you have separate lists of blacks and whites for promotion, any more than you have separate accommodations for blacks and whites for eating. Nothing will ultimately divide a society more than this kind of preference and this kind of reverse discrimination.[12]

Supreme Court Justice John Paul Stevens, who frequently votes with the liberal members of the Court, was so offended by a congressional enactment setting aside ten percent of public works contracts for minority contractors, that he compared it to the Nuremburg laws for its reliance on racial and ethnic identity.[13]

The Legal Issues

The constitutionality of governmental (constitutional limitations do not generally apply to private actions) affirmative action programmes involving race and gender-conscious goals and timetables or quotas seems quite firmly established. Voluntary private affirmative action plans also seem quite legal under the governing statutes. Language in the recent Memphis Fire Department case casts some doubt on whether federal statutory law permits a federal court to order such plans as a remedy for discrimination, but this latter situation seems to be the only situation in which such plans may be barred, and even that is uncertain for reasons to be discussed below.

There are four significant decisions.

1. The decision in *Regents of the University of California v. Bakke* represents a brilliant exercise in judicial statesmanship, engineered primarily by Justice Lewis F. Powell. In that case, the University of California Medical School at Davis had set aside sixteen places out of 100 for minority students. Allan Bakke, a white student, was denied admission because he did not qualify for one of the remaining 84 places; his grades and scores were higher than the average of the sixteen special admittees. He charged the University with racial discrimination against him.

Four Justices found the programme illegal under a federal statute and never reached the constitutional issue. Four other Justices—Brennan, Marshall,

Blackmun and White—ruled that the normally strict scrutiny applicable to governmental classifications by race—characterized frequently in other contexts as " 'strict' in theory and fatal in fact"[14]—was inapplicable when the classification was designed to benefit groups suffering from societal discrimination. These four suggested that the "middle level" test—which requires only that the classification bear a substantial relation to an important governmental purpose[15]—was properly applicable, and for these Justices, the sixteen-seat set-aside met the standard.

Justice Powell walked a middle line. He first insisted that all racial classifications—even those favouring minorities—must meet the exacting strict scrutiny standard. He then declared that eradicating the general "societal" discrimination relied on by Justices Brennan *et al.* was an unacceptable goal and that fixed quotas were an unacceptable means. He found, however, that for a university, ethnic and racial diversity *was* an acceptable objective and that a flexible, individualized programme *taking race into account* was an acceptable means. Thus, Allan Bakke was admitted because the Davis plan was struck down, but race consciousness in university admission was also allowed.

While statesmanship in any setting can always be criticized for shortcomings in logic, accuracy, candor, and the like (and Justice Powell's opinion can be, and has been, on all of these grounds), the judgment was truly Solomonic: while criticizing "rigid quotas" and allowing Allan Bakke to enter, the decision also permitted state universities to continue affirmative actions plans if they wanted to. A survey one year later found that the decision had not discouraged any affirmative action by schools and colleges. Moreover, in the course of his opinion, Justice Powell also approved various other preferential plans where prior discrimination had actually been found by an appropriate governmental body.

2. *Fullilove v. Klutznick* (1980). The significance of this latter point came out two years later in the minority set-aside case. During debate in 1977 on a public works bill, an amendment was attached requiring ten percent of the contracts to be given to minority business enterprises; such programmes have also become common on the state and local level. The minority set-aside was promptly challenged as discriminatory against white contractors, but six members of the Court, in opinions by Chief Justice Burger for three, and by Justices Powell and Marshall, had no difficulty upholding the programme as justified by the long history of discrimination in the construction industry. Justice Powell found that what might be called a "rigid" ten percent was still "reasonably necessary" enough to meet even his conception of the strict scrutiny test.[16] The plan also survived criticisms from Justice Stevens in dissent that the beneficiaries were not themselves necessarily victims of the discrimination—this was a future-oriented plan where, as in most such

programs, the beneficiaries of the remedy may not be the same as the victims of the discrimination.

3. *United Steelworkers, Inc. v. Weber* (1979).[17] In the private sphere, a 5–2 majority of the Court has upheld a voluntarily adopted craft training programme which allocated half the trainee slots to blacks. No constitutional issue was at stake because all the parties were private entities, but the Court has subsequently declined opportunities to distinguish or overturn such voluntary employment plans when adopted by city agencies, which, like the University of California Regents in *Bakke,* are subject to constitutional restraints.

4. *Firefighters Local Union No. 1784 v. Stotts* (1984).[18] Finally, in the *Stotts* case in June 1984, the Court rules that when it is necessary to lay off workers in a setting where a court had already ordered hiring goals and timetables, if there is an applicable seniority provision, seniority must be followed in the layoffs, even if that eliminates the gains for minorities achieved by the hiring plan.

This result, though deplored by many civil rights activists, was not unexpected. Although not always sacrosanct, seniority is nevertheless a hard-won goal for many workers, and is often indispensable to countering employer arbitrariness with respect to promotions, assignments and other employee benefits. For these reasons, the Supreme Court has frequently upheld seniority rights, particularly in the civil rights context.[19]

What shocked many, however, was a quite gratuitous two and a half page discussion of the general remedial powers of federal courts, which seems to announce that Title VII forbids federal courts from ordering goals and timetable hiring programmes even after a finding of discrimination: "[T]he policy behind § 706 (g) of Title VII, which affects the remedies available in Title VII litigation . . . is to provide make-whole relief only to those who have been actual victims of illegal discrimination",[20] is the way Justice White put it.

Until *Stotts,* the federal Courts of Appeal had unanimously ruled that in employment discrimination cases brought under Title VII of the Civil Rights Act of 1964, federal courts could order certain percentages of minority or female hiring or promotion.[21] Justice White's pronouncement, which was quite unnecessary to the result, as Justice Stevens emphasized, put a cloud on hundreds of orders going back to 1969, arguably affirmed by Congress in 1972 when it expanded Title VII, and never even questioned by the Supreme Court despite numerous opportunities over the last fifteen years to do so.

The Court's pronouncement on this issue is not a square holding, and it could be receded from in the next case without much difficulty. Even if that does happen, however, the opinion has created much confusion and uncertainty. It has removed pressure on employers and unions to hire and promote minorities and women, or to settle employment discrimination litigation. It has also encouraged the Justice Department ot try to open up many of the scores of decrees entered during the last fifteen years ordering such relief.

Mr. Abram's constitutional opposition to such plans is thus in no way justified by the Supreme Court's view of "the basic bedrock of the Constitution." Nor is the history cited by Assistant Attorney General Reynolds any better. In January 1984, he told an audience of pre-law students that the Fourteenth Amendment was intended to bar taking race into account for any purpose at all—"we fought the Civil War" over that, he told *The New York Times*. If so, he knows something that the members of the 1865–66 Congress, who adopted that amendment and fought the war, did not: less than a month after Congress approved the Fourteenth Amendment in 1866, the very same Congress enacted eight laws exclusively for the freedmen, granting preferential benefits regarding land, education, banking facilities, hospitals, and more.[22] No comparable programmes existed or were established for whites. And that Congress did not act unthinkingly—the racial preferences involved in those programmes were vigorously debated with a vocal minority led by President Andrew Johnson, who argued that the preferences wrongly discriminated against whites.[23]

The Moral Issues

But law is not always the same as justice. If the case for affirmative aciton is morally flawed, then sooner or later, the law must change. What then is the moral case against preferences for disadvantaged groups in the allocation of opportunities and benefits?

The arguments are basically two-fold: (1) hiring and other distributional decisions should be made solely on the basis of "individual merit"; and (2) racial preferences are always evil and will take us back to *Plessy v. Ferguson*[24] and worse. Quoting Dr. Martin Luther King, Jr., Thurgood Marshall, and Roy Wilkins to support the claim that anything other than total race neutrality is "discriminatory", Assistant Attorney General Reynolds warns that race consciousness has "creat[ed] . . . a racial spoils system in America", "stifles the creative spirit", erects artificial barriers, and divides the society. It is, he says, unconstitutional, unlawful, and immoral. Ms. Midge Decter, writing in the *Wall Street Journal* a few years ago, sympathized with black and female beneficiaries of affirmative action programmes for the "self-doubts" and loss of "self-regard" that she is sure they suffer, "spiritually speaking", for their "unearned special privileges". Whenever we take race into account to hand out benefits, declares Linda Chavez, the Executive Director of the Reagan Civil Rights Commission, we "discriminate", "destroy[ing] the sense of self".

All of this represents the rankest form of hypocrisy. Despite Mr. Abram's condemnation of "separate lists", the Administration for which these people speak uses "separate lists' for blacks, Hispanics, women, Republicans, Democrats and any other group, whenever it finds that politically or otherwise useful. For example, does anyone believe that blacks like Civil Rights Commission Chairman Clarence Pendelton or Equal Employment Opportunities Commission Chairman Clarence Thomas were picked because of the color of their *eyes?* Or that Linda Chavez Gersten was made the new Executive Director of the Civil Rights Commission for reasons having nothing to do with the fact that her maiden and professional surname is Chavez?

Perhaps the most prominent recent example of affirmative action is President Reagan's selection of Sandra Day O'Conor for the Supreme Court. Obviously, she was on a "separate list", because on any unitary list this obscure lower-court state judge, with no federal experience and no national reputation, would never have come to mind as a plausible choice for the Nation's highest court. (Incidentally, despite Ms. Decter's, Mr. Reynolds', and Ms. Chavez's concern about the loss of "self-regard" suffered by beneficiaries of such preferences, "spiritually speaking" Justice O'Connor seems to be bearing her loss and "spiritual" pain quite easily.) And, like so many other beneficiaries of affirmative action given an opportunity that would otherwise be unavailable, she may indeed perform well. Mr. Reagan's fickleness on this issue has become so transparent that he was chastized for it by one of his own true believers, Civil Rights Commission Chairman Pendleton.

In fact, there is really nothing inherently wrong with taking group identity into account, so long as the person selected is qualified, a prerequisite that is an essential element of all affirmative action programmes. We do it all the time, with hardly a murmur of protest from anyone. We take group identity into account when we put together political slates, when a university gives preference to applicants from a certain part of the country or to the children of alumni, when Brandeis University restricts itself to Jews in choosing a president (as it did when it chose Morris Abram) or Notre Dame to Roman Catholics or Howard University to blacks, when this Administration finds jobs in government for children of cabinet members. Some of these examples are less laudable than others. But surely none of these seldom-criticized practices can be valued above the purpose of undoing the effects of past and present discrimination. In choosing a qualified applicant because of a race preference we merely acknowledge, as Morton Horwitz has pointed out, "the burdens, stigmas, and scars produced by history . . . the injustices heaped on his ancestors and, through them, on him. The history and culture of oppression, transmitted through legally anonymous generations, is made antiseptic when each individual is treated as a separate being, disconnected from history."[25]

In some cases, moreover, group-oriented choices are necessary for effective performance of the job. Justice Powell in the *Bakke* case stressed the importance of ethnic and other diversity for a university, as a justification for taking race into account as one factor in university admissions. Such considerations are particularly important in police work, where police-community cooperation is indispensable, and the absence of a fair proportion of minority police in cities like Detroit and New York has not only hindered law enforcement, but has produced violent police-minority confrontations.

For these reasons, it is hard to take at face value this zeal for "individual merit", when it is group identity that determines so many choices on all our parts. As Justice Powell noted in *Bakke,* America is indeed "a Nation of minorities, . . . a 'majority' composed of various minority groups."[26] But as Burke Marshall has observed,

The Constitution generally, and the Fourteenth Amendment specifically . . . do not mean that racial, cultural, ethnic, national, or even religious identification must be exluded from the considerations that lead to actions by government officials, or legislatures, reflecting the pluralism of American society. They cannot mean, for example, that decisions on judicial appointments, political candidates, cabinet officials at all levels, or even bureaucrats in the instrumentalities of the state can never reflect racial, ethnic, cultural, or religious constituencies. If these considerations are valid for the political apparatus of government, they must also be valid, so far as the constitutional command is concerned, for other state decisions with regard to who is, and who is not, included in the discretionary allocation of benefits and power.[27]

Is it not discriminatory against whites or males, however, to deny them something they might otherwise have gotten but for the color of their skin or their gender? Is it true, as Brian Weber's lawyer argued before the Supreme Court, that "you can't avoid discrimination by discriminating"? Will racially influenced hiring take us back to *Plessy v. Ferguson,* as Pendleton and Reynolds assert? Were Martin Luther King, Jr., Thurgood Marshall, Roy Wilkins and other black leaders really against it?

Hardly. Indeed, it is hard to contain one's outrage at this perversion of what Dr. King, Justice Marshall, and others have said, at this manipulation of their often sorrow-laden eloquence, in order to deny a handful of jobs, school admissions, and other necessities for a decent life to a few disadvantaged blacks out of the many who still suffer from discrimination and would have few opportunities otherwise.

Can anyone honestly equate a remedial preference for a disadvantaged (and qualified) minority member with the brutality inflicted on blacks and other minorities by racist laws and practices? The preference may take away some benefits from some white men, but none of them is being beaten, lynched, denied the right to use a bathroom, a place to sleep or eat, being forced to take the dirtiest jobs or denied any work at all, forced to attend dilapidated and mind-killing schools, subjected to brutally unequal justice, or stigmatized as an inferior being. Setting aside, after proof of discrimination, a few places a year for qualified minorities out of hundreds and perhaps thousands of employees, as in the Kaiser plant in the *Weber* case, or sixteen medical school places out of 100 as in *Bakke*, or ten percent of all federal public work contracts as in *Fullilove*, or even 50 percent of new hires, cannot be mentioned in the same breath with the brutalities that racism and sexism inflicted on helpless minorities and women. It is nothing short of a shameful insult to the memory of the tragic victims of such oppression to equate the two.

Indeed, the real issue in all matters of equality and fairness is not reflected in the tautological "equal means equal" proclaimed by Mr. Abram. Rather, as H.L.A. Hart and so many others have pointed out, although the "leading precept" of justice "is often formulated as 'Treat like cases alike' . . . we need to add to the latter 'and treat different cases differently.' "[28] When some have been handicapped severely and unfairly by an accidental fact of birth, to treat such "different cases" no differently from others without that handicap is to treat them unjustly. It is not only on the golf course that it is necessary to consider handicaps.

But even if it is not discriminatory, is affirmative action unfair to innocent whites or males? Should a white policeman or fire fighter with ten years in the department be laid off when a black or a woman will less seniority is kept because an affirmative action decree is in force? Aren't those denied a job or opportunity because of an affirmative action programme often innocent of any wrong against the preferred group and just as much in need of the opportunities?

The last question is the most troubling. Brian Weber was not a rich man and he had to support a family on a modest salary, just like any black worker. A craft job would have been a significant step up in money, status, and working conditions. And *he* hadn't discriminated against anyone. Why should he pay for Kaiser's wrongs?

A closer look at the *Weber* case brings some other factors to light, however. Even if there had been no separate list for blacks, Weber would not have gotten the position, for there were too many other whites ahead of him anyway. Moreover, but for the affirmative aciton plan, there would not have been any craft training programme at the plant at all, for *any* whites. The white workers had been unsuccessfully demanding a craft-training programme for years, but they finally got it only when Kaiser felt it necessary to adopt the affirmative action plan.

Furthermore, even with the separate list, the number of whites adversely affected was really very small. The Kaiser plan contemplated hiring only three to four minority members a year, out of a craft work force of 275–300 and a total work force of thousands. In the first year of its operation, Kaiser still selected only a handful of blacks, because it also brought in 22 outside craftsmen, of whom only one was black. In the 1980 *Fullilove* case, upholding the ten percent set-aside of federal public works projects for minority contractors, only 0.25 percent of the total annual expenditure for construction in the United States was involved. In *Bakke,* only sixteen places out of 100 at one medical school were set aside for minorities. A new Boston University special admissions programme for black medical students will start with three a year, with the hope of rising to ten, increasing the minority enrollment at the school by two percent.

The *Weber* case discloses another interesting aspect of affirmative action plans. Because such plans can adversely affect majority white males, creative ingenuity is often expended to prevent this from happening. In *Weber,* a new craft programme benefiting both whites and blacks was set up; in the lay-off cases, time sharing and other ways of avoiding the dismissals—including raising more money—can be devised. So much for Mr. Reynold's worries about "stifling" creativity.

Strains can and do result, especially if deliberately stirred up. But strain is not inevitable: broad-ranging goals and timetable programmes for women and blacks were instituted in the Bell Telephone Company with no such troubles. The same holds true elsewhere, especially when, as in *Weber,* the programme creates new, previously unavailable opportunities for whites. Conversely, even if, as the Reagan Administration urges, the remedies are limited to specific identifiable victims of discriminatory practices, some whites may be upset. If a black applicant can prove that an employer wrongly discriminated against him personally, he would be entitled to the seniority and other benefits that he would have had but for the discrimination—with the Administration's blessing—and this would give him competitive seniority over some white employees, regardless of those employees' innocence. The same thing happens constantly with veterans and other preferences, and few opponents of affirmative action seem to be upset by that.

Among some Jews, affirmative action brings up bitter memories of ceiling quotas, which kept them out of schools and jobs that could on merit have been theirs. This has produced a serious and nasty split within the American civil rights movement. But affirmative action goals and timetables are really quite different. Whereas quotas against Jews, Catholics, and others were ceilings to limit and keep these groups *out* of schools and jobs, today's "benign preferences" are designed to be the floors that let minorities *into* a few places they would not ordinarily enter, and with relatively little impact on others. This distinction between inclusive and exclusionary practices is central.[29]

There is also a major confusion, exploited by opponents, resulting from the fact that we are almost all ethnic or religious minorities. Of course we are. And if it were shown that any minority is being victimized by intentional discrimination and that the only way to get more of that minority into a relatively representative portion of the work force or school is through an affirmative action plan, then these people would be entitled to such a remedy.

Group thinking is of course at odds with an individualistic strain that runs deep in American society. But individualism is only one strain among many. And what civil rights is all about, as many have emphasized, is an effort to undo a certain vicious strain of group thinking that established discriminatory *systems*. From *Brown v. Board of Education* on, civil rights decress have been aimed at dismantling racists systems against groups. Obviously, these racist systems hurt individual group members, and individuals bring the law suits, but even in *Brown,* the "all deliberate speed" remedy gradually dismantling the segregated school systems was future-oriented, with the particular plaintiffs not necessarily the actual beneficiaries: in many cases, only future classes of black children would be allowed in a school to be gradually integrated, not the particular plaintiffs. The same logic applies to systems of allocating jobs and other benefits that systematically discriminated against and exluded people because they were members of minority groups.[30]

For the fact is that the centuries of injustice have created deeply imbedded abuses, and the plight of black Americans not only remains grave, but in many respects, it is getting worse. The black unemployment rate—21 percent in early 1983—is consistently double that for whites and the spread is not shrinking. For black males, the rate—an awful 30 percent—is almost triple that for whites; for black teenagers the rate approaches 50 percent. More than half of all black children under three years of age live in homes below the poverty line. The gap between black and white family income, which prior to the '70s had narrowed a bit, has steadily edged wider, so that black family income is now only 55 percent that of whites. Only three percent of the nation's lawyers and doctors are black and only four percent of its managers, but over 50 percent of its maids and garbage collectors. Black life expectancy is about six years less than that of whites; the black infant mortality rate is nearly double.[31]

Although the situation for women, of all races, is not as bad, women generally still earned only 60–65 percent as much as their male counterparts, and in recent years black women have earned only 84 percent of the white female's incomes. The economic condition of black women, who now head 41 percent of the 6.4 million black families, is particularly bad. A recent Wellesley College study found that black women are not only suffering in the labour market, but they receive substantially less public assistance and child support than white women. The condition of female household heads of any race is troubling: 90 percent of the 8.4 million single parent homes are headed by women, and more than half are below the poverty line.

Affirmative action helps. For example, from 1974 to 1980 minority employment with employers subject to federal affirmative action requirements rose twenty percent, almost twice the increase elsewhere. The employment of women by covered contractors rose fifteen percent, but only two percent among others.[32] The number of black police officers nationwide rose from 24,000 in 1970 to 43,500 in 1980; that kind of increase in Detroit produced a sharp decline in citizen hostility toward the police and a concomitant increase in police efficiency. There were also large jumps in minority and female employment among fire fighters, and sheet metal and electrical workers.

Few other remedies work as well or as quickly. As the New York City Corporation Counsel told the Supreme Court about the construction industry in the *Fullilove* case, "less drastic means of attempting to eradicate and remedy discrimination have been repeatedly and continuously made over the past decade and a half. They have all failed." Where affirmative action is ended, progress often stops.[33]

An example from a state like Alabama illustrates the value of affirmative action quotas. Alabama, led by such arch-segregationists as George C. Wallace, had always excluded blacks from any but the most menial state jobs. In the late 1960s, a federal court found that only 27 of 3,000 clerical and managerial employees were black. Federal Judge Frank Johnson ordered extensive recruiting of blacks, as well as the hiring of the few specific identified individual blacks who could prove they were the victims of discrimination; these are, of course, the remedies currently urged by the Justice Department.

Nothing happened. Another suit was filed, this time just against the state police, and this time a 50 percent hiring quota was imposed, until blacks reached 25 percent of the force. Today, Alabama has the most thoroughly integrated state police force in the country, with 20–25 percent of the force black. A threat of such quotas in other agencies has also produced substantial improvements.[34]

Reasonable people will continue to differ about the appropriateness of affirmative action. Color blindness and neutrality are obviously the ultimate goal, and it was one of Martin Luther King, Jr.'s dreams. But it still remains only a dream, and until it comes closer to reality, affirmative action plans are necessary and appropriate. One cannot undo centuries of discrimination by simply saying "stop"—one has to take into account the harm that those centuries have brought, and try to make up for it. Otherwise, we in the United States will remain like Disraeli's "Two Nations."

First Fired: Which Should Decide?
Seniority or Affirmative Action

Seniority: *Firefighters* v. *Stotts* *

Justice White delivered the opinion of the Court. . . . The issue at the heart of this case is whether the District Court exceeded its powers in entering an injunction requiring white employees to be laid off, when the otherwise applicable seniority system would have called for the layoff of black employees with less seniority. We are convinced that the Court of Appeals erred in resolving this issue and in affirming the District Court. . . .

The difficulty with . . . (the Court of Appeals) approach is that it overstates the authority of the trial court to disregard a seniority system in fashioning a remedy after a plaintiff has successfully proved that an employer has followed a pattern or practice having a discriminatory effect on black applicants or employees. If individual members of a plaintiff class demonstrate that they have been actual victims of the discriminatory practice, they may be awarded competitive seniority and given their rightful place on the seniority roster. . . .

Here there was no finding that any of the blacks protected from layoff had been a victim of discrimination . . . it is inappropriate to deny an innocent employee the benefits of his seniority in order to provide a remedy in a pattern or practice case such as this.

---

* U.S. Supreme Court, *Firefighters Local Union No. 1784* v. *Stotts et al.* No. 82–206, together with *Memphis Fire Department et al.* v. *Stotts et al.* (June 1984).

First Fired: Which Should Decide?
Seniority or Affirmative Action

Affirmative Action, With Compensation for White Males: *Vulcan Pioneers* v. *N.J. Department of Civil Service* *

SAROKIN, District Judge:—This matter presents to the court one of the most difficult and troubling issues facing the judiciary today. Either by court order or consent decree, minorities have been hired as police officers and firefighters in major cities throughout the country. The clear purpose of such orders was and is to affirmatively correct the imbalances which have resulted from a history of discriminatory practices in the hiring and promotion of minorities.

Many of these orders, including the one here at issue, do not provide for the specific procedures to be followed in the event of layoffs. If the dictates of seniority are to govern, then minorities, being the most recently hired, will be laid off and the goals of affirmative action undermined. If, on the other hand, an attempt is made to protect such minority hires, then persons with greater seniority will be compelled to forfeit positions guaranteed by contract and statute. It is the tension between these two alternatives which renders the resolution of this problem so difficult.

The court, however, is convinced that adherence to strict contractual and statutory seniority requirements in determining who shall go and who shall stay cannot be permitted. The affirmative action plan embodied in the consent decree between the parties and the hirings pursuant thereto would be substantially eradicated thereby. The gains contemplated and those achieved would be lost. Furthermore, a municipality or the state would be able to avoid the effect of such an order or decree merely by withholding the funds necessary

---

* Reprinted from *Vulcan Pioneers* v. *N.J. Dept. of Civil Service, Fair Employment Practice Cases* 34 (19 May 1984): 1239.

to effectuate it. This type of unilateral action should not be permitted to thwart a judicial order or to justify the breach of a consent decree.

Affirmative action plans arose out of the recognition that this nation had oppressed its minority citizens, either purposefully or through the operation of more subtle social and economic forces. These plans seek more than to remove the nation's heel from the backs of minorities, but to reach down and to lift up those persons who have been deprived and discriminated against for centuries. The plans recognize the insufficiency of merely removing existing barriers. Affirmative action is necessary in order that historical imbalances and inequities not be prolonged well into the future.

Having recognized that obligation and acted upon it, are we to undo it in the face of economic reductions? Indeed, in hard economic times, it has always been the minorities who have suffered the most. It would be a dreadful step backwards to permit mass layoffs of minorities in light of the progress so recently achieved and so long in coming.

Changes in administration, changes in the composition of the Civil Rights Commission, indeed, changes in the government's position in this very litigation, should not alter the fundamental principles here involved. We cannot and should not retreat from our commitment to right the wrongs of the past. To permit layoffs based solely on seniority denies these principles and mocks the ideals of justice and equality which are the foundation of our Constitution and of the Civil Rights Acts.

By virtue of this determination, certain firefighters and police officers with greater seniority will be required to forfeit their positions. Were it not for the consent decree, these firefighters and police officers would be entitled to retain their positions under existing collective bargaining agreements and New Jersey civil service law. Though not themselves the perpetrators of the wrongs inflicted upon minorities over the years, these senior firefighters are being singled out to suffer the consequences. In effect, they are being required to hand over their jobs and paychecks to someone else. It is inconceivable that they can be asked to do this in the name of the public good, and yet not have the public assume the responsibility therefor. If we need to raze buildings to make way for a highway, to acquire land for a school or to obtain food to feed the poor, we do not simply take it from those who have it. What is involved in such cases is a taking of private property, and the Constitution requires that just compensation be paid.

Such a taking also occurs when the federal government, pursuant to civil rights legislation brings a lawsuit to enforce those laws and enters into a consent decree which adversely affects the contractual and statutory rights of private individuals. In such a situation, it is the federal government which must assume the resulting liability. It would be senseless to impose such liability upon the municipalities involved. Layoffs made in good faith, for economic reasons, may not be prohibited, for to do so would deny cities the right to reduce expenses. Moreover, if these municipalities could afford to pay just compensation, then they could afford to retain the workers. Requiring cities to pay persons whom they laid off because they could not afford to keep them would be ludicrous.

The court is therefore satisfied that the federal government must compensate senior firefighters laid off as a result of the application of the consent decree. The compensation to be paid is outlined below. However, the court recognizes that such compensation is small consolation to those who will nonetheless lose their jobs. Displaced senior firefighters and their families may well ask, "Why us?"

No truly satisfactory answer exists. Their perception of the unfairness visited upon them cannot be dissipated by a discussion of principle or of broad social goals. They cannot be expected to understand why they should pay for what others have wrought or why they should be singled out and forced to make an involuntary contribution to a cause not their own, no matter how worthy that cause may be.

If the analogy to taking for highway purposes is apt, then those whose homes are taken probably pose the same question. Compensation is not adequate reparation for the personal displacement and upset, and the need for a public corridor does not allay their personal loss. Affirmative action is also a highway of sorts. It provides an avenue of hope, a road to equality. However, to ignore the grief and anger of those who fall in its path is to be blind to a poignant reality of our times. One can only hope that those called upon to make the sacrifice will not permit it to escalate the very prejudice which it seeks to undo. They must recognize that affirmative action is likewise small compensation for those who are descendants of slavery and have continued to be the victims of insidious bondage for generations since its abolition. . . .

It is the intention of the court that, in the event of layoffs, the same proportion of minorities survive reductions in force as were employed prior to such reductions. Only to the extent the hiring goals were actually achieved shall they therefore be maintained. Those who are kept and those who are not will be determined in accordance with seniority to the maximum extent possible. It is only if this results in a disproportionate effect upon minority employees that an adjustment need be made, and such adjustment should itself reflect employees' respective seniority positions. Thus, as between two nonminority employees, one of whom must be laid off in order to maintain the proper proportion of minority firefighters, the least senior must go. Furthermore, the system here put in place by the court is, of course, meant to be temporary. When, in the course of time, minority firefighters attain the seniority rightfully theirs, this kind of relief will no longer be necessary, for they will then be laid off, in the event of economic hardship, in the proper proportions. In the meantime, however, a system is necessary that will protect the affirmative action plan now in place and just beginning to have its effect. . . .

The court also concludes that those firefighters who have or will forfeit their seniority rights as a result of the affirmative action plan discussed above ought to be compensated and that such compensation ought to come from the federal government. . . .

The amount of such compensation must, however, be "just." It is not intended to be a lifetime pension. Those senior firefighters who are laid off as a result of the affirmative action plan shall be under a duty to mitigate damages, by seeking to obtain other employment. Any claim for compensation shall be reduced by the amount of salaries or any benefits received as a result of such layoff. Moreover, the period of compensation shall end upon the attainment of other employment, but, absent exceptional circumstances, no later than one year from the date of layoff. . . .

This country owes a debt to its minority citizens to compensate them for generations of degradation and deprivation. That debt is being partially repaid by providing opportunities heretofore denied. To withdraw those opportunities now constitutes a denial of our democratic principles and a breach of faith to those who have fought and even died for them and to whom we promised that tomorrow would be better.

[Ed. Note: Judge Sarokin "reluctantly" reversed this federal district court ruling in June, 1984, shortly after the Supreme Court decided that during a budget crisis, layoffs by seniority could not be altered to protect affirmative action plans. Judge Sarokin stated that "cities or states bent upon discriminatory practices" now could "continue to do so under the guise of economic reduction" and "women and minorities will be the first to go." (New York Times 22 June 1984).]

First Fired: Which Should Decide?
Seniority or Affirmative Action

Affirmative Action, With Compensation for White Males*

Howard Glickstein _____

One possible way of conducting a layoff is to have a list of black males, a list of black females, and a list of white males, and then the persons would be laid off in proportion to their proportion in the general work force of the population. . . . The United Auto Workers suggested that if you are going to provide some special benefit to the victims of discrimination and that is going to affect some identifiable white males, it's only fair that the employer bear that burden because, after all, the employer did discriminate. And the United Auto Workers suggested that, in a layoff situation, if you decide to use some sort of proportional layoff and, as a result, some white males get laid off who would not have been laid off under the other method, then the white males should somehow be compensated for it by the employers. . . .

I think we should perhaps think . . . in terms of some sort of program, some sort of Federal program, that will somehow compensate the individuals who are going to be displaced as a result of some affirmative effort. For example, some years ago there was a great concern with automating the procedures on the New York waterfront, and there was enormous hostility by the unions to any sort of automation because that was going to result in many job losses. But finally, when some program which was heavily subsidized by the Government was developed which provided compensation for those people affected by the automation, that program was carried forward.

---

* U.S. Commission on Civil Rights, *Last Hired, First Fired* (Washington, D.C.: U.S. Government Printing Office, 1976). Excerpts of statements by Howard Glickstein.

Similarly, I think we have some program on the books at the present time that compensates businesses that suffer as a result of Government trade policies, where, as a result of some trade policy that favors products from foreign countries, some businesses suffer, that we have a program to compensate businessmen.

So what I am suggesting is that maybe there should be some sort of Federal program that is directly intended to deal with dislocations that occur as a result of implementing affirmative action programs, whether they are hiring programs or layoff programs.

A Preventive Remedy: Worksharing*

The controversy over seniority (and affirmative action) obscures the basic fact that employee layoffs themselves . . . may be forestalled or minimized by various means. . . . (Many) collective bargaining agreements . . . provide for "worksharing" (spreading the available work or hours of work). . . .

A task force appointed by the Governor of New York has considered subsidizing workers who accept a 4-day week by supplementing their wages with unemployment insurance benefits for the fifth day. . . . For example, any worker, whether public or private, who regularly earns $150 a week would get 4 days' pay of $120 under such a plan, plus an unemployment insurance benefit—half his or her regular pay rate—of $15.

Since the unemployment benefit is tax-exempt, the worker would pay lower Federal, State and city taxes, for a savings of $4 or $5 per week. Additional savings would result from a reduction in work-related expenses such as transportation and food. The Governor's task force estimated that the average worker's week would thus have a value of at least $141—and the worker would have an extra day off.

The proposal would avert layoffs that under usual seniority rules disproportionately affect younger persons, minorities, and women and enable employers to hold their regular forces instead of having to recruit new employees when their business improved. . . .

In addition to the proposed use of unemployment insurance to compensate those who work a reduced work week, another suggested incentive for worksharing efforts is tax relief for employers who maintain full benefits for workers who work less than full time under a worksharing plan. . . .

It must be emphasized that worksharing and other alternatives to layoffs are by no means permanent cure-alls for the problem of layoffs. As one study observed, "Where business conditions require a drastic cut in work force

---

* U.S. Commission on Civil Rights, *Last Hired, First Fired* (Washington, D.C.: U.S. Government Printing Office, 1977), 49–54.

size," and in an industry suffering long-term and apparently irreversible decline, the use of alternatives "will serve only to minimize or delay the impact of layoffs."

Nonetheless, as a 1975 conference in New York revealed, some form of worksharing is particularly well-suited for pieceworkers, hourly workers, salaried employees, and in manufacturing, service industries, and nonprofit settings such as universities and public employment. These include the industries and occupations employing relatively large numbers of minorities and women.

Notes

1.   Gregory Vlastos, "Justice and Equality," *Social Justice,* ed. Richard B. Brandt, (Englewood Cliffs, N.J.: Prentice-Hall, 1962), 31–72.

2.   Vlastos actually argues that *all* justified exceptions to equal distribution, those based on differences in merit as well as those based on differences in need, have a common equalitarian ground. If true, this claim would provide even stronger reason to reject the view that racial and sexual groups can qualify for distributive justice than what has been said so far. However, since Vlastos' argument concerning merit is rather intricate, and since the considerations already raised seem quite sufficient to disqualify those groups from deserving distributive justice, I will not pursue this point further.

3.   This conclusion is borne out by our intuitions in simple cases. If A is deprived of a month's social security benefits by a malicious clerk while B is deprived of a similar amount by a merely careless clerk, our reaction is surely that despite the clear difference in the clerks' intentions, both A and B deserve precisely what has been withheld from them, perhaps including interest, and nothing more.

4.   The argument of this section is related to, yet distinct from, an argument advanced by Robert Simon in his "Preferential Hiring: a reply to Judith Jarvis Thomson," *Philosophy and Public Affairs,* vol. 3, no. 3 (Fall 1974), 312–20. Simon contends that (a) it is not *obvious* that the preferential treatment of group members could serve to compensate a wronged group, and that (b) at least in the case of preferential hiring, this is unlikely because "preferential hiring policies award compensation to an arbitrarily selected segment of the group; namely those who have the ability and qualifications to be seriously considered for the jobs available" (315). My contention, by contrast, is that even if all the members of a particular disadvantaged group were compensated, the procedure would still be arbitrary in that it would stop short of compensating the equally deserving members of *other* disadvantaged groups.

5.   I have benefitted from helpful discussion of these topics with Michael Levin and William E. Mann.

6.   The Caste System: See William Ryan, *Equality* (New York: Pantheon Books, 1981), 140. The unemployment comparison between blacks with some college education and white high-school dropouts: See "Students, Graduates and Dropouts in the Labor Market," *Special Labor Force Reports, Monthly Labor Review* (October 1979). (Table reprinted in *State of Black America,* National Urban League, 1982.)

7.   Nathan Glazer, *Affirmative Discrimination,* (New York, Basic Books, 1975), 203.

8.   Housing discrimination. *Racism in America and How to Combat It,* U.S. Commission on Civil Rights (January 1970); J. and C. Feagin, *Discrimination, American Style* (Englewood Cliffs, N.J.: Prentice-Hall), chap. 4.

9.   Seniority and affirmative action. *Last Hired, First Fired; Layoffs and Civil Rights,* U.S. Commission on Civil Rights (February 1977), chap. 2.

10.   *University of California Regents* v. *Bakke,* 438 *U.S. 265,* 407 (1978).

11.   *Id.,* at 401 (Marshall, J., concurring).

12.   *New York Times,* 18 January 1984, p. 1, col. 1.

13.   *Fullilove* v. *Klutznick,* 448 *U.S.* 448, 534 n. 5 (Stevens, J., dissenting).

14.   G. Gunther, "Foreword: In Search of Evolving Doctrine on a Changing Court: A Model for a Newer Equal Protection," 86 *Harv. L. Rev.* 1 (1972).

15.   *Craig* v. *Boren,* 429 *U.S.* 190 (1976).

16.   448 *U.S.,* at 496–97 (Powell, J., concurring).

17.   443 *U.S.* 193 (1979).

18.   52 *U.S.L.W.* 4767 (12 June 1984).

19.   *International Brhd. of Teamsters* v. *U.S.* 431 *U.S.* 324 (1977).

20.   52 U.S.L.W., at 4772.

21.   *See* cases cited by Justice Blackmun, *id.,* at 4781, n. 10.

22.   *See, e.g.,* Act of 16 July 1866, 14 *Stat.* 173 (Freedmen's Bureau).

23.   *See* the discussion in Justice Marshall's opinion in Bakke, 438 *U.S.,* at 396–98.

24.   163 *U.S.* 537 (1896).

25.   M.J. Horwitz, "The Jurisprudence of *Brown* and the Dilemmas of Liberalism," 14 *Harv. Civ. Rts.-Civ. Libs. L. Rev.* 599, 610 (1979).

26.   438 *U.S.,* at 292.

27.   B. Marshall, "A Comment on the Nondiscrimination Principle in *'Nation of Minorities,'* " 93 *Yale L.J.* 1006, 1011 (1984).

28.   H.L.A. Hart, *The Concept of Law* 155 (1961).

29.   Marshall, *supra* note 18, at 1011–1012.

30.   *Id.,* at 1007–1008.

31.   These statistics are drawn from various sources, but the primary source is the Urban League's annual, *The State of Black America.*

32.   *Washington Post,* 20 June 1983, p. A3.

33.   *Wall St., J.* 10 August 1984, p. 31 (decline in minority government contracts upon termination of set-asides).

34.   Huron, "But Government *Can* Help," *Washington Post,* 12 August 1984, p. B1.

PART 8

WORKERS' SELF-MANAGEMENT

The Spring of Freedom: Spain 1936 *

Gaston Laval _____

On February 14 and 15, 1937 the Constitutive Congress of the Aragon Federation of Collectives took place in Caspe, a small town . . . which had been freed of the fascists by forces coming from Catalonia. . . . At that time collectivism was a reality and in full swing. In Graus as in many other places in Aragon application of socialism started with the organization of the agrarian Collective. Faced with the gravity of the situation. The revolutionary *Comité* dealt first with the most important and urgent needs. The harvest had to be gathered, the land cultivated and sown and maximum returns obtained from reduced efforts, seeing how many young men had been taken away by the demands of war. By the efforts of comrades of the U.G.T. and C.N.T., the old swing-ploughs drawn by a donkey were discarded, the strongest ranking animals were rounded up and set to work with the best ploughs on the land from which the boundary hedges had been grubbed up. The land was then sown with corn. The agrarian Collective was constituted on October 16, 1936 barely three months after the fascist attack. On the same day, the means of transport were officially collectivised though they had been in fact almost from the beginning. Other new steps were decided upon, in accordance with suggestions made by the two syndicates—the one socialist, the other libertarian. The socialisation of the printing industry was decided on on November 24. It was followed two days later by that of the shoe shops and bakers.

On December 1st it was the turn of the businessmen, doctors, chemists, blacksmiths, and locksmiths. On December 11th, that of the cabinet makers and carpenters. Gradually all the social activities entered the new organism.

The Resolution voted by the agricultural workers allows one to get a clearer picture of the basic outlines and general principles of the collectivisations

* Reprinted from Gaston Laval, *Collectives in the Spainish Revolution,* trans. Vernon Richards (London: Freedom Press, 1975), 83–112, by permission of the publisher. Copyright © 1975 by Freedom Press.

that followed, since in all cases their principles were more or less the same. This is the text:

"Agricultural workers, meeting in Graus on 16 Obtober, 1936 resolve as follows:

1. They join the general Community of all trades;

2. All the members join the Community of their free will; they are expected to bring their tools;

3. All the land of comrades entering the Community must be handed over to increase the common wealth;

4. When agricultural workers have no work to do, it is obligatory that they help in other trades which might have need of their labour;

5. An inventory in duplicate will be made of the land and chattels that have been brought to the Collectivity; one copy will be given to the owner of those properties and the other will remain in the hands of the Collective;

6. If for unforeseeable reasons the Collective were to be dissolved, each comrade will have the indisputable right to the land and goods he had brought to the Collective;

7. Members will nominate, at their meeting, the administrative Commission for their trade;

8. When agricultural workers have reached agreement on this latter point, they will have to nominate an administrative Commission composed of a chairman, treasurer, a secretary and three members;

9. This agrarian Collective will maintain direct relations with the communal Bank of all the assembled trades, which will be set up by the liaison *Comité;*

10. Workers who come to work collectively will receive the following wages: for families of three people or less, six pesetas a day; those consisting of more than three people will receive an additional peseta a day for each of them;

11. The wage can be modified according to the circumstances and at the suggestion of the administrative Commission of all the assembled trades;

12. Workers whose relatives do not belong to the Collective will receive wages to be established by the *Comité;*

13. The expulsion of a member of the Collective will have to be decided by the central Commission of all the trades, to which the agricultural section also belongs;

14. The members of the Collective undertake to work as many hours as the administrative Commission, in agreement with the local central Commission, will consider necessary, and it is vital that they should work with interest and enthusiasm.

Duly informed and in full agreement, the agricultural workers take cognizance of this Resolution."

This document as all the others of a similar nature—only in Alcorisa will one find an exception to the rule—was drafted by peasants who were not literate persons, and even made frequent spelling mistakes; one could also object to clumsiness in the drafting of the text, or to ambiguities in the terms used. Nevertheless the essential tasks are defined and practice would clarify and sharpen the thinking.

As a contribution to this clarification, it should be said that no collectivisation was carried out independently of the will of the people concerned. . . . But . . . the mayor was only a figurehead; he simply applied the decisions taken by the majority of the municipal Council which had to represent the Central government, to call up conscripts for the war, furnish identity documents, establish rationing for all the inhabitants of the village, individualists and collectivists. The Collective was only answerable to itself. . . .

The whole economic machine—production, exchanges, means of transport, distribution—was in the hands of twelve employees, who kept separate books and card-index files for each activity. Day by day, everything was recorded and allocated: turnover and reserves of consumer goods and raw materials, cost prices and selling prices, summarised income and outgoings, profit or loss noted for each enterprise or activity.

And as ever, the spirit of solidarity was present, not only between the Collective and each of its components, but between the different branches of the economy. The losses incurred by a particular branch, considered useful and necessary, were made up by the profits earned by another branch. Take, for instance, the hairdressing section. The shops kept open all day and operated at a loss. On the other hand drivers' activities were profitable, as was that for the production of alcohol for medical and industrial purposes. So these surpluses were used in part to compensate the deficit on the hairdressing establishments. It was also by this juggling between the sections, that pharmaceutical products were bought for everybody and machines for the peasants.

. . . (A) spring discharged in the depression of a large estate which its owner divided into parcels and let for rent. This jealous cantankerous man refused to allow people to go and drink the water because to reach it they had to take a path which crossed a hedge skirting a field and a small forest which were his property. Even his tenant farmers on hot days could not use it to slake their thirst. Nevertheless, quite frequently, and understandably, people disobeyed the owner's injunctions. So the chap had his way by having the orifice of the spring sealed off.

But the revolution changed the roles. Among the measures taken by the Revolutionary *Comité,* to the great joy of so many people, was the expropriation of the estate of that stiff-necked egoist and also the public enjoyment of the forbidden spring. It was decided to build, even through the hedges, a fine winding path down to the sparkling water; and the former proprietor had to take part in the work with those who had been his tenant farmers. When all was completed, and with that love which water arouses in Spain—and in so many other countries!—a marble plaque was placed above the sparkling jet. What I read, in golden letters, was: "The Spring of Freedom, 19 July 1936."

(In Fraga) as was the case everywhere, solidarity was extended in all directions. The members of ninety families who for various reasons such as illness, death of the principal breadwinner, etc. were condemned to poverty under the individualist society, were receiving the "credit" established for everybody. The militiamen's families were supported in the same way. A final achievement completes this story of mutual aid in action.

A number of old folk, men and women, abandoned by everybody, sad human flotsam of a society in which misfortune is one of the natural elements had come to Fraga from smaller and poorer villages. It was for these unfortunates that a *Casa de los Ancianos* (Old Folk's Home) was organised and at the time of my visit there were thirty-two of them staying there. They had rooms (or small dormitories), a dining room, a sitting room with a large open fire, the whole place was kept spick and span and reflected the warmth and cordiality of the welcome. . . .

I asked them about the way they were being treated. One of them summed up the view of all with the conciseness recommended by the Aragonese writer Baltasar Gracian, *Lo bueno, si breve, dos veces bueno* (the good, if brief, is doubly good) when he said: "We cannot complain neither of the food, nor the wine, nor the beds, nor of the love."

Why Should the Workplace Be Democratic?*

John Plamenatz _____

(In a community) citizens acting together might be just as competent, just as well informed and wise in reaching their decisions as elected representatives would be. There decisions would not be decisions for experts to take, though no doubt often better taken after listening to expert advice.

When we pass from communities to mere organizations, and in particular to productive enterprises, the case is different. Their essential purpose is not to look after the welfare of their members but to provide outsiders with specific goods or services. The rulers of a community, since their business is to lay down rules and to define standards that members of the community or some part of them must observe or meet in pursuing their purposes, or else to decide what services the community is to provide them, take decisions different in kind from those taken by the managers of productive and specific-service enterprises. Their business is a different kind of business. That, no doubt, is why we call it government rather than management, whereas we call the persons who run, say, a factory or a bank (or a chain of them) its managers rather than its governors or rulers. The business of managers is both narrower and more a matter for experts than is the business of government; the services or other benefits managers provide are highly specific, and they have to decide how best to provide them with the resources at their disposal. Managers do not, except within narrow limits, have to decide what services or benefits to provide; they do not have to decide between a wide variety of claims for benefits, of which only some can be satisfied. Most important of all in this context, the benefits they provide are not primarily for the members of the organizations they control. This is as much so when the

* © M E Plamenatz 1975. Reprinted from *Karl Marx's Philosophy of Man* by John Plamenatz (1975) by permission of Oxford University Press.

organizations are not profit-making as when they are, and as much so when they are public as when they are private.

Why, then, if productive and service enterprises differ so much from communities, should they too be democratic? Why should their members run them, or why should their managers be responsible to the members for how they run them? The case for popular government inside a community is, surely, different from the case for popular management in a factory or bank or army or administrative department. Only in small self-sufficing communities which are also multi-purpose productive enterprises, communities of the kind described by some of the Utopians, are government and management scarcely distinguishable, so that popular government is virtually also popular management. But we are now speaking of developed industrial societies.

Many people today, even when they are not socialists, agree that the private owners of an enterprise, or (as is more often the case) the directors nominally responsible to the owners, ought to be fairly strictly controlled in the uses they make of the resources at their disposal. Ordinarily, they favour this control, not because the responsibility of directors and managers to owners is often minimal, but because they believe it to be in the public interest. This control would, presumably, still be necessary in the public interest, even if the enterprise were owned by the workers inside it. Their owning it would not, in itself, bring it any more under 'public ownership and control' than if it were owned by shareholders who took its profits without working in it. Nor would it necessarily ensure that the enterprise was run more for the benefit of the community as a whole.

The claim that members of an autonomous community, if it is to a considerable extent self-sufficing, should collectively own the natural resources and instruments of production inside it, and should be free to use them as they think fit to their own best advantage, is at least plausible, even though also disputable.[1] The same (or rather, a similar) claim made for the workers in a productive enterprise or other such organization is not nearly as plausible. It may be in the public interest that the managers running such organizations should have a considerable autonomy, that they should not be too strictly controlled: but it is not obvious that this is any more so when the managers are the workers themselves or agents responsible to them. The interests of the workers in an organization, productive or not, can run counter to the public interest just as the interests of shareholders can. Even if it were true that the larger a social class, the less its interests (the interests shared by all its members) conflict with the public interest, it would not follow that the interests of small sections of a large class conflict with it less than do the interests of small sections of a smaller class. Nor is it obvious that the interests of separate organizations are less likely to conflict with one another when the organizations are run by their members than when they are not.

Socialists and anarchists too often speak as if this were obvious, especially when the members are manual workers.

Socialists who believe that justice requires that the profits of an enterprise (or what remains of them after paying taxes and providing for investment) should be shared among the workers in it need not hold that the workers should run the enterprise. A case still has to be made for their doing so. Besides, many organizations make no profits and do not provide goods or services paid for by the recipients. Some are run by governments, directly or indirectly, while others are privately controlled charitable corporations. Should they too be run democratically by the men and women who work in them? Can they be so, except to a limited extent, if they are to provide efficiently the services which it is their business to provide?

Of course, efficiency and the prevention of exploitation are not the only relevant considerations, and there are people willing to pay a considerable price in efficiency for other things. It also matters that the worker should be his own master at work, which nowadays he can seldom be on his own but only along with his companions at work. To many radicals this has seemed far and away the best reason for having industrial democracy or, as it is sometimes called, 'self-management'—presumably because it is held to be as desirable outside industry as in it. Self-management, so its champions say, may quite often promote efficiency but is also worth having when it does not. It enhances the workers' sense of their own dignity and weakens their sense of being at the mercy of events beyond their control.

I do not deny that these are great benefits, and may well be worth as much in many workers' eyes as substantial increases in material welfare. I merely inquire how far, and by what means, they are to be attained in advanced industrial societies.

No matter how much the workers run the organizations they work in, the decisions they take are the decisions of managers, and are restricted in many ways. Running a factory or bank, or even a branch of industry or commerce, is essentially different from running or controlling an economy, and the need to control the economy is not—as far as I can see—in any way diminished by putting the enterprises of which it consists under the management of the workers in them. Either the economy is effectively controlled, in which case the managers of enterprises, whether they are capitalists or workers (or their representatives), receive directives from the controllers of the economy; or the economy is not effectively controlled and the sense that the workers have of being at the mercy of events beyond their control is as great as ever. As the early socialists and Marx noticed, the capitalists too are at the mercy of events. Thus, in this respect, nothing is gained by putting the workers in the place of the capitalist, by ensuring that collectively they exercise his functions. On the other hand, if the economy is effectively controlled in the service of ends they understand and approve, their sense of being at the mercy of events is presumably diminished, even though they have no say in running the organizations they work in.

Marx and others have spoken of the workers' controlling 'production', and have presumably had in mind their controlling the economy as a whole and not just particular enterprises within it. But how, exactly, would the workers' control of 'the economy' differ from its control by a democratic state?[2] It could hardly be smaller in scale. Would it be less bureaucratic? It is not easy to see why it should be. If it were considerably decentralized, operating at several different levels, and at the same time reasonably efficient, it might need to be very bureaucratic, and the workers might feel about their delegates and agents pretty much as citizens do about their representatives in the 'bourgeois' democracies of the West.

Still, even if radicals have over-estimated the extent to which workers' control of the economy could be less bureaucratic and more genuinely popular than government is in the liberal bourgeois state, it may yet be the case that workers' control of the organizations they work in is both possible and desirable. There is still the claim that it makes them their own masters at work.

No doubt it does, in a sense. But the sense in which people who work together are collectively their own masters at work is different from the sense in which the individual farmer or craftsman or trader is so, and the difference is apt to be the greater, the larger the number of collaborators. When a handful of men and women run a farm or other small business together, their situation—though already significantly different from that of the farmer or craftsman who runs his business without partners—may still be such that the work of management is hardly separate from the work managed. Decisions about what to do and how to do it can even be taken by the workers while they are actually at work, or with only short interruptions in their work. Management is not then sharply separate from ordinary work.

But when the number of workers is large, the business of management, even though the workers do it together, has to be kept separate from the rest of their work. There must be times set apart for it. And if the workers, instead of doing this business themselves, elect representatives (even though from their own number), to do it for them, they have already ceased to be in the literal sense their own masters at work. Their work is in fact directed by others, though they have elected them to do the directing, and need not re-elect them.

In a large organization democratically run, even though some of the running is done by its members collectively, the sense of distance between managers and managed, between 'them' and 'us', is not wholly removed. Relations between them may be closer for being democratic—though not therefore always easier, as the experience of many a trade union proves—but the sense of distance remains. To be sure, the more relations between managers and managed are trustful, the readier the rank and file of the organization are to think and speak of its official policies and decisions as 'ours' rather than 'theirs'. But relations are not always the more trustful for being democratic; and the extent to which they are so may vary considerably from one type of organization, from one sphere of action, to another. If there were good reason to believe that, on the whole, citizens trust their rulers the more (or 'identify' with them the more readily) the more democratic the political system, this would not justify our concluding that the same is true of armies, that soldiers are the more likely to trust their generals, the more an army is democratically organized. Armies, no doubt, differ greatly from political systems, but then so too does industry, even when it operates on a large scale. I do not deny that democracy can, and often does, enhance the sense of community between 'them' and 'us', and that it may do so in industry as well as in politics. I say only that we cannot take it for granted that it will. If it were to do so in industry, that of course would be a great advantage, and one perhaps worth buying at a considerable cost in efficiency.

But this is by no means the only advantage that champions of workers' management have hoped to gain from it. They have complained of the monotony and 'uncreativeness' of labour under capitalism, and have looked to workers' management for a remedy for these ills. For my part, I do not see how it can be a remedy for them, except to a small extent. To be sure, management is, or can be, a 'creative' activity, and as much so (if not more) in large as in small organizations. But it is so, to any considerable extent, only for those who take the initiatives, who make the proposals, or who mobilize opposition to them, who do the talking in whatever bodies take the major decisions. Even where these decisions are taken by the workers or members collectively, most of them (if the organization is large) are mere listeners and voters. Their role is not unimportant, but also it is not exactly 'creative', as the role of a leader may be said to be. And if the workers elect representatives to make the major decisions for them, their role as mere electors, though still important, is even less creative. All or most of the workers in an organization can take a creative part in managing it, only if two conditions hold: if the organization is small and they all take part in making the major decisions.

Work, even in the largest organization, can of course be so organized that a great part of it is done by teams of workers who are left to themselves to get on with the jobs allocated to them. How far this can be done must vary greatly with the character of the work in question. Perhaps, if there were more workers' management in industry, or more management responsible to the workers, work would be more often organized with this end in view;

though this is by no means certain. In any case, even managers not responsible to the workers, whether they were appointed by private owners or by some public authority, might find it conducive to efficiency and to good labour relations to encourage autonomous teamwork where it was technically possible. Already, there is a good deal of it in some industries. Even foremen appointed from above often find it expedient in practice to consult the men they work with. Democracy comes easily to collaborators when they are few and leadership calls for no long training or rare skills, especially when the collaborators all belong to the same social class. Actually, it often comes easily enough, under these conditions, even when they do not belong to the same class, as many a person who has served in a small detachment of the armed forces can testify.

Workers seem not always to share the aspirations for their class of the radicals. Often, they seem to care less about managing the businesses they work in than about being well organized to get good wages and conditions of work, and other concessions, from their employers and the government. Radicals sometimes put this down to their being affected by 'bourgeois' ideas or diverted from ambitions they would otherwise have by 'bourgeois' tastes and comforts. But many of the ideas and tastes that critics of bourgeois society call bourgeois are no more bourgeois than proletarian. These critics exaggerate the extent to which workers adopt the habits and standards of more affluent classes. A hundred years ago most middle-class families kept servants and few of their womenfolk went out to work, whereas working-class families kept no servants and many of their womenfolk took work outside the home. Today most middle-class families are in these two respects like working-class families, and yet—to the best of my knowledge—there are no sociologists (not even radical ones) arguing that the bourgeois are being 'proletarianized'. Why should a higher standard of living and more schooling lead to the 'embourgeoisement' of the workers, when doing without servants and women going out to work do not lead to the 'proletarianization' of the middle classes? These two classes may well be more alike in important respects than they used to be. But why speak of these changes as if they involved the cultural assimilation of either of these classes by the other? I suspect that sociologists and political theorists speak of these changes (or of their effects) as *embourgeoisement,* or the cultural assimilation of the working by the middle classes, for no better reason than their occurring in a society they have learnt to call *bourgeois.*

Whatever the cause, the workers in the West seem less concerned to manage the organizations they work in than to defend their interests against those who manage them, whether the organizations are in 'private' or in 'public' hands. They want to be well paid, to have decent working conditions, to be fairly treated by their employers, and to be well organized to press their demands on the management and also on government when it intervenes in industrial disputes. They also want social benefits of various kinds, not only because they are the better for having them but also because increased security strengthens their hand in their dealings both with employers and with the government. They want to be well placed to make agreements which seem to them just and to their own advantage.

That the work that most people in an industrial society do to earn their livings is dull is a fact that just has to be accepted, as Marx himself recognized in his later years. No doubt, much of the work done in more primitive societies is also dull, or would seem so to men and women brought up in our society. What people find dull varies with their tastes and aspirations. Yet manual work today, if it is as dull as it used to be (and perhaps duller), is also, on the whole, less arduous and much better paid. Office work is dull, too, for the most part, calling for skills easily acquired, and is often repetitive.

I doubt whether workers' management would do much to make manual or routine office work seem less dull to those who do it; which is not to deny that it might be desirable for other reasons. I suspect that most workers in the industrial countries, whether capitalist or not, are more concerned that the economy and the organizations they work in should be efficiently run, so that they can benefit from this efficiency, than that they should take part in running them. They may well doubt whether their taking part in running them would increase their efficiency. Yet experience has taught them that they must be strongly organized, industrially and politically, to ensure that they get a larger share of the wealth created by greater efficiency. On the whole, and not only in the capitalist West, they seem keener to get their share of the benefits that come of this increased efficiency than to take part, either directly or through representatives, in organizing it.

The worker who is most obviously 'creative' is the artist, the poet, or the thinker, who produces what is uniquely his own and is recognized as such by others. Creative, too, is the inventor, who conceives of new instruments and methods, and the reformer, who introduces new social practices or standards. But most men are not 'creative' in this sense, and it is not obvious that they need to be in order to be happy. 'Creative' in a secondary (or different) sense of the word is the craftsman who exercises skill and judgment in producing something well made, and the organizer who does so in directing the work of others. Though there are many people who do creative work of this kind, there are many more who do not. It may well be that most people are capable of this second kind of 'creativeness', though in developed industrial societies few have much scope for it at work. They are not craftsmen and they do not direct the work of others, or not at a level that calls for much skill and judgement. If there were workers' management in the enterprises or organizations they work for, their part in it—though by no means unimportant, any more than the electors' part in a political system—would scarcely deserved to be called creative. If they are to have much scope for creative activities, it must be—as Marx recognized in the third volume of *Capital,* when he contrasted the realm of freedom with the realm of necessary labour—in their leisure hours.

That being so, and if they really want (as no doubt many of them do) opportunity to be 'creative', would they not be well advised to care more about being well paid for the work they do, having a shorter working day and better conditions at work than about workers' management in industry?

Democracy in the Workplace*

Robert A. Dahl _____

Although political theorists who favor worker participation have often emphasized its potentialities for democratic character and its beneficial effects on democracy in the government of the state, a stronger justification, one with a more Kantian flavor, seems to me to rest on a different argument: *If* democracy is justified in governing the state, then it must *also* be justified in governing economic enterprises; and to say that it is *not* justified in governing economic enterprises is to imply that it is not justified in governing the state.

I can readily imagine three objections to this argument. . . . I address these objections in turn.

Property Rights

As to property rights, transferring control over the decisions of a firm to its employees, it might be objected, would violate the right of owners to use their property as they choose. . . . If a right to property is understood in its fundamental moral sense as a right to acquire the personal resources necessary to political liberty and a decent existence, then self-governing enterprises would surely not, on balance, diminish the capacity of citizens to exercise that right; in all likelihood they would greatly strengthen it. Even if property rights are construed in a narrower, more legalistic sense, the way in which a self-governing enterprise is owned need *not necessarily* violate such a right. As we shall see, it could entail a *shift* of ownership from stockholders to employees.

* Reprinted from Robert Dahl, *A Preface to Economic Democracy* (Berkeley: University of California Press, 1985), 57–58, 111–33, by permission of the publisher. Copyright © 1985 by University of California Press.

Are Decisions Binding?

Do economic enterprises make decisions that are *binding* on workers in the same way that the government of the state makes decisions that the citizens are compelled to obey? After all, laws made by the government of a state can be enforced by physical coercion, if need be. In a democratic state, a minority opposed to a law is nevertheless compelled to obey it. But a firm, it might be said, is nothing more than a sort of market within which people engage in voluntary individual exhanges; workers voluntarily exchange their labor in return for wages paid by the employers. Decisions made by the government of a firm and by the government of the state, however, are in some crucial respect more similar than this classical liberal interpretation allows for. Like the government of the state, the government of a firm makes decisions that apply uniformly to all workers for a category of workers: decisions governing the place of work, time of work, product of work minimally acceptable rate of work, equipment to be used at work, number of workers, number (and identity) of workers laid off in slack times—or whether the plant is to be shut down and there will be no work at all. These decisions are enforced by sanctions, including the ultimate sanction of firing.

Have I now understated the difference? Unlike citizens of a state, one might object, workers are not *compelled* to obey managerial decisions; their decision to do so is voluntary. Because a worker may choose to obey the management or not, because he is free to leave the firm if he prefers not to obey, and because he cannot be punished by management for leaving, some would argue that his decision to obey is perfectly free of all compulsion.

But an objection along these lines exaggerates the differences between a worker's subjection to decisions made by the government of a firm and a citizen's subjection to decisions made by the government of the state. Take a local government. A citizen who does not like a local ordinance is also "free" to move to another community. Indeed, if a citizen does not want to obey her country's laws, she is "free"—at least in all democratic countries— to leave her country. Now if a citizen were perfectly free to leave, then citizenship would be wholly voluntary; for if a citizen found "voice" unsatisfactory, she could freely opt for "exit." But is not "exit" (or exile) often so costly, in every sense, that membership is for all practical purposes compulsory—whether it requires one to leave a country, a municipality, or a firm? If so, then the government of a firm looks rather more like the government of a state than we are habitually inclined to believe: because exit is so costly, membership in a firm is not significantly more voluntary or less compulsory than citizenship in a municipality or perhaps even in a country.

In fact, citizenship in a democratic state is in one respect more voluntary than employment in a firm. Within a democratic country, citizens may ordinarily leave one municipality and automatically retain or quickly acquire full rights of citizenship in another. Yet even though the decisions of firms, like the decisions of a state, can be enforced by severe sanctions (firing), unlike a citizen of a democratic state, one who leaves a firm has no right to "citizenship" (that is, employment) in another.

Like a state, then, a firm can also be viewed as a political system in which relations of power exist between governments and the governed. If so, is it not appropriate to insist that the relationship between governors and governed should satisfy the criteria of the democratic process—as we properly insist in the domain of the state?

Let the firm be considered a political system, one might now agree. Within this political system, however, cannot the rights of workers be adequately protected by labor unions? But this objection not only fails to meet the problem of nonunion workers (who in the United States compose about 80 percent of the workforce); it also implicitly recognizes that in order to protect some fundamental right or interest, workers are entitled to have—have a right to—at least *some* democratic controls. What, then, is the nature and scope of this right or interest? To say that its scope is limited by an equally or more fundamental right to property runs afoul of our earlier analysis. On what grounds, therefore must the employer's *right* to democratic controls be restricted to the conventional (but by no means well-defined) limits of trade unions? Is this not precisely the question at issue: Do workers have a fundamental right to self-government in their economic enterprises: If they do have such a right, then is it not obvious that, however essential conventional trade unions may be in reducing the impact of authoritarian rule in the government of a firm, an ordinary firm, even with a trade union, still falls very short of satisfying the criteria of the democratic process?

Does the Strong Principle of Equality Hold?

. . . The democratic process is justified by . . . a strong principle of equality: With respect to all matters, all the adult members of the association (the citizens of a government) are roughly equally well qualified to decide which matters do or do not require binding collective decisions. Those who participate shall decide which matters the demo (the citizenry) is best qualified to decide for itself; which matters, in the membership's view, the demos is not qualified to decide for itself; and the terms on which the demos will delegate a contingent and recoverable authority to others.

But if (this) strong principle does not apply to business firms, then the case for self-governing enterprises is seriously, perhaps fatally, damaged, while the case for rule by the best qualified—the "guardians" to use Plato's term— is correspondingly strengthened. The government of large American corporations, I suggested earlier, could be seen as a form of guardianship. Although managers are nominally selected by a board of directors, which in turn is nominally chosen by and legally accountable to stockholders, in reality new managers are typically co-opted by existing management which also, in practice, chooses and controls its own board of directors (Herman 1981). Guardianship has also been the ideal of many socialists, particularly the Fabians. In this view the managers of state-owned enterprises were to be chosen by state officials, to whom the top managers were to be ultimately responsible. In most countries, in fact, nationalized industries are governed by some such scheme. One could easily dream up still other meritocratic alternatives.

Thus in theory and practice both corporate capitalism and bureaucratic socialism have rejected the strong principle of equality for economic enterprises; explicitly or by implication they uphold guardianship. Because of the overwhelming weight of existing institutions and ideologies, probably most people, including many thoughtful people, will find it hard to believe that employees are qualified to govern the enterprises in which they work. However, in consideration whether the strong principle of equality holds for business firms, it is important to keep two points in mind. First, while we may reasonably compare the ideal or theoretically possible performance of one system with the ideal or theoretical performance of another, we cannot reasonably compare the actual performance of one with the ideal performance of another. Although a good deal of the discussion of self-governing enterprises that follows is necessarily conjectural, my aim is to compare the probable performance of self-governing enterprises with the actual performance of their current principal alternative, the modern privately owned corporation.

Second, . . . the strong principle of equality does not require that citizens be equally competent in every respect. It is sufficient to believe that citizens are qualified enough to decide which matters do or do not require binding collective decisions (e.g., which matters require general rules); of those that do require binding collective decisions, citizens are competent to decide whether they are themselves sufficiently qualified to make the decisions collectively through the democratic process; and on matters they do not feel competent to decide for themselves, they are qualified to set the terms on which they will delegate these decisions to others.

Except in exceedingly small firms, employees would surely choose to delegate some decisions to managers. In larger firms, they would no doubt elect a governing board or council, which in the typical case would probably be delegated the authority to select and remove the top executives. Except in very large enterprises, the employees might constitute an assembly for "legislative" purposes—to make decisions on such matters as the workers choose to decide, to delegate matters they prefer not to decide directly, and to review decisions on matters they had previously delegated as well as the conduct of the board and the managers in other ways. In giant firms, where an assembly would suffer all the infirmities of direct democracy on an excessively large scale, a representative government would have to be created.

Given the passivity of stockholders in a typical firm, their utter dependency on information supplied by management, and the extraordinary difficulties of contesting a managerial decision, it seems to me hardly open to doubt that employeees are on the whole as well qualified to run their firms as are stockholders, and probably on average a good deal more. But of course that is not really the issue, given the separation of ownership from control that Adolf Berle and Gardiner Means called attention to in 1932 in *The Modern Corporation and Private Property*. A recent and much more systematic study reports that 64 percent of the 200 largest nonfinancial American corporations are controlled by inside management and another 17 percent by inside management with an outside board, or altogether 81 percent of the total, with 84 percent of the assets and 82 percent of the sales (Herman 1981, table 3.1). Although the percentage of management-controlled firms might be less among smaller firms, the question remains whether workers are as qualified to govern economic enterprises as managers who gain their position by co-option—thus producing a sort of co-optive guardianship.

This question raises many of the familiar and ancient issues of democracy versus guardianship, including the grounds for believing that the putative guardians possess superior knowledge about what is best for the collectivity, and also superior virtue—the will or predisposition to seek that good. It is important therefore to distinguish knowledge about the *ends* the enterprise should seek from technical knowledge about the best *means* for achieving those ends. As to ends, the argument might be made that self-governing enterprises would produce lower rates of savings, investment, growth, and employment than society might rationally (or at least reasonably) prefer. As to means, it might be contended that self-governing enterprises would be less likely to supply qualified management and for this and other reasons would be less efficient than stockholder-owned firms like American corporations.

Ends: Savings, investment, growth, and employment. How then would a system of self-governing enterprises affect savings, investment, employment, and growth? For example, would workers vote to allocate so much of enterprise earnings to wages that they would sacrifice investment in new machinery and future efficiencies? Would firms run democratically by their employees be more shortsighted than firms run hierarchically by managers? American corporate managers are frequently criticized nowadays for an excessive emphasis on short-run as against long-run returns (e.g., Bluestone 1980, 52). Would self-governing enterprises accentuate the sacrifice of deferred to immediate benefits, to the disadvantage and contrary to the collective preferences of their society? If so, would not the particular interests of workers in an enterprise conflict with the general interest?

Purely theoretical analysis by economists, whether critics or advocates of worker-managed firms, is ultimately inconclusive. Advocates of self-management agree that in contrast to conventional firms in which managers seek to maximize total profit for shareholders, the worker-members of self-governing firms would seek to maximize the per capita income of the members. In view of this, some critics reason, members would have no incentive to expand savings, production, employment, or investment unless the effect were to increase their own per capita earnings; and they would have a definite incentive not to do so if they expected that by doing so they would reduce their own earnings. These critics therefore conclude that in some situations in which a conventional firm would expand in order to increase returns to shareholders, worker-managed firms would not.

Advocates of self-governing firms reply that in an economy of self-governing firms, the problem of employment is theoretically distinguishable from the problem of investment and growth. In the theoretical scenario just sketched out, expanding employment is a problem only at the level of the individual firm. At the level of the economy, however, it would be dealt with by ensuring ease of entry for new firms. If unemployment existed and enterprises failed to respond to rising demand for their product by expanding employment, new firms would do so; hence both investment and employment would increase. As to investment, except in the circumstances just described, members of a self-managed enterprise would have strong incentives to invest, and thus to save, whenever by doing so they would increase the surplus available for distribution to themselves (cf. Jay 1980, 17–27; Schweikart 1980, 73–74, 103–106).

In the real world, however, these comparisons between theoretical models do not take us very far. As Peter Jay remarks:

So far we have been comparing the rational investment behavior of workers' cooperatives with the rational behavior of idealized capital enterprises working according to textbook optimization. If we actually lived in the latter world, we would hardly be considering the problem discussed in this paper at all.

(*Jay, 20*)

Turning then to the domain of practical judgment, it seems likely that in the real world, self-governing enterprises might stimulate as much savings, investment, and growth as American corporate enterprises have done, and perhaps more, because workers typically stand to incur severe losses from the decline of a firm. If we permit ourselves to violate the unenforceable injunction of some welfare economists against interpersonal comparisons, we can hardly deny that the losses incurred by workers from the decline of a firm are normally even greater than those investors suffer; for it is ordinarily much easier and less costly in human terms for a well-heeled investor to switch in and out of the securities market than for a worker to switch in and out of the job market. A moderately foresightful worker would therefore be as greatly concerned with long-run efficiencies as a rational investor or a rational manager, and perhaps more so.

This conjecture is supported by at least some cases in which, given the opportunity, workers have made significant short-term sacrifices in wages and benefits in order to keep their firm from collapsing. They did so, for example, at both Chrysler Corporation and the Rath Packing Company. And when workers won the company their incentive to sacrifice in order to save it is all the stronger. As a worker in one of the plywood co-ops put it, "If things get bad we'll all take a pay cut. You don't want to milk the cow, because if you milk the cow, there's nothing left. And *we* lose the company" (Zwerdling 1980, 101).

Perhaps an even more relevant example is that of Mondragon, a complex of more than 80 workers cooperatives in Spain. During a period in which the Spanish economy was expanding generally, the sales of the Mondragon cooperatives grew at an impressive rate, averaging 8.5 percent from 1970 to 1979. Their market share increased from less than 1 percent in 1960 to over 10 percent in 1976. The percentage of gross value added through investment by the cooperatives between 1971 and 1979 averaged 36 percent, nearly four times the average rate of industry in the heavily industrialized Basque province in which Mondragon is located (Thomas and Logan 1982, 100–105). Moreover, when a recession in the Spanish economy led to declining profits in 1981, "investment [was] squeezed, but the workers [were] prepared to make sacrifices to keep their jobs, digging into their own pockets to keep the balance sheets in shape" (*The Economist,* 31 October 1981, 84). Members chose to contribute more capital rather than cut their wages. Thus the members of one co-op voted to increase their individual capital contributions by amounts that ranged from $570 to $1,700, depending on wage level. Nor have the self-managed enterprises of Yugoslavia on the whole followed the theoretical model advanced by critics of self-management. Though the causes are complex, with some exceptions they have not sacrificed investment to current income but, on the contrary, have maintained very high levels of investment.

A final observation on the problem of savings, investment, employment, and growth: The introduction of self-governing enterprises *could* be accompanied by the creation of new investment funds operating under democratic control. Although a system of self-governing enterprises of the kind suggested in this chapter differs in crucial ways from the proposals for wage-earner funds advanced by the Swedish Social Democratic party, that proposal is relevant because of its emphasis on funds for investment. Often called the Meidner Plan after its author, Rudolf Meidner, who developed it with his colleagues in the research bureau of the national trade union organization or LO (Meidner 1978), the proposal was adopted by the LO in 1976 and, in altered form, by the Social Democrats in 1978. As revised by 1980, the proposal would require the largest firms—altogether about 200 companies— to set aside each year 20 percent of their profits in the form of "wage-earner shares" that would carry voting rights. As a result, ownership of these firms would gradually pass to the employees. At a 10 percent rate of profit, for example, wage earners would gain majority ownership in about thirty-five years.

However, the wage-earner shares would not belong to individual workers, as they do in employee stock ownership plans, nor to the workers of an enterprise collectively. Instead, the shares and therefore the voting rights would be transferred to various national and regional funds, which would be governed by representatives elected by wage-earners—*all* wage-earners, it should be added, not only those employed by the 200 or so contributing firms. A firm's employees would never control more than 20 percent of the voting rights in their own firm, whereas an increasingly larger share would accrue to one of the representative bodies. With a powerful, unified, and inclusive trade union organization and a history of success in using centralized national bargaining to equalize wages and a centralized government to socialize incomes, the Swedish labor movement and the Social Democratic party are disposed to favor a more centralized solution than the sytem I am suggesting. The important point, however, is that the funds are intended not only to provide "economic democracy" but also to ensure a greater supply of capital for investment.

Much closer to the idea of self-governing enterprises described here is a proposal introduced in Parliament by the Danish Social Democratic party in 1973 (Ministry of Labour 1973). The proceeds of a payroll tax covering most Danish firms (about 25,000) would be divided in effect, in two parts. One part—the smaller—would go to a national investment and dividend fund that would be used both to strengthen Danish investment and to provide a social dividend to Danish workers. Virtually every worker would receive certificates from the fund in an amount proportional to the number of years worked but not to the employee's wage or salary. The certificates would be nonnegotiable, but an employee would have the right to withdraw the value of his certificates after seven years or at age 67; upon death their value would be paid to the employee's estate. The other and larger part of the proceeds from the payroll tax would remain in the firm as share capital owned collectively by the employees, who would vote as enterprise-citizens, that is, one person, one vote. The employees' share of capital, however, and thus of voting rights, would not be permitted to increase beyond 50 percent—presumably a provision to reassure private investors. Like the Meidner Plan in Sweden, the Danish proposal is intended to achieve several purposes: greater equalization of wealth, more democratic control of the economy, and, definitely not least in importance, a steady supply of funds for investment.

Thus it is not inconceivable that workers might enter into a social contract that would require them to provide funds for investment, drawn from payrolls, in return for greater control over the government of economic enterprises. If self-governing enterprises proved to be better matched to the incentives of workers than hierarchically run firms, and thus more efficient, a system of self-governing enterprises might be a prescription for economic growth that would surpass even Japan's success—and leave recent American performance far behind.

Means: Managerial skills. A disastrous assumption of revolutionaries, exhibited with stunning naivete in Lenin's *State and Revolution,* is that managerial skills are of trivial importance, or will arise spontaneously, or will be more than compensated for by revolutionary enthusiasm. The historical record relieves one of all need to demonstrate the foolishness of such an assumption. The question is obviously not whether self-governing enterprises would need managerial abilities, but whether workers and their representatives would select and oversee managers less competently than is now the case in American corporations, which are largely controlled by managers whose decisions are rarely open to serious challenge, except when disaster strikes, and not always even then (Herman 1981). If a system of self-governing enterprises were established it would be wise to provide much wider opportunities than now exist in any country for employees to learn some of the tools and skills of modern management. One source of the Mondragon cooperatives' success lies in the prominence they have assigned to education, including technical education at advanced professional levels. As a result, they have developed their own managers (Thomas and Logan, 42–47). In the United States, at least, a significant proportion of both blue and white-collar workers, often the more ambitious and aggressive among them, aspire to supervisory and managerial positions but lack the essential skills (see, e.g., Witte 1980). Efficiency and economic growth flow from investments in human capital every bit as much as from financial capital, and probably more (cf. Denison 1974). A system of self-governing enterprises would be likely to heighten—not diminish—efforts to improve a country's human capital.

If in the meanwhile skilled managers are in short supply, self-governing enterprises will have to compete for their services, as does Puget Sound Plywood, a worker-owned cooperative. The president and members of the board of trustees are elected by and from the members, who all receive the same pay. However, the president and board in turn select a general manager from outside the membership "because he can command pay that is far in excess of what he could realize as a shareholder [i.e., as a worker-member]. . . . The qualifications for being a general manger are not what one would normally gain from working in a plywood mill. So we usually employ the best person we can find in the industry" (Bennett 1979, 81–82, 85).

Means: Efficiency. Unless self-governing enterprises were less competent in recruiting skilled managers, they should be no less efficient in a narrow sense than American corporations at present, And unless they were more likely to evade the external controls of competition and regulation, they should not be less efficient in a broader sense. I have suggested why it is reasonable to expect neither of these deficiencies to occur.

Yet if self-governing enterprises can be as efficient as orthodox firms, why have they so often failed? As everyone familiar with American and British labor history knows, the late nineteenth century saw waves of short-lived producer cooperatives in Britain and in the United States. Their quick demise convinced trade union leaders that in a capitalist economy unionism and collective bargaining held out a much more realistic promise of gains for workers than producer cooperatives. In both countries, and in Europe as well, labor and socialist movements largely abandoned producer cooperatives as a major short-run objective. Most academic observers, including labor economists and social historians, concluded that the labor-managed firm was a rejected and forlorn utopian idea irrelevant to a modern economy (e.g., Commons et al. 1936, 2:488).

In recent years, however, a number of factors have brought about a reassessment of the relevance of the older experience (cf. Jones and Svejnar 1982, 4–6). These include the highly unsatisfactory performance of both corporate capitalism and bureaucratic socialism, whose failings have stimulated a search for a third alternative; the introduction and survival—despite severe difficulties—of self-management in Yugoslavia; some stunning successes, such as the U.S. plywood cooperatives and the Mondragon group; formal economic analysis showing how a labor-managed market economy would theoretically satisfy efficiency criteria (Vanek 1970); growing awareness of the need to reduce the hierarchical structure of the workplace and increase participation by workers in order to increase productivity; and the seeming success of many new arrangements for worker participation, control, or ownership in Europe and the United States.

In sum, it has become clear that many failed labor-managed firms had been doomed not by inherent weaknesses but by remediable ones, such as shortages of credit, capital, and managerial skills. Moreover, in the past, producer cooperatives have usually been organized in the worst possible circumstances, when employees desperately attempt to rescue a collapsing company by taking it over—often during a recession. It is hardly surprising that workers may fail to save a firm after management has already failed. What is surprising is that workers' coorperatives have sometimes succeeded where private management has failed. For example, it was from the failure of privately owned companies that some of the plywood co-ops started (Berman 1982, 63).

I have also mentioned the Mondragon producer cooperatives in Spain as an example of success. They include their nation's largest manufacturer of machine tools as well as one of its largest refrigerator manufacturers. During a period of a falling Spanish economy and rising unemployment, between 1977 and 1981, employment in the Mondragon co-ops increased from 15,700 to about 18,500 (Zwerdling 1980, 154ff. and *The Economist,* 31 October 1981, 84). Unless they are denied access to credit—the Mondragon complex has its own bank (Thomas and Logan, 75–95)—self-governing enterprises have a greater resiliency than American corporations. For in times of stringency when an orthodox private firm would lay off workers or shut down, the members of a self-governing enterprise can decide to reduce their wages, curtail their share of the surplus, if any, or even contribute additional capital funds, as at Mondragon. As these and other cases show, self-governing enterprises are likely to tap the creativity, energies, and loyalites of workers to an extent that stockholder-owned corporations probably never can, even with profit-sharing schemes (cf. Melman 1958).

Although rigorous comparisons of the relative efficiencies of labor-managed and conventional corporations are difficult and still fairly uncommon, the best analysis (Jones and Svejnar 1982) of a broad range of experiences in a number of different countries appears to support these conclusions: participation by workers in decision-making rarely leads to a decline of productivity; far more often it either has no effect or results in an increase in productivity (see also Simmons and Mares 1983, 285–93).

Notes

1. It is disputable because natural resources are very unevenly distributed among autonomous communities, so that the naturally poorer ones can be self-sufficient

only at the cost of a low standard of living or else, if they rely heavily on foreign trade, may be at a great disadvantage compared with the others.

2.   Ordinarily, when we speak of 'the economy', we have in mind certain kinds of activity (those we call 'economic', usually without being quite sure where to draw the line between them and non-economic activities) in so far as they take place within the confines of a state, or can be controlled by its government. But Marxists and other radicals look forward to 'the disappearance of the state', and it is not clear how extensive in their eyes the economy controlled by the workers is to be.